JANICE LaROUCHE was the first management/career consultant to apply the new awareness of women's needs to practical strategies in career planning and advancement. She established her nationally acclaimed "Workshops for Women" in 1968, and since then has been recognized as having revolutionized the field of career counseling by understanding that women have unique problems, and finding specific solutions to help women achieve their optimum earning potential and career ambitions.

Janice LaRouche has appeared frequently on national radio and TV and has been featured in major news media from *The New York Times* to *Forbes Magazine* to *Glamour*. In her own career she has worked as a social service executive, a director of management and staff training, a member of the faculty of the American Banking Institute, and a columnist for *McCall's*. Currently, in addition to her work as a career counselor, she is a faculty member of the New School for Social Research.

REGINA RYAN is the head of her own independent book producing company. The former editor-in-chief of Macmillan Adult Books, she was the first woman ever to hold that position in a major hardcover publishing house. Prior to that, she was an editor for many years at Alfred A. Knopf, Inc. Ms. Ryan lives and works in New York City and Connecticut. She is married to the novelist Paul Deutschman.

"Owning this book is like having your own personal career counselor sitting on the shelf anticipating problems and knowing just how to help you solve them. LaRouche and Ryan have written the most comprehensive work Baedeker of this or any decade—and they've done it with *heart*."

‑TY COTTIN POGREBIN
tor, Ms
thor, FAMILY POLITICS

GH00806317

This book is dedicated to the countless women who never had the chance to be what they could be, and to all those who have fought to give women that chance.

We would like to thank Paul Deutschman for his invaluable aid and counsel during the writing of this book; Seymour Jacobson for his unfailing good humor and supportiveness; Page Cuddy for her enthusiasm and her real understanding of what we were trying to achieve; and Nellie Sabin for her incisive and thoughtful editing.

Working Woman: Strategies for Survival and Success

Janice LaRouche
& Regina Ryan

UNWIN
PAPERBACKS

LONDON SYDNEY WELLINGTON

First published in paperback by Unwin® Paperbacks, 1985
Reprinted twice in 1985, and once in 1986.
Fifth impression, 1988
Unwin Paperbacks is an imprint of Unwin Hyman Limited

Unwin Hyman Limited
15–17 Broadwick Street, London W1V 1FP

Allen & Unwin Australia Pty Ltd
8 Napier Street, North Sydney, NSW 2060, Australia

Allen & Unwin New Zealand Pty Ltd with the Port Nicholson Press
60 Cambridge Terrace, Wellington, New Zealand

British Library Cataloguing in Publication Data

LaRouche, Janice
  [Janice LaRouche's strategies for women
  at work[. Working woman : strategies for
  survival and success.
  1. Women, Employment – Manuals – For women
  I. [Janice LaRouche's strategies for women
  at work]   II. Title   III. Ryan, Regina
  IV. Strategies for women at work
  331.4

  ISBN 0–04 440313–5

Although the case histories in this book are based on my work as a career counselor, both the names of the participants and the details describing them – the industries, job descriptions and titles – have been changed so that the actual identities will not be recognisable. In addition, the stories themselves are often composites of several different occurrences.

Printed in Great Britain by Cox & Wyman, Reading.

CONTENTS

CHAPTER 2
I'M HAVING TROUBLE WITH MY BOSS   17

CHAPTER 3
STRATEGIES FOR MOVING UP   79

CHAPTER 4
BUILDING THE RIGHT IMAGE   171

INTRODUCTION

A Personal Statement by Janice LaRouche

This is intended to be a handbook for women in the workplace. It is organized and written so that it can be used as a guide and reference source of practical, concrete, and strategic advice that will help women solve their problems on the job and get what *they* want out of work.

While many women are out in the workplace today, most of them are still vastly underpaid and underutilized; they are doing the scut work, and their time and abilities are going to waste. They are exploited.

The women's movement is fighting to end this exploitation by forcing open the doors to equality, but it is very hard, even today, for most women to act on this equality, to function as equals in the day-to-day situations of their own lives. Nonetheless, as the doors open, each woman, herself, individually, must be able to walk through them.

My hope is that this book will help women see and seize opportunities, learn to think strategically, and take their rightful, equal places in the business world.

In large part, *Strategies for Women at Work* grew out of my own personal experience.

In the late sixties, small feminist consciousness-raising groups were springing up throughout the country. That history-making era coincided with a kind of personal liberation of my own. At that time, my son was old enough to go to a boarding school that he very much wanted to attend, and by then I was earning enough money to send him. My marriage had broken up some years before, when my son was still a baby, and thereafter I had been responsible not only for his care, but also for supporting the two of us. I had felt hopelessly unprepared for any such challenge. I had had no profession, no college degree, and almost no knowledge of what a career involved or what the business world was about. And worst of all, I was psychologically unprepared. It had never even occurred to me that I would ever be responsible for myself financially or emotionally or in any other way. I did not respond to the challenge with optimism or strength. Indeed, I was overwhelmed by the responsibility for myself and my child. I cried easily. I felt abused and resentful, betrayed by the world.

The one thing that I did understand was *why* I was in this position—why I was so wiped out. I had been a strong believer in women's equality ever since my early teenage years, and had long been aware of the fact that women didn't get an even break. Thus, I didn't take my inadequacy personally—and that began to give me a lot of hope.

Despite all my handicaps, I managed to carve out a career. It was a painful struggle, and an on-the-job training program, but, bit by bit, I learned to be strategic. I learned to negotiate, to be assertive, and, gradually, to be independent, step by step by step.

Through these long years, I had two strengths going for me. One was my feminism. The other was a good feminist friend who was a master strategist and who understood how discrimination against women was internalized. He understood and was sympathetic to the impairments women suffered, so, over and over again, as I confronted problems, he was able to help me see two essential aspects of each issue: first, that the particular problem was not of my making—that whatever defects I had were not innate in my being and that I was indeed a victim; and second, why the problem was so difficult for me to confront, or even to recognize.

His analysis took the burden off me. ("Of course it's hard for you to tell people what to do. A woman isn't supposed to be the boss. Women are supposed to accommodate," he would explain.) And once I had gotten off the defensive, I could begin to hear the strategic advice he was giving me—and begin to approach the problem at hand with some assertiveness and with as much cleverness as I could muster.

By 1968 I had carved out a successful career in my chosen field. For the first time in many years, I could claim some hours of the day for myself. I became active in the women's movement and met up with all these bright, energetic, young feminists. Most of them were not even thinking about developing careers for themselves.

They thought, discussed, and acted with the highest political consciousness, determined to break down the walls of prejudice that kept all women segregated in—and even excluded from—the workplace. And that, to a considerable degree, was accomplished.

But once the political battle against discrimination was in part achieved, once the doors started to open—or, at least, were left ajar for us to push our way in—there were new issues to confront. We had to learn the independence in thought and action that had always been the province of men. We suddenly had to *be* equal. We had to meet the challenge of achieving personal independence through financial independence and equality in the workplace—the challenge of developing our own careers. These were entirely new issues.

I had already discovered on my own, through a bitter, hard struggle, the crucial role that work played in a woman's life. Now I had the idea that I could help these women in somewhat the same way my friend had helped me. I wanted to pass along what I had learned and what had worked for me. I thought of a career workshop that would provide women with a forum where they could learn what they had missed out on by growing up female in our culture. They had been deprived of all the "natural" things that men learn through *their* growing-up process, as well as the things men are exposed to every day at the office or in the plant, the vast experience they accumulate through their contact with each other, the strategies, the wheeling and dealing, the knowledge of what to do and how to do it.

As it turned out, I was the first person to bring a feminist perspective to the field of career development.

When I told some of these young feminists my thoughts about a career workshop, they leaped at the idea. Within a matter of weeks, they were dealing with long-standing problems, getting out of trouble, becoming motivated, establishing new goals, obtaining raises and promotions. The women in that first group moved forward fast, from hippy drop-out to anthropologist, from clerk to art director, from public relations copywriter to political analyst. It was the beginning of new lives for them—and a new career for me. Soon thereafter, I founded Workshops for Women, and have been counseling women in the same way, full-time, ever since.

I envision *Strategies for Women at Work* as an expansion of the career workshop idea. My purpose is to help you solve your specific on-the-job problems on a day-to-day basis—to provide you with a "what to do, when" handbook.

We will be looking at a wide range of on-the-job problems that have come up through the years in the workshops. We'll examine the difficulties my clients faced (with, of course, identities disguised), and then the solutions that they and I, together, devised.

These solutions embody a way of thinking that may not be familiar to you, but I expect that as you read the book, you will acquire a bag of tools that you can then reach into and apply to many different situations. My hope is that you will come away with a whole new method of analyzing and solving your work problems strategically.

Men and women have many similar problems on the job, but women have to face, and try to surmount, the problems caused by discrimination and prejudice. In addition, women by and large are handicapped by their upbringing; they are not prepared for the difficulties they encounter at work.

Of course, there are exceptions. Some women do very well. They seem to have a natural ability, but more likely, as some studies have suggested, they have atypical backgrounds. But the majority of us have to learn how to solve job problems through experience, experiments, and mistakes—painfully have to work out ways and means that many men and these few women come by "naturally."

The fact that I've been helping women to solve these workplace problems should not be taken as an indication that I personally approve of things as they are. I don't—but that's beside the point here. This is the world that exists in business, and while many people, including women, are working to change the existing order, you still have to learn to function in this world. What I'm trying to do is help you make the best deal you can for yourself.

Essential to the strategies we will be working out in this book is the basic premise that you have to learn to be independent. This happens through a series of steps. You don't go from dependence to independence in one easy step or with one flash of insight, just as you don't go from being a child to being an adult in one magic moment.

Achieving independence and equality is not easy. My hope is that by reading and using *Strategies for Women at Work,* you'll find a method, a way of approaching problems, that will help you attain these goals.

JANICE LaROUCHE
September 17, 1983

HOW TO USE THIS BOOK

This volume is designed to be used as a handbook. It is organized problem by problem, as women typically present them. The solution to each problem contains three elements:

1. An analysis of the dynamic of the workplace and the people in it—what's really going on—which is often mysterious and baffling to women who are inexperienced in this area.
2. For those of you who have that problem, an analysis of what might be standing in the way of your finding or implementing a solution. This includes a discussion of the particular block or barrier to effective action that you, as a woman, might have acquired simply by virtue of having grown up in our culture.
3. Specific, concrete solutions to resolve the problem—the strategies (your overall plan) and the tactics (what you can do tomorrow morning, even down to the words to use).

Bear in mind that *finding the right strategic move has to do with understanding the workplace; using the solution has to do with understanding yourself.*

It would be wise to read this book straight through the first time; you'll gain an overview, and you'll learn new ways—a method—of thinking about problems and approaching solutions. However, this volume can also be used as a reference work—a look-it-up sort of book. If you want to locate your particular problem at the moment, look through either Appendix A (a detailed and descriptive complete table of contents) or Appendix B (a topic-by-topic breakdown and cross-referencing guide) in the back of this volume. Look for the heading or subheading that most clearly articulates your problem.

As you read the book, it's important to understand that the same problem can occur at different levels in the business world. A secretary can have the same problem in her own context that a vice president would have in hers. In such cases, one strategy may serve to solve the specific problems of both. It's a good idea, therefore, to read the case histories with an eye to abstracting the core of the problem and the solution.

I will be presenting some very specific solutions to problems. Don't take them too literally. Situations vary in their details; there are fine points of difference. *You have to use your instincts. A solution has to feel right in your particular situation.*

One final point: throughout the book, we have made the boss a man and the employee a woman. We did this quite consciously—for the sake of clarity. We wanted to avoid the confusions that arise when the boss is a "she" and the employee is also a "she." But nevertheless, it's also a reflection of reality. Most of my clients are women—and even today, most of their bosses are men.

IS IT WORTH IT?

In this book, I've made an assumption: that for women, the importance of getting a career established has moved from a nonexistent or subordinate place to the first priority in their lives. It is becoming clearer that in today's world the work you do provides the substructure on which everything else—an interesting life inside and outside the office, financial security, and even the quality of personal relationships—depends, much as it does for a man. No longer can a woman rely on another person (if indeed she ever could) to provide her with a lifelong guarantee of loyalty, emotional and financial support, and a life-style and milieu based on the other person's occupation and status.

Once you accept this reality—that your life is in your own hands—the need to establish a career becomes clear. Thus, for women, work can no longer be thought of as transitory or stopgap, something to be avoided or abandoned if possible. Rather than just "going to work" or "getting a job," a woman today has to make a commitment to a career and to developing all the skills and attributes that will make her career materialize—the independence, the assertiveness, the strength, the strategic sense.

For most women, this means, in a certain sense, becoming what they are not. It requires a qualitative change in how they function and how they think, a task which can be an enormous struggle.

Is the struggle worth it? I can't blame you for asking yourself this question, since the difficulties and obstacles women have to surmount in the workplace are formidable. But I don't think you have much choice in the matter. The risk of *not* developing a career can be overwhelming. Whatever you want your life to be, it's up to you to get it. Nobody else is picking up the tab on a long-term contract.

Fortunately, the rewards for accepting responsibility for yourself are great—and tangible. You can see and feel them, and people around you can see and feel them. First and foremost, you are earning your own way.

Then, there's also the element of self-fulfillment. You have more chances to develop your potential, because you are in a broader arena with many choices. You are no longer dreaming of What Might Have Been but of What Is Now Possible. Moreover, you are being paid for these personal gains. You are given tangible evidence of your value to others. At the same time, you are creating a better future for yourself. By virtue of the skills and know-how you are accumulating, you are giving yourself more options as you grow older.

But, most important, there is the basic payoff: you develop the confidence of knowing that you can take care of yourself. You become an equal and independent person. Being grown up is a satisfying state—that's why women throughout the world are struggling for equality.

Many working woman today are experiencing these rewards—but are they paying too high a price for them? Does this commitment bring problems? Obviously, it does; any course of action brings problems. But rather than weigh up a list of the pros and cons of developing a career—which seems absurd under the circumstances—let's deal here with the objections, the points of doubt, that are sometimes brought up:

• *There isn't much net gain financially.* This argument is frequently used to justify staying home, but I believe it takes a completely shortsighted approach to both the individual woman and her circumstances—both in the job and in her personal life. It assumes that the high cost of going to work (baby-sitters, clothes, lunches, carfare, etc.) and the amount of income that the woman earns are fixed figures. For the woman with a family, the costs decline as time goes on. And for the woman who is developing a career— just as for the man who is developing a career—greater knowledge and skills usually bring greater income.

• *Your boyfriend or husband resents the life-style. You're asking him to pitch in on the chores. Moreover, most of the time, you are not available to play.* I think that when a man complains and a woman feels guilty that she is not providing enough, she projects her guilt and concern about her failing as a woman, thus leaving the way open for him to feel justified in his complaint. The scenario runs something like this. He complains. She wavers, hesitates, becomes defensive, apologetic, angry—because she's afraid that she's not giving him the life he wants, and that she is responsible for his moments of disappointment. Moreover, she feels that he is absolutely not able to tolerate this disappointment, and will ultimately leave her for another, more accommodating woman. Women typically feel that if they can't satisfy a man's desires—whether for food, or a nice home, or sex, or favors, or amusement—the man will go elsewhere. It doesn't occur to a woman who feels like this that just being who she is could well be her main attraction.

The woman who truly values herself believes that she is offering something important and valuable to her partner in the time that she does spend with him. If she thinks he's lucky to have her, he'll be more inclined to think likewise.

• *There isn't enough time for your children.* For most women with careers and families, this is a given truth—it comes with the territory. In effect, you are holding down two jobs, and there are just not enough hours in the day or sufficient energy in your body and mind to give your children all they need and all that you'd wish to give them. One way to handle this, which helps both you and your children, is to bring your children in on the problems—as well as the solutions. You don't tell them what you've decided—or what you and your husband have decided—for them. Instead, you discuss the situation—whether about business trips, after-school activities, shopping for tonight's dinner, or whatever—*en famille*. In that way, the kids benefit and you (or you and your husband or consort) benefit. When children see the need and how they can be really helpful, it gives them self-esteem and importance that children are not generally accorded in our culture.

If children are given responsibility in ways that they can handle, that responsibility will be a positive factor in their growth and development. (There are many good books which can help you with this.) The family will miss out on certain things but it will gain others. Moreover, kids grow up and the rough years pass.

If you feel the need and if it's possible, take off some time during these rough years or hire some outside help to tide you and your children over. Taking time off may disadvantage your career, but being slowed up is not a major problem. There are many factors that go into career success beyond the amount of uninterrupted time spent on the job.

• *You have no time for yourself.* When you make decisions to do one thing, you automatically knock other things out of the running. People who love their work don't usually have this kind of resentment, so there's a good case for trying to move to a level of work that's compatible with your abilities and interests. If you enjoy your work but are overwhelmed by the sheer number of hours it demands, you may have to learn to be more strategic. (Read on!)

• *You are outpacing your boyfriend or husband.* The concern here is that the man will feel demeaned. If you haven't resolved this issue for yourself, you cannot help your mate resolve it. If you believe that your success in one area of your life—your career—makes you a superior person, you will contribute to any predisposition he might have to feel demeaned. You have to ask yourself if *you* have some inner need to establish your superiority. If you do, you will probably select the competitive arena in which you shine and establish that as the true measure of a person's worth and importance. If that's not the case—if you can shift away from that self-aggrandizing criteria—then you can respect people for their own unique qualities and achievements, and everyone around you, including your mate, will sense your respect. When you clearly communicate that career success is not your measure of a successful person, then you are not contributing to the problem, and the issue should diminish and may even dissolve.

You can always fantasize about how wonderful things would be if you weren't working—the grass is greener in the other pasture. It's easy enough to feel the pain of a present reality and fantasize the pleasures of a nonexistent one. What I've tried to do in the following pages is show you the clear and basic rewards of a career: that you can provide for your critical needs yourself, be your own person, and, ultimately, live a better life.

Chapter One

BLOCKS TO SUCCESS

CONTENTS

Introduction

1. The Morality Block
2. The Virginity Block
3. The Honesty Block
4. The Efficiency Block
5. The Play-It-by-the-Rules Block
6. The Put-Yourself-Down Block
7. The I-Have-Trouble-with-Authority-Figures Block
8. The Dependency Block
9. The Waiting Block
10. The Helplessness Block
11. The Work-Is-Like-Family Block
12. The Helpmate Block
13. The Modesty Block
14. The Security Block
15. The Competence Block
16. The Compliance/Aggression Block
17. The Perfection Block
18. The If-You-Can't-See-It, It-Isn't-Work Block
19. The Competition Block
20. The I-Hate-to-Fight Block
21. The Empathy Block
22. The Ambivalence Block
23. The Like-Me Block

INTRODUCTION

Women who work are well aware that they generally have a harder time of it than men. Not only do women often have to be better than men to get to the same place, but in addition, many working women seem to run up against difficulties, rough spots, and painful occurrences far more often than men do.

The problems women encounter in the workplace arise from three basic causes: first, from prejudice, which everyone knows about—but which does not always operate in ways you might think (more about that later); second, from women's unfamiliarity with how business works at higher levels—which results in some common female blind spots (as we shall see throughout this book); and third—the subject of this present chapter—from women's cultural conditioning and upbringing.

In all cultures, children are encouraged to enter into the activities and take on the personalities that will fit them for their ordained adult roles. They learn what is expected of them as they observe and imitate and listen to the people who take care of them. They also learn through the subtle approval and disapproval of their actions by those around them.

Although this process doesn't operate like a cookie factory, turning out perfect replicas with each press of the button, little girls, by and large, still grow up learning to be what the world around them hopes they will be—wives, mothers, and homemakers—and, by and large, they are discouraged from those activities that would better prepare them for a future in the workplace.

Although many girls these days are expected to have careers, it is nonetheless almost always with the hope that the future will bring them an easier and better life than they might be able to provide for themselves.

Thus, women are steeped in notions of "feminine" behavior patterns, mind-sets, and emotional expectations that are often irrelevant, inappropriate, and damaging to their own career interests. Such obstructive behavior patterns—or blocks—can prevent them from implementing the required solutions to their job problems.

I have run into dozens of these blocks over and over again through the years in my counseling work with women. But I've learned that once a woman becomes aware of the particular blocks that stand in her path, as well as why they exist, she is usually able to surmount them and move on to the solutions and strategies that her job problems require.

So before we get into the discussion of the solutions, tactics, and strategies that are at the heart of this book, we will examine together the major blocks that most commonly handicap women so that you can think about how they might apply to you—and what you, personally, can do about surmounting them.

These blocks are often closely related, but you'll find that each one focuses on a different aspect of behavior that stops women from realizing their full potential. To see how these blocks affect women's actual job situations, look at the listing of topics in Appendix B.

1. THE MORALITY BLOCK

Women tend to make moral judgments from a frame of reference that blocks their understanding of and movement in the workplace. They judge workplace practices using family and friendship values, putting human needs above all. But businesses and even social service agencies have another dynamic that must be, if not accepted, at least understood. Money, power, and growth constitute their bottom line. Before making moral judgments, career-oriented women need to understand, first, *how* the system works, and, second, *why* it works the way it does. It is not enough to stand aside and judge it. Women must develop leadership strength, assertiveness, and strategic ability—the very qualities we've been taught not to have—in order to influence the system, to change it, and to function professionally within it.

2. THE VIRGINITY BLOCK

Closely related to the Morality Block is the Virginity Block. Conditioned to play a "feminine" role of exaggerated innocence, women often feel compelled to express shock and disbelief at the ways of the business world. The need to display our spotless purity is a holdover from the days when women were cherished for their chastity and goodness. At work, this naive attitude —manifest in expressions of dismay—doesn't win respect, but rather cuts women off from sources of information. Responding with a nonjudgmental attitude will better serve women as they seek to learn the ways of the work world, after which they can evaluate those ways and decide when and when not to adapt to them.

3. THE HONESTY BLOCK

Women entering the work world often insist upon a high degree of openness in themselves and others. In addition, they understand the importance of being in touch with feelings and being able to express these feelings. Although candor and emotional honesty can be valuable assets in personal relations, "letting it all hang out" in a work setting can be unwise, inappropriate, and often damaging. In order to achieve their goals in the workplace, women need to be selective about the specific truths they reveal —and to choose their words wisely.

Not only must women learn to measure the effect of what they say and do, but they must also become sensitive to the value of business information. Since, in the past, women's discussions and ideas had little to do with whether money was made or lost, women tend to share ideas and information too easily. They are often less guarded than they need to be in the competitive arena of business. Being able to control your communications in a careful way—revealing only what you want to reveal—is not only necessary for self-protection, but also implies the ability to keep confidences, shows independence, and, ultimately, inspires trust.

4. THE EFFICIENCY BLOCK

Women often think that efficiency in business is based on some sort of flow chart that diagrams the shortest distance from A to B. Coming from the home, where they are both planners *and* doers, they have not had experience with getting things done through complex channels of power. While running the shortest course from A to B might be the ideal, it's rarely possible in business, where work gets done through an intricate set of relationships enmeshed in the realities of human quirks, resistances, skills, and lack of skills. But goals can be achieved by recognizing and working through these channels. It is not through the formal organizational chart that you get work done, but through the informal structures which you can influence—and can even set up yourself.

5. THE PLAY-IT-BY-THE-RULES BLOCK

In business, women tend to take the apparent rules literally, instead of grasping the often different set of principles by which work structures really operate. Men, who learn early in life that there are always two sets of rules—and when which apply—adapt more easily to living with both overt and covert rules. Trained for leadership, boys are encouraged to be autonomous and self-reliant. Defiant little boys who refuse to submit, who make their own rules, are admired for displaying courage, independence, and manliness. But girls, raised for a subordinate role, are applauded for being obedient, for following rules, for being respectful, for being "good." Women must break out of this prescribed mold and learn to evaluate the rules for themselves. Only then can they can become sensitive to the *real* rules of the game and learn to deal with the two levels of workplace reality.

6. THE PUT-YOURSELF-DOWN BLOCK

When something goes wrong, women, much more than men, tend to blame and criticize themselves. Even when things are going well, women consistently underrate their own abilities. They find it difficult to present themselves in the best light, feeling more "honest" when they share their self-doubts and self-criticisms with others. Honesty, for many women, takes the form of a self-deprecating statement. They have been so battered by the sexist messages in our culture that they have absorbed, at some deep level, the notion of their own inferiority. In "honestly" delivering negative statements about themselves, they are simply mirroring our society's disparaging view of women. This inner demoralization is one of the most subtle and insidious effects of sexism. When women say about themselves what their detractors say about them, the nefarious deed is done—the chauvinists have won the day. Women must move toward seeing their strengths and abilities more objectively so that they can present themselves authoritatively, in a manner that inspires confidence and commands respect.

7. THE I-HAVE-TROUBLE-WITH-AUTHORITY-FIGURES BLOCK

In the process of putting themselves down, women are often pushing others up. Women have internalized the prejudices of our society and, overly critical of themselves, they tend—just as erroneously—to idealize others. They see themselves as weak, and those in authority as powerful and strong. The less they believe in their ability to do things for themselves, the more they need to believe in the power of others to do things for them. But when *you* have so little power and *they* so much, they—the authorities—become awesome. They, not you, seem to have the power to alter your life. With so much at stake, some women are frightened into speechlessness, while others, enraged by the feeling that someone else has so much control over their future, lash out.

This unrealistic view of authority creates a major barrier for women: it prevents them from having the kind of productive, team relationships with higher-level people which are so necessary to moving ahead in business. When women realize that one source of their overreaction to authority stems from their having absorbed society's view of women as lesser creatures, they will be better able to see authority figures more realistically. And when women start seeing themselves as the major power in their own lives, they will no longer be intimidated by the power of others.

8. THE DEPENDENCY BLOCK

Women, taught to envision their fate in someone else's hands, often fail to take initiative in the workplace. They tend to see themselves as reporters of problems, not solvers of problems. They are likely to feel unable to do on their own what needs to be done—to make final decisions without consulting or getting the approval of a higher authority. This inability to rely on oneself, this need to lean on others, creates a serious obstacle that must be surmounted if a woman wants to move ahead at work. Its source lies in childhood: while everyone immediately recognizes the disastrous consequences of overprotecting a boy, girls are routinely pulled back to safety and the protection of the home. They arrive at adulthood without having had the opportunity to take the gradual steps toward independence that are necessary to becoming a self-reliant, self-sufficient adult. Women must learn to count on themselves, and as they do, they will begin to reap the considerable rewards of strength and autonomy.

9. THE WAITING BLOCK

Women who equate passivity with feminine desirability will often wait for things to happen rather than take steps to *make* them happen. Whatever they may aspire to, they're not about to make the first move, the first call, the first overture. Their resistance to taking aggressive action can amount to virtual paralysis at work, where very little gets done without a great deal of enterprise. While these women imagine that waiting is appropriate and will somehow get them ahead, just the opposite is true. By not pursuing opportunities, they only lose opportunities.

10. THE HELPLESSNESS BLOCK

When things go wrong at work, many women feel helpless. Surrounded as they are by the twin realities of male power and female powerlessness, they tend to see others as responsible for what has happened. But that gives the power to someone else, and at the same time robs you of your own resources. It stands in the way of figuring out what you can do to turn the situation around. Women must learn to take responsibility for whatever happens. They must avoid succumbing to the childlike feeling that things are out of their hands, and instead take advantage of every opportunity to develop and exercise their power. Even if the other person *is* fouling up, or the company *is* being unfair, or the boss *is* being stupid, it doesn't mean you are blocked from success. In fact, if you accept the challenge of setting things right, you may look very good in comparison.

11. THE WORK-IS-LIKE-FAMILY BLOCK

All too often, women hope to find approval and acceptance from a boss or a company that only a family can give. Traditionally oriented toward family relationships, women must learn a different level of relating on the job, both asking and giving different kinds of cooperation and support than are appropriate in a family situation. And if women expect too much, they typically give too much as well.

12. *THE HELPMATE BLOCK*

In the past, the female role—in business and in the family—has been to provide the support that helps *others* move to center stage. Women have played the subordinate to others' starring performances, the support role to their lead roles. Playing the traditional helpmate is a hard habit to break. Not only is it ingrained in us as the truly feminine way to be, but it is also part of a deal: I help you become successful, and you take the ultimate responsibility for my welfare. Many women, instead of focusing on what they can get out of the workplace, typically spend much of their energy looking for opportunities to give. Yet seeing themselves in this way—as givers, not takers; as helpers, not leaders—stops women from figuring out the real needs of a situation and how best to respond. It stops them from taking initiative and accepting responsibility. And it prevents them from doing what's best for themselves and for their own careers. To give up the support role means giving up the hope of getting support. It means learning how to support yourself. It means developing inner independence, and acting on it.

13. *THE MODESTY BLOCK*

While men often spend a good deal of energy placing themselves in positions of maximum visibility, women (as mentioned earlier) usually wait passively, just hoping to be noticed. They want credit for what they do and often feel resentful when someone else—their boss or their peers—gets it instead. But they feel immodest in calling attention to their achievements and therefore they often fail to communicate their competence. This tendency to stay in the background is a deeply ingrained part of women's cultural conditioning, and it prevents women from learning the all-important skills of self-promotion.

14. THE SECURITY BLOCK

Historically, women have opted for security. Responsible for the lives of others, yet not having their own fate in their own hands, they traditionally have faced risk and change with foreboding. Women today still don't have the full measure of confidence and courage that comes from exercising one's abilities to the utmost. As a result, they too often settle for modest positions they can count on, for jobs they can handle with ease, rather than setting their sights higher. Until women give up their preference for safe and clearly defined work situations, there is no possibility of their moving into or handling positions of real responsibility.

15. THE COMPETENCE BLOCK

Sometimes what gets in women's way is their own good work. Women are conscientious. They work long and hard at learning to be good at their jobs and at developing technical competence. What they are then surprised and angry to discover is that technical skill, while necessary, is not by itself rewarded with promotions. Deprived of the opportunity to learn about the world of business, women have been generally unaware that the higher one goes in the workplace, the more one's success depends on combining competence with political ability, a sense of strategy, and human relations skills. Women bitterly resent the painful discovery that instead of being rewarded for their competence, as they thought they would be, they have to start all over again. They have to master abilities that they know little about and that are difficult to learn. Women who wish to advance at work must overcome both their limited view of on-the-job competence as well as their anger at having been misled about the ground rules. They must get past their misperceptions about the value of competence by itself and the resentment that stands in the way of their reaching for new and broader kinds of competence.

16. THE COMPLIANCE/AGGRESSION BLOCK

Although most women today realize that they must break out of the compliant behavior patterns traditionally equated with femininity, many women are finding that this is easier said than done. Accustomed to going along with others' desires, some find it impossible to change their behavior.

Others may shed their compliant ways, only to move abruptly to aggressive behavior. Their pent-up anger shows through, and not only do they fail to get what they want, but they alienate others in the process. Then their secret belief that women's assertive behavior will be met with rejection is confirmed, and they collapse back into the safety of submissive behavior. But the reaction they've gotten is not due to their assertiveness, but to their hostile aggressiveness. Women must seek every opportunity to practice assertion, not only to get it right, but also to avoid building up explosive anger. Once they are able to be assertive, they will be able to make strategic decisions about being either assertive or aggressive or compliant, depending on the situation. Until you are able to assert, you don't have that choice.

Women must also understand that assertiveness is neither a masculine nor a feminine quality, but the characteristic of an effective human being. Assertive behavior is based on a true sense of equality, a respect for yourself as well as for others. It represents a self-assured, consistent statement of your position without the need to attack or denigrate the position of others. Asserting yourself while respecting others is a very good way to win respect yourself.

17. THE PERFECTION BLOCK

Many women demand perfection of themselves and of others at work. They edit every word, monitor every action in a time-consuming, inhibiting, and ultimately self-defeating effort to do things "just right." And when they are discovered to be less than perfect—when they are criticized—they take it hard. This striving for perfection is a natural reaction to the messages of a society that regards women as inferior. Left with the feeling that they have so little to offer, women put tremendous importance on doing things flawlessly. They see perfection as their only passport to success and status. Women must move toward accepting themselves as fully competent and reject—with every fiber of their being—any and all notions that they are inferior. When a woman really believes she is an equal human being with as much to offer as anyone else, then she can accept her flaws—and the flaws of those around her—as normal and natural, as the reality of life. And this, in turn, will free her from any counterproductive obsession with perfection.

18. *THE IF-YOU-CAN'T-SEE-IT, IT-ISN'T-WORK BLOCK*

Women tend to get anxious when work assignments don't yield visible re-sults, such as a specified number of papers written or projects completed. In the past, women's work has always been highly tangible; a woman's day was counted a success if the baby was cared for, the sheets folded, the dishes washed, the dinner on the table. Women were close to the product—they were front-line, hands-on doers. Thus, they often fail to perceive the importance of work that lacks that degree of concreteness. Yet the higher up one gets in the workplace, the further one gets from the actual product, from results that can be stacked and counted. For instance, while women tend to see the social side of work as wasting time, it may well be an essential aspect of the job. And to many women, leisurely think-time is suspect as well, though it may be the most productive—and ultimately, the most profitable—labor of all. Women must begin to rely on their ideas and their creativity—and when they begin to be valued for their thinking, they must let go of their anxiety over not producing visible, measurable achievement.

19. *THE COMPETITION BLOCK*

Women tend to withdraw from competition on the job, preferring instead to "just do my work." They are caught in a psychological no-win bind. When they see themselves as inadequate, they find competition too frightening; they back off for fear that they will lose, and that in losing they will expose their inadequacy. When they see themselves as strong, as having the advan-tage, they back off for fear that they will win, and that in winning they will humiliate their competitors. To become comfortable with competition, women must become less concerned about whether they win or lose. They must learn that competition in the best sense means playing the game—win *or* lose—and not abandoning the field to your rivals. It means developing the skills that will keep you in the running and that will give you the re-wards of your own development. The more you grow and strengthen, the less you will fear being done in—and the less likely you are to *be* done in. And when you win, remind yourself that you are not the cause of your com-petitor's problems. How competitors react—whether they are humiliated and angry, or philosophical and undaunted—has to do with the kind of people they are. If a competitor has potential and confidence, he or she will be able to see that there are many opportunities in this large world. And if you lose, the same applies to you.

20. THE I-HATE-TO-FIGHT BLOCK

If women find it difficult to compete, they find it even harder to fight. Taught that their very survival depends upon their being pleasant, soft, quiet, and approved of, women are uncomfortable challenging others. The images of the woman who argues—the bitch, the shrew, the harridan—are ugly and shrill, the very opposite of sweet femininity. To be unfeminine, we are taught, is to be totally undesirable, and thus we are intimidated and driven back into compliant silence.

Not only do women dread being seen as "bitches" or "shrews," but because they lack experience with arguing and fighting, they are frightened by anger. They fear the destructiveness of their own rage and they fear the retaliatory rage of others. They imagine their anger will be met with total rejection, or even actual physical abuse. While it's no wonder that women by and large continue to rely on agreeableness as their insurance policy, they must realize that being agreeable may in fact ensure failure at work. Being overly accommodating undermines the image of strength required for success in the workplace. Women have to start risking arguments. They have to learn how to fight. And they have to see that arguing—in appropriate ways and for the right issues—can win them respect and rewards.

21. THE EMPATHY BLOCK

Accustomed to relating to people on a purely personal level, women often get overly involved in the personal problems of those with whom they work. While it is critical for women to be responsive to their children's problems, that degree of responsiveness is misguided in the workplace. Women have to understand that their power to help someone in a work setting is limited. That is not to say that women should shut off their feelings for others: their ability to empathize with others is a quality to be valued. They do, however, have to be able to function objectively and effectively—something they will be better able to do if they accept the fact that they cannot always be the solution to other people's problems.

22. THE AMBIVALENCE BLOCK

While men understand that they are responsible for their own futures and must work for a living, many women feel that they have a choice. When the work is mundane or the rewards are small, when the going gets rough or the pressure grows, they dream of being rescued, of being able to withdraw to an easier life at home. Yet they know that life at home, while solving some problems, brings others—isolation, or boredom, or unfulfilled potential. Caught on this edge of ambivalence, women stop short of a full commitment to their work. They must understand that although staying home seems to offer welcome alternatives—autonomy, peace, protection, freedom—what seems to be a way out is actually a way into dependency. The idea of choice is an illusion. As mentioned earlier, women today can no longer pin their hopes for lifelong support and protection on a fragile bond to someone else's success and benevolence. They must be able to support themselves both financially and emotionally. And to do that, they have to make a firm commitment to work, and to confront and solve the problems that arise, rather than retreating to illusory dreams of the safety of the home.

23. THE LIKE-ME BLOCK

Too many women tend to gear their behavior in the workplace to the approval or disapproval of others. They seem to have an excessive need to be liked, to be approved of and loved—and this serves as a validation of themselves. They are, ipso facto, "worthwhile." Conversely, if they are disapproved of, disliked, unloved, then they are in the same measure "worthless." Thus, they tend to act as if accommodating others' wishes will bring sure approval and rewards, while asking for something or turning people down or inconveniencing them will result in disapproval and punishment. This is actually far from reality. True, you may not be liked at a given moment, depending on your action at that particular moment. But you are disliked or liked on the basis of the sum total of many things having to do with your many qualities—and as a result of other people's reactions to that totality.

Why is it that so many women have this like-me hang-up? I think it's because traditionally the entire unfolding of a woman's life depended on her being approved of by others. She lived in a truly small world, one with limited opportunities and unlimited prejudices. All too often, her only way to make a comfortable place for herself in this world depended on her winning the approval and affection of others.

Happily, the world has become a much larger place for women. It is time for us to get rid of the anachronistic feelings that used to help us get by, but today simply serve to limit and undermine us.

Now, with this understanding of the particular way in which women are raised, let's go on to analyze and solve typical problems that arise on the job.

Chapter Two

I'M HAVING TROUBLE WITH MY BOSS

CONTENTS

Introduction

INTRODUCTION

Troubles with the boss are not only the most common—and potentially hazardous—of work problems, but they also seem to be the most baffling to those who find themselves caught in this unhappy situation. Typically, what I find when someone comes to me with a "boss problem" is this: my client, the employee, has been working with commitment, integrity, creativity, loyalty, efficiency—all the qualities one would value most in a worker and, for that matter, in a human being. The boss, however, is growing more and more critical of her. He* doesn't seem to value these qualities; indeed, he seems to reject the best she has to offer. He may prevent her from getting information, or disregard her ideas, or fail to clarify his instructions, or use her time wastefully. Whatever form it takes, he's hindering her. She's trying everything in her power to do her job well—the very job he hired her to do—and he is not letting her function. She may even redouble her efforts to please him, but nothing helps. He continues to push her and her contributions aside, becoming more remote and less helpful. Usually, by the time she comes to me, she has decided the situation is hopeless. His behavior is irrational. She sees him as either threatened, or psychologically unbalanced, or incompetent, or sometimes all three. Her friends have advised her to move on, to go someplace where her good talents and energy will be appreciated.

At the same time, certain though she is of the boss's shortcomings, she doubts her own capabilities. Could the problem lie with her? Is she failing in some way? Is he responding negatively because of something *she's* doing wrong?

She swings back and forth on the question of who is to blame, sometimes making a strong case on her side ("Nobody can work with him! Nobody likes him.") and sometimes coming down hard on herself ("I don't

*As explained previously, we have made the boss male and the employee female throughout this book for the sake of clarity.

19

have the experience," "I'm not creative enough," "Maybe I should be doing more.").

.   This chapter is not designed to fix the blame, but to help you, through a better understanding of what has been happening and why, get out of the quandary you are in, and then to work out new strategies that address the real problems involved.

Of course, it's possible that your boss *is* impossible. You might indeed be well-advised to leave your job. But, on the other hand, if you become a clever strategist, he will become less difficult to deal with. A good strategist is not easily victimized, either by a tyrant or by a nincompoop. In fact, the more clever you are, and the more independent and politically astute you are, the more the boss's ineptitude or shortcomings can actually work to your advantage.

Asking you to compensate for your boss's shortcomings—if indeed that is what is wrong—may seem unreasonable. You may resent having to spend time and emotional energy dealing with his irrationality in order to give him the gift of your labor. But when you think about it, what's so unfair about asking you to become more clever, more independent, more politically astute? It's only unfair if you see him as the leader and yourself as instruction-taker. Of course, it is unfortunate that the boss is not responsive to your legitimate needs, but in any case, you're in no position to change him.

Once you stop demanding that the boss have qualities he doesn't have, you've taken a giant step toward solving your boss problems. The second step is to work around his shortcomings and develop those abilities that enable you to do your job with or without his help.

This idea is hard to accept if you see the taking of full responsibility as overwhelming. As seen in Chapter 1, women often have a difficult time believing that they can and should be their own main source of strength. This difficulty must be confronted head on.

You, yourself, must and can be the source of all solutions, as you will see in this chapter. Your problems are really *your* problems and must ultimately be solved by you. *You* have to decide when it's possible, practical, and politic to use the boss as a resource to solve a problem, and when to turn elsewhere. When you have that kind of independence, you won't be victimized by the boss's failings, real or imagined.

I have not taken up women bosses as a separate issue because the following chapter is mapped out to deal with categories of difficulties that any boss, male or female, may present—the angry boss, the threatened boss, the procrastinating boss, etc. You may find that in your experience, women bosses are more of one thing or another. More women, for example, may feel threatened by the people under them, or may keep too much control over their staff's work. A higher proportion of male bosses may be disorganized or undermining. While it's difficult to know whether the generalizations people often make about bosses represent stereotypical thinking or do indeed reflect reality, it does seem reasonable to assume that both men and women bosses would reflect the differences between men and women in general—differences that have to do with growing up in very different ways.

1. MY BOSS IS NOT AVAILABLE

Why a boss has time for some people but not for you • What can sour your relationship with your boss—and how to salvage it • How to make yourself invaluable • The reluctance to stick your neck out when you are uncertain • Getting your good ideas off the ground

"My boss is not available. I can't get in to see him, or when I do, he's on the phone or shuffling papers. He seems less and less interested in what I have to say." I hear this complaint constantly. Sometimes my clients will state it baldly, just as I've phrased it above. Or sometimes they'll use vaguer language, mention that the boss has been less communicative lately, or that he's been constantly tied up with important things and too busy to see them. There's often an element of *change* that I pick up when I listen to women who have this complaint. The boss listened *once*. He *used* to communicate; *at first,* he was accessible.

Clearly what has happened is that the employee, hired in the best of faith and high hopes, has disappointed or dissatisfied the boss, and as a result he has begun withdrawing his attention.

Most of the time what has occurred is that the employee has been using the boss's time in a way that is unproductive or unpleasant—from the boss's point of view. She's been asking too many questions, seeking too much guidance, or interrupting at the wrong times with the wrong issues stated in an unclear way. From the employee's point of view, there are good reasons for her behavior. After all, there's a job she's supposed to be doing, and certainly the boss is the only one who can tell her what he wants. But to the boss's mind, she's wasting his precious time. He hired her to save him time and effort. Instead, she keeps over-involving him. She isn't taking his problems away, she's adding to them.

If you're having difficulties with an inaccessible or increasingly unresponsive boss, the way to improve the situation is to make him view time spent with you as a worthwhile investment for him. Try to show him that when he spends time with you, it pays off because ultimately it *saves* time for him. It may be that he uses his time badly, and your time is exceptionally well-spent. But that's not the point: we're looking at the situation as *he* sees it.

Start by saving his energy, even if accomplishing this means expending more of your own. Efficiency is not the name of the game, not when it takes *his* energy to save yours. He doesn't see the value of your efforts as equal to his, whether they are or not. He'll invest some effort, but he wants a big return. If he doesn't get it, your relationship will falter. So don't go into your boss's office and say, "What are the priorities this morning?" or, "How should I take care of this?" Go in and say, "I did this," or, "Today I'm calling and telling X we've reached our decision and how we would like him to proceed." Use your meetings with your boss to deliver reports of decisions and accomplishments. Don't ask him to do your thinking. Instead, *report* your thinking. (He'll let you know if he differs.) And don't ask him for information that you can get from others, even if he happens to be the handiest or the most experienced person around. By keeping informed through other channels, you'll protect your image of being bright and on top of things. Elementary questions, after all, are neither impressive nor interesting.

Sometimes an employee isn't even aware that she's creating time burdens and boring interactions for her supervisor.

Kathleen's Story

One of my clients, a researcher working for a scientific foundation, got on well with her boss at first, but after a few months she began to feel overlooked and ignored. Her job was to help her boss choose projects the foundation might do well to support, and then get in touch with the project directors, suggesting the foundation's interest and asking them for more detailed information. The first part of her job—writing up thoughtful, extensive reports for her boss that thoroughly described various appropriate projects—went very well. But after she'd been on the job a few months,

Kathleen realized she was having more and more trouble accomplishing the second part of her assignment—getting in touch with project directors. Her boss had ceased listening to her, had stopped responding to her reports with specific instructions about which projects to pursue. Indeed, her weekly reports were piling up on a bookshelf behind his desk.

I asked Kathleen some careful questions about how she was writing up her reports. It turned out she would list and then describe in no particular order the projects she was recommending. "Here is a memo on some exciting new projects," she'd write on top. "Which shall I get going on?"

No wonder her boss didn't get back to her! He had to read through dozens of pages in which only undigested information, never any opinion or judgment, was presented. Rather than doing work for him, my client was actually giving him extra work—and difficult, demanding work at that. Not only was she alienating the boss by doing this, but, as women often do, she was abdicating the most hazardous part of her job: making decisions which were central to the agency's function—as opposed to the less risky, fact-gathering aspects of the job on which she had been concentrating her efforts. *She avoided the judgment part of the job because it was risky, but then her boss avoided her and her cumbersome reports.*

I pointed out to Kathleen that what she could do was make her own choices, then indicate these and her reasoning at the start of her weekly report. She could begin by saying that, while she was providing information on, say, ten new projects they might support, she herself favored number one or number eight, and why. Did he agree? Should she pursue these two? Armed with all her research, *she* was the one who was intimately acquainted with the projects. She could think the matter through, make a judgment, and present her recommendations, building a logical case for them and laying out the information clearly and simply. The chances were that he would respond. All that would be required of him would be to follow her logic and see if he agreed or disagreed. "Here's what I think we should do and why" is easier to respond to than "What should I do?"

Her boss needed time for his own responsibilities—that was what he'd hoped to gain when he'd hired her. He trusted her judgment, or he'd never have given her the job. What he'd wanted was her ability to evaluate and offer opinions, not merely her ability to gather facts.

Soon after we discussed the situation, Kathleen started making her reports in the fashion I advised. And shortly afterward, her boss was promptly answering her memos and reports. He'd put a check next to her "I favor number eight," and write tersely, "Go ahead!" Or else he'd note,

"Not innovative. This was done in California two years ago." Whether he approved or disapproved of her suggestions, he was getting back to her quickly now. He had moved from avoidance to responsiveness, sometimes even meeting with her to thrash out the decision. She'd made her input worthwhile. Now their meetings paid off for him.

So before you write off the boss's availability, ask yourself:

- Do you ask your boss a lot of questions?
- Could you have gotten answers to your questions yourself?
- When you meet with your boss, are the problems you present so complex that he has to take a great deal of time to figure them out? Or do you present problems simply?
- Do you simplify his decision-making by offering appropriate and valid suggestions?
- Have you taken the problems as far as you can? Or are you afraid to risk giving an opinion or making a judgment?
- Do you accomplish a lot in a small amount of time when you meet with him?
- Do you leave him more informed after a meeting with you than he was when the meeting began?
- Does your boss shift topics? Is he more concerned about issues other than the ones you bring up? Are your priorities his priorities?

If time spent with you pays off for your boss, you can count on his reappearing. *A boss always finds time for the most valuable people on his staff.*

2. MY BOSS DOESN'T GIVE ME DIRECTION

The key step in moving from an assistant position to a directing position • How to initiate your own projects

Unless you were hired to do routine work, your chief value lies in the extent of your ability to direct yourself. If you want to advance your career, you have to be able to take initiative, and learning how to do that begins here, with the solution to this problem.

Since society has not traditionally viewed women as leaders, women resist seeing themselves in that role. Some of us even have problems in leading ourselves. We look to other people to structure our work; we pull at the boss for more direction. A woman who recognizes herself in this description has a serious problem that must be overcome if she wants to move up into a managerial position. Indeed, the most difficult transition for a woman is the move from an assisting position to a directing position.

To me, the complaint that the boss doesn't give you enough direction seems misguided—you couldn't have a better opportunity. Your basic training for the role of full responsibility is learning how to direct yourself in any situation. You need a go-ahead from your boss for your selected course of action, but that's *all* you need. You've got to go full steam on your own. This doesn't mean acting without regard for the boss's thinking, but it does mean you must not be dependent. If you don't like doing things this way, that is your problem, not his. If you think he's not cooperating, figure out what to do next as if you were the boss.

Cynthia's Story

Cynthia's boss said, ''Maybe you should be working on the Steiner account.'' He mentioned that Mme X, the head of the European division, was planning a trip to America. Cynthia was a junior account executive in a high-powered public relations firm, and this assignment represented a good chance for her to show her stuff. She knew that she could use Mme X—a very dynamic, attractive, and articulate woman—to get important attention for their product. Time passed, however, and nothing more was said about Mme X's trip. Cynthia began to worry that it had fallen through—and with it, her chance to make a splash for her product and herself. I suggested that instead of sitting and waiting, Cynthia should go ahead on her own and do what she could to make the trip happen. She should decide when, in her judgment, the best time for the trip would be, how long it would take to set up a schedule, how urgent the need was, etc. It was a new way of working for her, but she went ahead, thought it through and then phoned Mme X in Europe and persuaded her to come, describing the need, suggesting the best time, and detailing what her visit would accomplish. *Cynthia* made the project a reality; she didn't need her boss's direction.

As a precaution, just before she made the call to Europe, Cynthia checked out her plan with her boss—not to ask his permission, but to give him a chance to veto her ideas if he disagreed.

This is what is meant by those newspaper ads that advertise: "Wanted: Self-starter with initiative." And it's precisely this quality that bosses fear women don't have. You have to prove you can get going—and keep going—on your own if you want to make the transition to a full directing position.

But, you may ask, what's the boss there for? Isn't giving direction his job? Not necessarily. The "hands off" boss expects you to understand and implement policy. He expects you to achieve your goals without subtracting time from his work. Those who are not able to do this will lose out. He'll promote the people who can.

If you do happen to have a nondirective boss, don't resent him. Instead, take the opportunity to practice self-direction for your next job.

3. *MY BOSS DOESN'T TEACH ME A THING*

Why a boss leaves you on your own • When it doesn't pay to express dissatisfaction • How the idealized family model interferes with a woman's initiative • How to learn what you need to know to get the job done • How—and when—to get your boss involved in your education

The teaching aspect of a boss's role is usually limited to a few words here and there. If you seem to need much more than that, the boss will most likely avoid you. When you start your job, he'll probably show you around, make some general remarks about the work, respond willingly to a few well-considered questions, and then hope to be finished with you, at least until he's sure you're good enough on the job to warrant his taking out time from his own day to acquaint you with the more intricate aspects of the company, the field, or your own position.

An experienced manager teaches slowly, and only after he's determined that someone is worth the investment. He'll ask himself, "Can she produce? Will she stay with the company? Should I bother spending time showing her the best ways to do things when I'm not yet sure if I really like and respect her?'' He won't be interested in teaching an employee more than the basics until he's made up his mind about these questions.

It's a Catch-22 situation, since very often an employee feels that she can't produce, or do the job properly, unless the boss starts explaining things. If this is your problem, you may feel embittered, or even hopelessly lost. But if your boss senses this, he'll react negatively to you, and perhaps even conclude that he doesn't like you, or that he needs someone with more knowledge or initiative than you seem to have. He'll decide not to invest time in training you, but instead will look for someone better to replace you.

There are underlying factors involved here. It seems to me that the dilemma you are involved in flows from the fact that girls growing up were encouraged to stay close to home. Their lives were circumscribed by the family. The larger world was presented to them as both more frightening and less accessible than it was to men. So women as adults made virtually all their demands on those who were part of their small household world— their lovers, husbands, and children. But things are different today. Women are no longer expected to be timid about the world outside the home, and the outside world is an increasingly available resource. Yet in some ways, when a woman feels hopeless and helpless because her boss isn't giving her enough information to do her job, she's falling back on the old nuclear family model of relationships. She's being fearful of the larger world, or thinking it's inaccessible, and hoping a nearby man—in this case her boss—will satisfy all her needs. But the nuclear family was never a particularly appropriate model for the workplace, and it is less so as women move beyond the office wife role.

Therefore, if the boss does not fill in your knowledge gap, find out how to do the job for which you were hired without asking him for help and without letting him know how confused you feel. If you can't use him as a resource, move quickly to find another. Build business relationships near and far. Develop a network of people who can fill you in. You may need to invest time and money in this process—you may need to hire experts, or take courses or even private lessons in time management, organization, speech writing, editing, accounting, physics, whatever it is you must know to do your job well. Use *every* resource you can think of. The more worldly you are, the more you'll be able to pare down the questions you'll have to ask your boss. He'll then know that you're a person who learns a lot and learns it fast—just what he's been waiting to see before investing his training time.

4. MY BOSS DOESN'T UNDERSTAND MY WORK

How bosses survive without knowing anything • How the nature of the work changes as you move up • More ways to look good • How to deal with a boss who expects too much work in too little time • The bottom-line argument

When people say this to me, my first thought is: why should he? As you see it, when you need help, he's the logical person to ask for it. But people can't give you what they don't have, and it's quite common for bosses not to have a clear understanding of how certain chores or responsibilities in their own departments are performed. They are either out of touch with the actual performance details or were never involved with them. Chances are you know this, and what you're really saying is that a boss *should* understand the job. But again, why should he? The belief that he should stems from your own unfamiliarity with how management works. It is a common female blind spot that results from the fact that far too few women have achieved middle- and upper-management positions. Many simply don't know how such positions work—but they do know, from experience, that supervisors in lower echelons are selected directly from the ranks and have intimate experience and excellent performance records with the details of company operations. Actually, the higher you go, the less you need to know about operational details.

Not only does a boss not have to understand your job, but chances are he'd appreciate your not telling him too much about it. He's counting on you to understand it, and to give him only the wrap-up he needs. It's true that he makes decisions about it—he tells you what to proceed on, as well as what to neglect or soft-pedal—but he absorbs just what he needs to know in order to make those judgments. So if his decisions are off the mark, then and only then should you attempt to "explain" your job to him. And even then, you should avoid getting down to nitty-gritties.

This is a challenge, but it can be accomplished if you think of your task as being like that of acquainting a shareholder with a company's year-long activities through the presentation of a three-page brochure. Keeping it simple will not only please your boss, but will also upgrade your skills as a communicator and clarifier.

Let me give you an example. I've had several clients who have complained, "My boss doesn't understand my job, and he wants me to do it in one-third the time it actually takes." I've always suggested to my clients that, rather than spell out to their bosses the exact tasks that fill their hours, they should talk about the end results of their activities. For example, if the boss objects to the length of time you spend on the telephone with clients, you might say something like, "I talk to each client an average of twice a week. That's thirty-four minutes per client. But our billings are running $17,000. As I see it, that's a worthwhile investment. The clients are happy; they're sticking with me; there's very little turnover."

If the end results are impressive, your boss usually won't press you about your methods.

5. THE BETTER I AM, THE MORE WORK MY BOSS PILES ON

When you're doing too much • The need to feel needed • Evaluating your own performance • How to say no without getting fired • When it's to your advantage *not* to refuse work • Moving up by doing more

Most bosses, under pressure themselves, are ready to take advantage of the woman who can't say no. It's a common problem: women typically find it difficult to say no to a boss. They're afraid they'll lose the boss's admiration, or even lose their jobs. While that may happen, it's more likely that women who can't say no are underestimating their own value, and thus, in over-giving, are in fact selling themselves short.

Here's a classic situation: you perform well; the boss appreciates you and gives you more work. You're flattered and you feel needed. (Your boss may be playing on your need to be flattered, or your need to be needed.) You do the new work happily. Now the boss can't get along without you— you're indispensable. And you believe you're valued because you always say yes. Now you think your job is secure only if you continue this pattern. At this point, if you take a stab at turning down extra work, and your refusal is met with disapproval, your belief is set in cement.

It shouldn't be. If your work is valuable, and your relationship with your boss is good, the risk of turning down extra work is small. If you believe in your value, you won't panic at the thought of negotiating your own needs. It's only if you feel you're easily replaceable that you'll overdo things. Of course, it's hard for women to have confidence, since their contributions have so often been devalued, but you must learn to be objective about your strengths and to avoid accommodating every request.

In order to evaluate the real risks of refusing work, you need to be in touch with your uniqueness. You probably have many thoughts about yourself—some in direct conflict. You may feel that you're not very special—if you turn the boss down he'll find someone else—and at the same time feel that you really do an exceptional job, that there's no one quite like you.

Think the two attitudes through. Try to evaluate clearly your contributions, and the quality and quantity of your work. Then you're ready to negotiate your situation.

When you're clear about your value, and you're ready to say no to extra work, be sure to present your objections in terms of *loss of productivity for the boss*. Don't say, "With all this extra work, I have no time for my family." The boss won't care. He can't afford to—the pressure of his position pushes against his humanitarian impulses. Do say, "I will take on these new duties, but project X will be delayed. We won't be able to recoup our expenditures until I have time to do the follow-ups." You can use your own need for relaxation *if* you present it as it relates to his needs: "I need to relax fully in order to produce fully. One reason I get so much done is my ability to concentrate totally. I work hard and I play hard. I don't waste time on the job, because I meet my other needs in the same concentrated way after work." By providing these arguments against taking on more and more and more work, you're reminding him of the value of your contributions—and you're positioning yourself as cooperative, but not a cooperative slave.

Of course, you have another choice, too. If you can learn something from the new work, do it. You can use the situation to develop new skills and/or the importance of your role. If your boss is increasing your responsibilities, you are, in effect, being promoted. The extra work gives you a toehold on the next rung of the ladder. Your first move is to find ways to get rid of the work that doesn't help your case, but if you have to do the old *and* the new, do that, too, for a while. Then capitalize on your expanded responsibilities by consolidating your position with a new title and matching salary. One way to move up is to over-give and then collect the debt—but don't forget to collect! Don't just let yourself be exploited. Let the boss know you can do it all, but that it works against his interests if you're *stuck* with it all. As you prove your efficiency, use that efficiency to indicate your value, and to demand more staff under you and more money in your paycheck.

6. MY BOSS CAN'T DELEGATE RESPONSIBILITIES

How to change his view of you • Four reasons your boss won't share the work • How to get the good assignments by teaming with your boss instead of competing • Telephone protocol

There are several reasons why a boss, even a very busy one, won't delegate responsibilities to employees. Before you can decide what strategies to use to get more work, you have to figure out what the boss's motivation for denying it to you is. Maybe he doesn't have confidence in people, or women, or you—or even himself. If he doesn't have confidence in himself, he might hoard work to prevent competition. If he lacks confidence in women, you'll have to prove you're one in a million (that's how the chauvinist sees female talent: as the exception to the rule). To do this, you may have to overcome his view of you as a go-fer instead of a charge-taker.

But whether your boss lacks confidence in women in general or *you* in particular, you've got to find a way of letting him know that you can function independently. He may see you as a good follower, but one who needs a lot of direction. You've got to show him you're on the ball. And you've got to instill this idea in his mind frequently. Tell him you've checked the statistics on such-and-such, and that you've contacted so-and-so. Tell him you'll be reviewing the forms that are coming up for the meeting six days from now. Show him you're on top of every problem he's already handed over, and anticipate the problems he hasn't thought of. People won't know that you can take full responsibility until you demonstrate it. Take note of the times your boss trips you up or beats you to the punch. Each time that happens, he wonders if you can handle things on your own.

Now, let's say he's holding on to the tasks because he sees this as the only way to hold on to his job. His department is standing still, or just not growing, and he doesn't want to delegate himself out of a job. Even in this case, there are strategies you can employ. For example, work on ideas to broaden the scope of his division's activities. Create more room for both of you.

Still, it may be that the boss knows you can do a good job, and his job is not threatened. Nevertheless, he doesn't turn tasks over to you. There are many valid business reasons for this seemingly mystifying behavior, among them:

- There's a better chance of a successful outcome if your boss does the job himself.
- The boss knows that some business contacts will be offended if the highest-ranking person doesn't deal with them.
- The boss wants to do the things he enjoys doing.
- He wants to do the prestige jobs—the tasks that elevate his status, his position in the field, or his position with his own management.

I had a client whose job was to obtain book excerpts for a major magazine. Her boss, the editor-in-chief, was rarely concerned with which books she requested for examination from agents and publishers, as he trusted her judgment entirely. But every once in a while he'd snatch the job back. He himself would make a phone call and contact an agent or publisher, asking to see a certain book himself. Often it was a book the excerpt editor was herself planning to request, and she felt miffed by his intrusion into her domain.

I asked my client what the books the editor-in-chief personally tracked down had in common. It turned out that invariably they were written by exceedingly famous authors. I pointed out to my client that there were probably two reasons her boss got into her act from time to time: either the deal was too big or too important to risk, or there was a certain prestige or interest in his having the opportunity to talk personally with a famous author.

What can an employee do in a situation like this? Actually, she can gain from it, if she understands that the boss's interference is flattering—an indication of the importance of her work. I would try to work as a team with the boss, long before he could snatch the big deal away from me. Instead of trying to hoard the work—competing with him and resenting his intrusion —I'd invite him in at the appropriate stage of the negotiations. I'd suggest that *he* make the necessary calls, or ask if he'd *like* to make the calls. The more on target I am, the more I clue the boss in, the more I invite him in at the appropriate moment, the more likely it is that he will reciprocate by including me, by giving me information and inviting me in and keeping me in at every stage of the deal.

In every field there are glamour or snob appeal tasks, and it's a mistake for an assistant not to recognize this. Then, too, there's a hidden protocol in every field—who talks to whom is very important. For example, I know that on occasion an assistant of mine has been miffed when I've made my own phone calls to set up appointments with people in top management, since usually she sets up appointments for me. But I also know that, trivial as it may seem, the president of a major corporation might be offended if I had an assistant telephone him instead of talking with him myself. My reason for doing this task myself is not to take work away from my assistant, or to experience a brush with glamour, but to observe protocol and to avoid offending an important contact.

7. MY BOSS UNDERMINES MY AUTHORITY AND DOESN'T BACK ME UP

Keeping your authority intact • Strategies to get the boss to team with you instead of working around you • When your staff bypasses you • What to do when a client goes over your head

This can do you in fast. As soon as people see you're not the real decision-maker, that you don't have influence or power no matter what your title, they'll stop listening to you. The problem snowballs. Your boss sees that people don't respond to you, and so feels compelled to intervene further.

Why would the boss be party to a process that makes you ineffectual and makes more demands on him? There could be many reasons, from thoughtlessness to a compliant nature, from an unconscious need to control to a calculated move to hold on to the reins. If your boss actively encourages people to come directly to him, he's squeezing you out. This is the way he keeps himself a general—and you a private. But maybe his reasons for not supporting you have nothing to do with you, or are not calculating at all. Often overlooked are the commonplace reasons: he's just gotten some new information that has made him see the issues in a new light, or maybe he routinely bends under the pressure of the latest argument he's heard, or perhaps he's come up with a new or better idea.

Maybe he's just forgotten to let you know. If it happens once in a while, you can let it go by, but watch out—it's critical to maintain direct authority.

Even if you are able to see why the boss changed his mind, he may put you in an embarrassing position in relation to others in your company or industry. His reasons for not supporting you may be perfectly innocent, but he still causes you trouble. You have a lot at stake in having your decisions respected, and when they're overthrown your influence is threatened. When a boss interferes with your authority, whatever the reason, it undermines that authority. He has made your word unreliable.

Although it may sound impossible, you need to control your boss. You need to find strategies that will align him with you as an authoritative team, thereby controlling his impulse to bypass—and thus diminish—you.

Linda's Story

Linda, a project director for a computer software house, would give her client companies the number of hours they had contracted for and, for the sake of good client relations, would even throw in some extra hours of consulting time. When her boss objected to the extra hours she gave away, she stopped being so generous. Yet when clients raged to the boss about kinks in the system and asked him for more free time from Linda, he always knuckled under. So, of course, the clients began to go over Linda's head. Her new strategy is to continue offering clients the gift of a few extra hours, but now she makes it clear that this is a favor that she has the power to give, and that additional hours on any unresolved problems will have to be paid for. When a job draws to a close and a client begins to make special requests, she goes right to her boss—to explain her proposed gift and its limits, and to tell him of the appeal that the client will predictably make for extended time. But instead of criticizing the client for pressuring her for free time, she builds up his case. By putting it in the most favorable light, she's stepping in on the client's side. She explains how dissatisfied the client is. She describes the unrealistic promises the sales department had made in order to lure the client into the deal. Together, she and her boss, as a working team, decide what to do, hashing out the pros and cons. If the answer is no, Linda tells the client. At the same time, the boss is well-armed to back up her refusal. He is no longer vulnerable to the client's best arguments because he's already heard them from Linda. If her boss agrees to the concession, she presents the good news as a valuable favor that she has the authority to give or to withhold.

If you want to prepare the boss to back you up, here's the strategy to use: *always pass along your opponent's best arguments.* If you don't, if you present his case weakly or in a bad light, of course your boss will understand your point of view—but then, when your adversary presents his strong arguments, your boss will be impressed and back up your adversary instead of you. That's how you are party to the undermining of your own authority.

Here is another course of action you can use when your boss reverses your decisions. This one is for situations in which the boss weakens your control over those who work under you. Tell your staff that they *must* work directly through you, that you have an open door for their problems, but that you won't tolerate having them impose on your boss's time. Follow up all infractions. If either anyone working for you or your boss crashes your rule, never let it slip by. Speak to them quickly, reminding them of the appropriate avenues for dissent. But be sure you've made out a very strong case ahead of time with your boss for this position.

Your strong argument should be that if others see the boss as a court of appeal, they'll be in his office every minute. And when they're not actually in his office, they'll still ignore you, and thus the work will suffer. You've got to remind your boss that this is a critical issue, and that if he wants you to take responsibility, he has to support your authority. Suggest that he refer people to you, and that if he then wants to discuss the situation, he speak to you privately. Show him how that's the only way you can get your job done.

And if the whole problem is caused by doubts about a woman's ability to establish authority, your very insistence will help him resolve those doubts.

8. MY BOSS IS THREATENED BY ME

How to recognize when he's really threatened • How and when to
minimize the threat • If you do want to depose him

This is a commonly heard explanation for a deteriorating relationship,
but it is not always a correct explanation. People often feel that when the
boss hoards information and responsibilities, he's afraid of competition—
afraid that they're learning too much too fast, that they're making him look
bad, that they might even get his job. Maybe so, but it could be the opposite: he's not confident they can do the job at all—they require too much
direction or instruction. Or he's sized them up as limited—not worth the
trouble.

How can you tell if the boss feels threatened by you, or the opposite—
lacks confidence in you? How can you tell whether he feels you're too good
or you're not good enough?

In part it depends on the boss's background and experience. It's unlikely he feels threatened if he has technical skills that you don't possess, or
if he's functioning in different territories. For example, even if you outpace
him at actual tasks, if he has the political contacts that get the contracts,
he'll feel secure.

But if your skills and abilities are almost as good as his, or if you have
even more to offer than he does, or if his political connections are bad, or
his performance is slipping, or he's frightened or paranoid, it's possible he
will feel threatened. He'll want you to do well on his behalf—in fact he'll
need you all the more—but if he's afraid you'll show him up, he might
solve his problem by excluding you. If you want to minimize the competitiveness, remember that, for the most part, bosses don't feel threatened by
the excellence of their staff members as long as the staff teams with the boss
in such a way that *he* gets credit for their good performance. It's only when
he sees his staff as competing for credit that he'll move against them. So
if you think your boss feels threatened by you, examine your own behavior.

It's possible that instead of throwing your lot in with his, and hoping to
progress as a team, you have a secret agenda. It's possible that although
you're working with him and for him right now, you're hoping that very
soon you'll be someplace else—in his place, or even above him—so you're
not giving your boss your ideas. You're not working *through* him but are

trying to get credit in order to make yourself more visible to his bosses or to people outside the company.

If this is so, then yes, it's quite likely that your boss senses your defection, and astutely perceives a real threat. If you do want to depose your boss, be cautious. If you see him as a loser and can't work creatively with him, don't tip him off to your competitiveness. If, for example, you want to withhold an idea—do it in a way that he can't suspect. If you want to be visible to your boss's boss, do it carefully or you'll be boxed out before you have your chance to box out your boss.

9. MY BOSS EXCLUDES ME FROM MEETINGS AND INFORMATION

Meeting protocol • Business secrets • Why exclusion is a greater problem for women than for men • How expressing your moral judgments and human empathy can cut you off in the workplace • Ways to get yourself included

You know you could function better if you had more information. You want to learn more so you can do more. What could make more sense than that? But this isn't the way the boss views the situation. He's worried about cost. He's weighing up the expense of sending an employee around to meetings against the price of losing her labor on daily chores. Or else he's perfectly happy with having her do exactly what she's doing now, and never learning or doing anything more. Probably nothing will change unless she can point out an advantage to him in her becoming more familiar with the inner workings of their company or industry, or more conversant with the broader considerations of various issues.

If you're having this problem, you should work up a good case for your boss which shows why you should be at meetings. The case must be put so that he sees how *he* would benefit, not how *you* will benefit. You can't say, "I want to go to that meeting so I can learn more."

Spell out how your learning will benefit the boss. Say, "If I attend the vice president's strategy sessions, and get an early fix on our approach to the client's problems, I can begin drafting proposals immediately. It will save time. It will also save the vice president's time—he won't have to have special meetings to fill me in, and I will have a better understanding of the decisions. The quality of the proposals will improve."

Even so, he still may not want you present at the meetings. People want, like tennis players, to play with better players. Unless the boss sees you as a valuable contributor, he'll worry that too much time will be wasted listening to, or explaining to, the uninformed, and that there'll be too many oars in the water. But also important (and, more important to some), there's a certain status about meetings. If everyone gets to go, then the status is lost. The boss, much as he may see advantages to himself in having you present, may nevertheless have to deny your wish in this status-conscious society, because if you get invited, his higher-level peers may feel offended.

And there are other reasons you may be excluded. While the more you know about a situation, the better the job you can do, there are situations in which a boss quite properly has information that he doesn't want to share with you. In corporate settings, this is often because the best way to deal with difficulties is precisely that: not talking about them. The very process of airing things changes subtle political issues. In addition, certain business secrets, like those having to do with contracts and prices, are best known by the fewest people.

Of course, this secretive air in business can be particularly hurtful to women, who are often excluded *because* they're women and therefore considered not trustworthy or too naive. Men believe that women place moral and human considerations above business issues, that women are not as "tough" as they are. Well, they're sometimes right, and if you want to be included, you will have to be careful about when and how you apply moral judgments. If your boss thinks you're judging him negatively because you feel morally superior, he will not want you at meetings. Self-righteous critics are not welcome.

One of my clients ran into such a situation when her boss confided in her that in order to sell a customer on his company's capabilities, he had taken credit for work done by another company. My client was inwardly shocked, but she didn't say a word. Her boss viewed his outright lie, his grabbing credit for work his company didn't even do, as a clever trick, while she saw it as a dirty trick. But if she had reacted with the shock she felt, she would have cut off her pipeline of valuable information.

Here's a tip: if you are a storehouse of information, if you take the time to bone up on things, if you try to anticipate developments and stay on top of everything, then people will *want* you to come to meetings.

And another tip: practice speaking so that people will want to hear what you have to say. If you can present information clearly and simply—with a pointed story here and an amusing twist there—people will *want* to listen to you.

10. MY BOSS PROCRASTINATES AND WON'T MAKE DECISIONS

Why your boss procrastinates • The wisdom of delayed action • How to move your boss along • When to take the initiative yourself

You do your work thoroughly and quickly, you're on the ball, and yet the work winds up sitting endlessly on the boss's desk. Your colleagues are pressuring you. The client, the supplier, *everyone* is pressing you with deadlines. But the boss brushes you aside.

It's possible that the boss procrastinates in getting back to you—in letting you know how or when or on what to proceed—because you haven't made the choices simple and clear enough for him to be able to shoot back an answer without much effort. But sometimes you've been doing things just right, writing memos to which he can respond succinctly and quickly, getting your details from others, coming to him only for his comments or final approval. Yet, still he delays. Or doesn't respond.

Why? Why do bosses procrastinate? The most common reason is fear: the boss is *afraid* of making a decision. He has learned to survive by not sticking his neck out. Indeed, he may pay a big price if he does. So he chooses inaction.

What should you do? Your position is untenable: you can't get him to move, yet you're being judged on *results*.

First of all, you need to stop being critical of his seeming cowardice and try to determine the dangers he apparently perceives. What are they? What exactly are the repercussions that worry him? See if you can figure them out. Become the kind of person who obsessively explores all the possible dire consequences of a particular move and let him see that you're not pushing blindly ahead, heedless of the dangers he worries about. When you report to him, indicate that you've thought through the possible dire consequences of a decision, balancing them against the consequences of inaction. ''The system is not as streamlined as it could be, and the field staff will grumble about extra paperwork. Still, I think it's more important to get the new system installed. Top management is beginning to look at the costs of the delays.''

He is frozen by fear. You must counteract this and resolve his doubts as you've resolved your own—through reason. You'll not only be getting him to move ahead, you'll also be giving him a good role model—*you*—as well as a way to sell the proposal to his boss, just as you're selling it to him.

What about the procrastinating boss who eventually makes decisions but habitually does so at the last possible minute?

Women have traditionally been locked into the narrow sphere of implementing other people's decisions, and have consequently learned to pride themselves on their speed, efficiency, and accuracy. As a result, they tend to be intolerant of procrastination. They view delaying as the result of laziness or neurosis, and their perception of a boss's procrastination has a moralistic ring: "I'm a planner; he does everything at the last minute.''

There can be value, however, in waiting until the last minute to make a decision, and wisdom in using all the time available to gather thoughts, opinions, and information. When you're dealing with complex problems, it takes time to weigh all the pros and cons. Decision-making is not an organized process—new thoughts keep coming, stimulated by the environment in which one works. The procrastinating boss may not be as foolish as he at first appears to be!

There are other explanations for procrastination. Maybe the boss has priorities, and you're not catching on to them; all you see is your own territory. Or he's juggling a number of projects, trying to select the most important ones. Often procrastinators start a project (to see how things shape up) and stop (things don't look so good), and pursue a variety of projects before they settle on a winner.

Some procrastinators are faced with *your* problem: someone higher up in the hierarchy is a habitual procrastinator. Or—the best of all possible reasons for procrastination—they know that in time the problem or the project might disappear. Many people accustomed to having a desk full of papers realize that once in a while things happen without their having to do anything, because time itself will cause projects to be scrapped, problems to be solved.

And there are even more reasons for procrastination. Your boss may be overly identified with his product, his work. He may have the you-are-your-product syndrome. It's common. Many people procrastinate because their work is never good enough to reflect their view of themselves. They're overly involved in how people see them, and everything they do has to enhance their image. They live with the fear that if the product is not first-rate, people will think that *they* are not first-rate. The procrastinator finds that thought intolerable. He's not so much afraid of making a mistake as of being perceived as less than the best.

Your boss may simply be resisting your pressuring him to make a decision. Some procrastinators interpret responsibilities as demands. "I'm not going to do it because *you* want me to," they seem to say. It's as if they're in a power struggle with a parent. They resist anything they *should* do as if it's a demand that comes from a mother or father.

If your boss is a habitual procrastinator, what can you do?

- Keep him informed of deadlines.
- Try moving projects ahead on your own, while acquainting him with your decisions, and see if he stops you.
- Keep giving him status reports. Don't drop projects until you are sure he has—permanently.
- In general, proceed as independently as possible.

11. MY BOSS IS OVER-CONTROLLING, AND INTERFERES IN EVERYTHING I DO

Is he interfering or supervising? • If you and the boss have different ideas about how to do things • When to go along and when to argue • How to reassure the boss by showing you have things under control

Is your boss simply controlling, or really over-controlling? If he interferes because he doesn't like what you're doing—the results you get—I'd say he's attempting to influence the process so that he gets the results he wants. He's just doing his job. He's in control of the situation.

In this case, you have to decide whether or not he has something to teach you about how to get the results he wants. You might try to convince him that things will work out your way. But if he doesn't agree, that's it: it's his way or out. Only when you do things his way will he relinquish control.

On the other hand, if your results are good, if things are going well and he's *still* always looking over your shoulder, he's over-controlling. You're successfully taking charge, and he's acting as if you can't. It's a major problem. He's acting like a parent with a child—you—and like a bad parent, at that. It's demoralizing, a motivation damper.

Here I'd take a stand. I'd point out that he doesn't have to concern himself with my methods since I'm giving him what he wants.

You'll have to speak up. But before you do, try to figure him out, just as you would the procrastinating boss. He's probably afraid of something. Find out what it is that he's so worried about; why he feels that he has to watch over you and guide your every step.

Alma's Story

Alma, the publicity director of a large oil company, supervised a staff of fourteen people. Out of the blue one day, her boss suddenly demanded that from that time on the entire staff had to be in the office by 9 A.M. Alma was angry at the boss's interference in her operation, and thought it inadvisable to press her staff to show up by nine. It had been her experience that the people under her worked very long hours whenever there was a reason to do so—for example, whenever they were putting together conferences or working on press kits. They'd come in at eight in the morning and work without complaining right through the evening to meet their deadlines. But she knew that her people were willing to stay long and late when the workload required it because when things were slow, she was relaxed about the hours they worked; they were under no injunction to be in by 9 A.M. exactly.

Her boss, however, saw things differently. The sight of empty desks at 9 A.M. triggered his anxieties. Would the work get done? How does the department look? Are we getting our money's worth out of these people? Are they going to be coming in later and later? He needed reassurance. So, when Alma's boss began complaining about laxity on her part, she pointed out to him that the staff had met seven deadline emergencies in four months. She also pointed out to him that whatever the negative aspects might be of finding the office relatively empty at nine, the advantages of having people willing to work late when the need was critical were greater. More was accomplished by her method of giving people time flexibility than would have been accomplished by tightening the reins. She added to her regular reports a rundown on hours worked—a constant reminder that the company was getting what it needed. She showed him she was in control of the situation, and by keeping him informed, reassured him that *he* had control.

Although the temptation is to withhold information in order to keep the boss off your back, in actuality, it works the other way: the more information you give a controlling person, the more he feels in control—and the less he'll bother you.

12. MY BOSS IS DISORGANIZED

Blaming the boss versus taking responsibility yourself • Why some women have trouble handling a social or business situation on their own • Why you must—and how you can—move from dependence to independence

While having a disorganized boss can be extremely difficult to deal with, the more dependent you are, the more serious the problem is. If you feel you need him to guide you, and he's too disorganized to cooperate, you feel overwhelmed. You analyze the problem as being due not to your dependency, but to the chaotic conditions he's created. To prove your point, you note, ''Nobody can work with him.''

Check out your statement. Is there an exception? If there is, it might give you a clue to finding a way to work with the disorganized boss. Of course, some people's disorganization is much more severe than others. But the perpetual challenge of being successful in the workplace is to find your own creative and independent way to deal with all sorts of individuals and situations. As soon as you cast blame, you introduce a diversion that leads you away from finding unique, innovative solutions. So your first effort should be to try to make your projects work, by hook or by crook. You can even use the boss's disorganization to your advantage. His very carelessness will soon suggest to you a host of ways in which you can broaden your responsibilities. And chances are he'll be enormously relieved when you say, ''X is pounding on the doors to get the figures. I think I can pull them together by Thursday, and calm him down, if you'd like me to take care of it.''

The more you get the project under your own wing, the better you'll be able to cope, given the disorganized boss's tendency to scatter and lose information. If you don't resist taking responsibility, you won't resent becoming super-organized. Some people resent doing the boss's work, but in this situation, it's the only way to do yours. It may not be fair, but if you're achievement-oriented, you'll take the extra hurdles in stride.

If the boss keeps losing material you give him, make copies of everything before presenting it. Make several sets. Every time you go into his office to discuss the problem, bring your own set and a set for him with you. Don't count on his having the material at hand. When you're expecting him at a lunch appointment with a client, don't count on him to remember it—check with his secretary to see that it's in his book. A couple of days before the lunch, remind him about the appointment, using that opportunity *not* to let him know how disorganized you think he is, but to show how well-organized you are. Say, "I thought I'd make a reservation at Lucrezia's for Wednesday's lunch with Carolyn Tracey," or, "Here are some notes I've drafted that might be helpful at Wednesday's lunch." And if he doesn't show up, be prepared to take over. Don't act as if the important person is not there.

Many women are fearful, even panicky, when the men they are counting on socially cancel out at the last minute. Such distress comes from a woman's feeling that she won't be accepted or that she cannot handle a social situation alone. It's related to women's fears that they are somehow unimportant, that it's the men in their lives—their lovers or husbands or bosses—who are the valuable people, the ones their guests want to see. Men become social crutches, badges, passports to validation. The need to be accompanied by a man, which has its basis in our history, still lingers, and many women feel uncomfortable alone in social and business situations. But our abilities have raced ahead of this outmoded dependency. You don't need the boss to impress the client. He probably can, but if he's not reliable, take on the job yourself. Bring in the overview, the special resources, the good news, whatever your boss would have pulled out of his hat. Now *you* are important by virtue of doing the job. You may not have the same information or style that your boss has—but use yours, whatever it is, to make the meeting worthwhile. Sooner or later you must learn to function independently. You might as well begin to practice now.

It's important to avoid being punitive toward a disorganized boss (and chances are you'll be less likely to react this way if you shift to independent activity). Don't try to make him feel negligent or guilty. Don't say, "But you were the one who lost the minutes of that meeting!" Most likely he's been disorganized all his life, and lots of people have tried without success to change him. Simply supply what he's lacking, as effectively as you can.

And watch out. What you perceive as disastrous might be working out very well for the boss. His disorganization, while unpleasant, may not trouble him at all. So don't over-organize your boss. When one of my clients approached her boss with a mammoth chart to maximize everyone's efficiency, he walked away saying, ''Sometimes the best ideas are no ideas.'' While the boss's methods might not satisfy some people, he doesn't care, as long as his methods work for him.

13. MY BOSS IS A PERFECTIONIST—WE DO THE SAME WORK OVER AND OVER

When being a perfectionist works • How to relax the perfectionist and get him off your back • How—and when—to take a stand • Presenting the bigger picture • Publicizing yourself • If you've slipped up

When a boss demands performance at an unreasonably high level that is not in keeping with the realities of today's world, it may be that he has a personality defect. It may be that he's incapable of seeing forests and can only concentrate on trees. But some demanding bosses can see major issues as well as minor details. Some demanding bosses have just decided that being demanding works for them.

Before you conclude that your boss goes overboard about details, ask yourself whether he's losing sight of the broad picture—and failing—or keeping track of all the pieces and moving ahead. If his nit-picking is doing him in, bide your time. There will soon be a job opening—his job. But if he's succeeding by virtue of paying careful attention to detail, why shouldn't he continue? People are wise to use their own strengths. Not everybody works in the same way. If it's in his nature to be a perfectionist, and if he's succeeding in his career, you may as well buckle down and give him the kind of job he wants. If he sees his perfectionism as part of his success, he won't appreciate your undermining it. To you, he may seem uptight, but if he's got a good track record, he's right to feel confident about judging which details are important. You need to grasp his criticisms, learn from him, and let him know you accept his high standards. It's an interesting matter of style. Some people take rifle shots: they select their targets, aim very carefully, and usually hit. They count on quality. Others use buckshot. They're not meticulous. They count on quantity—something will work. They play a numbers game. And many people combine both of these opposing styles to varying degrees.

Often it isn't simply a case of the boss being a perfectionist by nature. It's possible he's acting this way because in his view you're not doing an adequate job. If the boss rehearses you a dozen times before he lets you have lunch with a client, there may be something you're doing that's making him nervous. Examine your work. Concentrate on your evaluation before concluding that perfectionism is just his nature. Ask yourself whether or not you've grasped your boss's sense of priorities, style, language, taste. Try to see the flaws that he sees.

If your work has been excellent and well-received by others, however, and your boss always finds a meaningless flaw, then that's his way, and you have to learn to cope with it. Try to refocus him on goals. Remind him that the relationships with clients that he was worried about are in fact working, that you're getting exactly what was planned. Recall for him the client who just referred another agent to your company, with the specific recommendation that he work with you. Reassure him: "I've brought in $20,000 in new business just this month." Draw his attention to your accomplishments and end results in order to get the less consequential details in perspective.

Self-publicizing—assuming you're right about what a good job you've done—usually relaxes the perfectionistic boss, who's irrationally overconcerned about errors. Anxiety keeps him from seeing the reality: that you are producing excellent results for him. If you keep reminding him about how good the results you've been getting are, his need to perfect every little detail will diminish.

If your boss does catch you in errors, don't get into a "but" contest. Reassure him by accepting the criticism and correcting your errors.

14. MY BOSS REJECTS ALL MY IDEAS

How to evaluate the worth of your ideas • When a good idea is a bad idea • Power politics • What to do with a surefire idea • When to bail out

Many women enter the workplace thinking a good idea is a good idea, and that's that. If an idea looks as if it might make money, or streamline the operation, or solve a problem, they can't wait to propose it, and so they are totally mystified when the boss doesn't cheer at their obviously creative contribution.

When he doesn't implement their idea, or at least praise it, they think less of the boss. They decide he doesn't have vision or energy or interest— that he's just putting in his time. They don't understand that ideas are a dime a dozen, even good ones. Many bosses resent ideas, even good ones, because they've heard a million of them.

What counts to a boss is how well an idea fits into the total picture, and how feasible it would be to implement. If he's sitting on top of a dozen unfinished projects, he won't be very enthusiastic about starting another one. Who's going to move it along?

Many people can come up with excellent suggestions to improve departmental efficiency, or win new clients, or develop a new product, but even more important is getting the suggestion through red tape and making it feasible by obtaining financial backing for it and finding the time and personnel to deal with it. If your suggestions are backed by practical ways to make them work, you'll get a hearing. Your track record counts here. Don't be too eager to show your creativity, or to move in too fast with bright ideas that will be rejected. Go slowly. Your task, at least at the outset, is to build credibility by presenting carefully thought out ideas that are balanced against the demands of other priorities and are backed up by strategies for implementation.

Politics often stand in the way of acceptance of even a terrific idea. A woman will say to her boss, "Listen, I've got a great idea! Since we're having trouble with that project, why don't we move it through the marketing division?" And then she'll feel that her boss is foolish, or lazy, or uninterested in success when he turns down her suggestion. Well, maybe the head of the marketing division is her boss's worst enemy, or strongest competitor. He won't discuss that with her; she has to figure it out. Her suggestions have to be in line with his political strength. If he's not well-positioned in the company, for example, he'll reject her ideas because he knows he's on the losing team, and the big boss rejects all *his* ideas.

There are a host of other reasons that cause bosses to reject ideas. Let's say a boss is being pressed to cut expenses. He cannot afford to look bad by pursuing an idea—your idea—if it involves spending money to save money or to earn money. In this circumstance, while your idea is good for the company, it isn't good for him. It becomes a good idea for him only when you can resolve his need to look cautious about expenditures.

Or let's say your boss thinks, "Our department's buried under projects." Or that he even thinks, "This idea is going to create a lot of new work for me, just when I was planning on getting my workweek reduced to four days until fall."

If you're not getting support for your ideas, stop and figure out why they're getting rejected. One TV producer, whose job was to present ideas, came to me because her boss was not only unresponsive to her creative and important suggestions, but, even worse, he was becoming generally negative toward her. When we analyzed the ideas that he did accept from other people, it became clear to us that he liked to work with "safe" themes rather than with controversial or innovative material—and her ideas were always of the latter sort. Moreover, there was no reason for him to change. He had a responsive audience; the ratings were good. Thus my client's proposals conflicted with his basic strategy.

But maybe your idea *is* terrific, and the people around you are simply unable to see its value. I can call on my experience here. Years back, I had an idea that could solve a major problem that was plaguing the hospital for which I worked. But I hesitated to present the idea to my boss. He was a handsome, middle-aged man who often as not analyzed hospital administrative difficulties with the statement, "The trouble with this place is that there are too many female directors." While he liked having young, attractive women around, he saw the more mature, highly experienced female directors as petty, middle-aged troublemakers. Since I qualified as a middle-aged female director, I was fearful that my creative solution to this major problem of the moment would be disregarded. I knew that because of his prejudice he wouldn't give me a fair hearing. So I came up with the stratagem of proposing my idea *first* to the executive director's best buddy, the head of security (a man whose department was directly involved with the problem), and together we went to the executive director with the idea. I took a backseat during the meeting. And, as I had anticipated, my boss—once the idea was presented to him by a respected strong man—was easily persuaded of its soundness. After it had been approved, I played the lead role in implementing it, and there was never any doubt that the idea was mine.

If your ideas are really good but your strategic efforts to put them across fail, here's a tip for a last resort: you can always present them during an interview for a new job and impress your potential new employer with your outstanding capabilities.

15. MY BOSS EXPECTS ME TO DO HIS JUNK WORK (OR DIRTY WORK)

How to get the boss to want you to do more important work • When doing the dirty work pays off

The homemaker's traditional role has been to provide the support systems for the ambitions of other family members. She managed the services, the meals, the clean and pressed clothing, all the back-up that was necessary to enable the students to go to school, the wage-earners to go to work. The new woman thinks more in terms of an equal distribution of those support services that make activity outside the home possible. Her goal is to provide all members of the family, *including* herself, with time to develop and perform a role in the larger world. She has spear-headed a move away from the traditional division of labor within the family toward the development of similar or unisex roles for all household members. She has tried to get away from—or at least divvy up—the repetitious household work.

The supervisor in an office is not interested in divvying up boring or distasteful work equitably. Starting with the things only he can do, he adds the tasks he wants to do, and hires others to do the rest. He tries at all costs to avoid junk work (boring tasks), and dirty work (distasteful ones). And he has management's authority to do this. If your boss is in the habit of passing such duties on to you, you have to decide when it's to your advantage to go along with his plan, or when it might be better to protest.

Let's look first at how to get rid of junk work. The more important your own projects are, the less likely it is that your boss will tell you to pick up his boring work. But until you've positioned yourself as being *too* valuable to interfere with, you may have to go along with his requests. Later, once you're positioned, you can show him that he is the one who loses out when he takes you away from your work. Then you and he can sit down together to find a better solution to his problem.

Dirty work is another matter. You may actually find that the more valuable you've shown yourself to be in this arena, the more your boss will rely on you to do his dirty work. One of my clients was given a series of exciting

new assignments by her boss, assignments that made her job far more interesting and responsible. But one of her first tasks in her newly upgraded role
was to inform a colleague that the desirable assignments she had just gained
were no longer to be handled in her colleague's department.

It was painful. My client and the colleague had been friends. My client
was furious that her boss himself didn't do the informing, the dirty work of
explaining that he had taken the goodies away from one person and given
them to another.

I pointed out to my client that this wasn't the kind of thing her boss liked
to do. He, like many people, had trouble delivering bad news. He loved to
tell people when they were promoted, but he dreaded having to fire them.
In fact, he was a very compliant person. And as a result, he'd looked for his
opposite in his senior staff. My client, a strong, assertive woman, had
seemed perfect. Indeed, it was precisely because she was much tougher
than he that he had decided to advance her to a position where she could do
his managerial dirty work. Consequently, it would be foolish for her to refuse it. He wanted her precisely because she was good at it! Viewed in this
positive light, she had gained an opportunity to learn an essential managerial skill: demoting people without destroying their self-confidence, their
loyalty to their work, or their good working relationship with her.

16. MY BOSS IS ALWAYS CRITICIZING ME

Self-confidence under fire • Doing things the boss's way • When
the boss refuses to clarify his criticism • When a criticism is dead
wrong • Working smarter, not harder • Learning how to analyze
and evaluate criticism • How to handle criticism productively
• When to leave

If you're not giving the boss what he wants, take heed; you may be on
your way out. But even when the situation has gotten pretty run down, you
can reverse it fast. When women feel disapproval, they usually try to set
things right by working harder—but if the criticism has nothing to do with
work quantity, you'd do better to work less and think more. Figure out
what the criticism is really about.

If you live under the weight of constant criticism, your self-confidence
may be eroding. Part of you believes you're as inept as your boss says you
are, and you grow more and more unable to understand or adapt, and less

and less able to resolve your differences. It's absolutely essential to try to get this situation under control. If you don't, your life is bound to be miserable. Since you'll probably get fired if things continue the way they're going, you can't lose by experimenting with new strategies. Learning how to evaluate and handle criticism is crucial to the boss-subordinate relationship.

Try facing the fact that you may have to do things the boss's way, however much you don't want to. You can attempt to change his mind, but if you can't, you've no choice but to let his way prevail. If criticism makes you rebellious, you're in trouble. But if you see criticism as part of the learning process, you can turn it to advantage. This doesn't mean you can't discuss differences with your boss; it just means accepting the fact that he has the deciding vote.

If the criticism you're receiving is vague, you can ask for clarification. Often, however, you won't get any answer. Then, you have to be a detective.

Stephanie's Story

Stephanie's boss hinted several times that something was awry with the production department, finally saying outright: ''The vice president of production feels things aren't going well.'' She was puzzled. She'd only met the production V.P. once. What was her boss talking about? She tried to get further information, but her boss clammed up. She was puzzled and annoyed. Why wouldn't he spell out the problem so she could correct it?

Actually, her boss was being smarter than she realized. If he gave her all the details of the complaints against her, he couldn't be sure what she'd do with them. She might go to the people involved and cause further trouble. No matter how much he personally liked Stephanie, getting his job done depended on the cooperation of a lot of people, and he was smart enough not to get into trouble with them. Besides, the details of the difficulty were irrelevant to him. He was concerned simply with the fact that the people in production weren't happy with Stephanie.

Generally speaking, a boss is not a good parent who wants everyone to get a fair shake. He's not interested in a hearing and a just verdict. He simply wants things to work—with a minimum of effort. And he knows that, for whatever reason, some people work out on the team, and some people don't. His view is self-centered: he'll investigate only if it's to his advantage. So I advised Stephanie to be the detective. She would have to figure out the meaning of the mysterious criticism herself.

She had one clue. The problem area was production. Was she failing to meet the production department's deadlines? Intruding on their territory? Not cooperating with their requests? Did she have friends in production, or enemies? Stephanie and I decided on a possible reason the V.P. of production had criticized her. Being new to the job, she had been so concerned about being efficient and businesslike, so anxious about getting enough work completed, that at times she had been abrupt. Perhaps they saw her quick, efficient manner as bossy, even imperious.

Stephanie experimented with a change in style. She spoke more considerately, less intensely, made requests instead of demands. She no longer took the cooperation of the production department for granted. Less than three weeks later, her boss praised her for a project, gave her some new assignments, and mentioned that the production V.P. had commended her.

It's very important to evaluate the seriousness of any criticism. If it comes frequently, or from high up, or is broad in scope, don't let it go. It is necessary to analyze the criticism immediately and take quick corrective action.

Now suppose the criticism is very specific, and dead wrong. Deliver your challenge to your boss's point of view assertively. That's your responsibility. What good are your ideas if you can't present them persuasively? But if you consistently lose—and the criticism persists—you have an important decision to make. Either you move to doing things the boss's way or you leave.

Perhaps you're being compulsive when he wants you to be impulsive, or impulsive when he wants you to be painstaking and cautious. So of course he's critical of you. What you've got to do is figure out not only *what* he wants done, but the *style* in which he likes things done. Then, do the work his way. If you can't, if you consistently see the boss's criticism as off base, you're working for the wrong person. You and he will never respect each other.

17. MY BOSS DOESN'T GIVE ME PRAISE
OR RECOGNITION

Why the need for praise? • What the real rewards should be
• Evaluating your performance yourself • Flattery as manipulation • Making yourself look good • Why the boss won't say
thank you • Teaming with the boss for shared credit

Why should he? And why do you need it? In the workplace, praise customarily comes in the form of a paycheck. Many people don't understand this. They believe that they ought to be getting, and that they even need, complimentary, encouraging evaluations of their performance. It's an attitude that seems to be instilled into them by our very culture, which nourishes reliance on praise. Teachers and parents offer praise as if it were essential for learning. We constantly say to our children, "Good, fine, that was really nice," whether it's because the kids have taken their first steps, or said their first words, or learned to ride a bicycle. It's as if we can't acknowledge the drive of the child to press forward in the natural course of her or his development without our help. Everything a child does is critiqued: it's judged good, bad, or better, evaluated, measured, graded, thus setting the state for the need to be encouraged with someone else's words.

Reliance on external praise affects both sexes. But women, whose worth is traditionally devalued, seem to need more reassurance than do men. This doesn't mean that men are filled with self-confidence, but that women, like blacks or any group that has been discriminated against, are less sure of themselves and their worth.

In addition, men have a better understanding of the customary rewards of the workplace—money, promotion, opportunity. Until women absorb the essence of the workplace environment, they remain dependent on praise for validation. One of my clients came to me because she had received so little praise she thought her job was threatened. During the course of analyzing her situation, I discovered that she had just received a substantial salary increase. Although she hadn't grasped it, she was on her way up, not out.

Not only is praise unessential, it can also be a trap. In exchange for praise, many women will stay far too long and work much too hard at low-paying tasks far below their ability. It's not unusual to find a woman working for peanuts for a boss who exploits her labor by giving her a daily ego fix of "you're wanted and needed" instead of the perks and dollars most men would surely demand. And, sadly, it's also not unusual for a woman to give unfailing loyalty and competent support to the development of her boss's career—only to be passed over or abandoned with little more than a thank-you. Starved for recognition and the need to be important in a world where men are the big shots, women can too often be manipulated with flattery.

With understanding, you can get rid of the need for external approval. You can evaluate and approve or disapprove of yourself. Whether you have a boss who over-flatters or under-praises, try evaluating your own performance. How does what you're doing now compare with what you were doing a month ago? Are you learning, growing? Do things make more sense to you now than they did before? What are the problems and objectives of your work? Are you making headway?

If you don't have a boss who gives positive feedback, assume that his evaluation of your work conforms to yours unless you hear otherwise. And once in a while, let him hear your appraisal of your own work. Don't assume he knows what's happening. Highlight your achievements for him. Let him know you've increased efficiency, solved a knotty problem, reduced friction—give a fact, tell a story. But don't brag. Submit the facts. "I signed up two new buildings this week. One was a particularly hard sell." Go on to your interesting story. Don't give your evaluation of the achievement, but tell your story and let him draw the conclusion. Praise doesn't have to emanate from the boss. It's just as useful when it emanates from you, provided, of course, that you've been evaluating yourself realistically, and as a more giving boss might.

If your boss doesn't give praise because he's afraid you'll ask for rewards—for a raise—you can at least set the stage with your reporting system and self-praise, letting him know that *you* know you're worth more.

If he doesn't give praise because he's too competitive, and your successes make him feel less adequate, give him credit; report your success as a team.

18. MY BOSS BLOWS HOT AND COLD—
I DON'T KNOW WHERE I STAND

How to determine if your boss's mood swings have to do with you, or him • How to handle mood swings in a businesslike way • Why women tend to see themselves as responsible for others' moods • The danger of overreacting to the cold treatment • How to tell when the cold shoulder does mean trouble

"One day he's nice, the next day he doesn't say a word to me." With a boss like this, it's important to decide whether he's trying to tell you how he feels about your work, or whether he's a moody type who dumps his personal problems onto everyone. He may not be satisfied with you. But on the other hand he may be a person whose moods swing regularly and are affected by many factors. When he interprets the people in his environment as valuing and accepting him, when he perceives himself as successful, he's happy, and he soars. When he interprets the people in his environment as rejecting, he sees himself as worthless, and he sinks. His feelings can shift from minute to minute, and be affected by such things as *his* boss not saying good morning.

While your boss's opinion of himself changes, your opinion of him can be consistent. The danger to you lies in keying your moods to his—in reacting to his ups and downs. You don't have to be entrapped in his distorted self-appraisal. Maintain a constant stance toward him based on business needs, your evaluation of his strengths, and your evaluation of the strengths of the relationship. This doesn't mean being insensitive or unaware. It does mean being objective.

Of course, objectivity is difficult. Women tend to take on undue responsibility for how other people feel. And many of us have an exaggerated sense of our ability to affect the moods of those around us. We believe we really can make other people happy or unhappy. I don't subscribe to this notion. I believe that while sometimes one can, momentarily, make someone happy or unhappy, our power over others' feelings is—alas—very limited. People have their own natures, and tend to return to their own essences even though they may, indeed, believe that others are responsible for their moods. Unfortunately, women are all too ready to accept the blame and to see themselves as responsible for other people's unhappiness. If you refuse to take that responsibility, you won't panic when the boss grows cold. You can maintain a balanced acceptance of him and of your relationship with him. And your balance—your objectivity—may even prove helpful.

Gail's Story

Gail was a client of mine who was totally thrown by her boss's mood swings. She overreacted to her boss's unpredictable moodiness: when her boss was cold, she pulled away because she felt pushed away. She stopped setting up their once frequent, informal get-togethers. It was unfortunate, because in a sense she was creating another rejection for her overly sensitive boss. I advised Gail to define and establish the parameters of the relationship herself rather than cooling off in reaction to his cold climate. She started by restoring the most productive aspects of their past relationship, stopping in at the boss's office almost daily with a bit of news or a friendly word, and every now and then suggesting a relaxed catch-up meeting at lunch—the kind of lunch they frequently used to share. She rebuilt the relationship by repeatedly putting the boss in contact with her strengths, his own strengths, and interesting and important matters. Instead of reinforcing the boss's negative feelings about himself by backing away, her unwavering respect for the boss and their collaboration stabilized their relationship. Gail did not permit herself to be rejected. She responded to the real needs of the situation.

Nevertheless, if you have a boss who brings his moods into the workplace, who makes unreasonable or unfair business decisions on the basis of how he's feeling that morning, you have to gauge the situation day by day, hour by hour, and decide how good your chances are, in the light of his mood, to have your ideas accepted. So become a student of his moods and time your proposals accordingly.

In general, when your boss is in a bad mood, don't put him on the spot by asking what's wrong. Even if he wanted to tell you, or understood it himself and *could* tell you, it's inappropriate to ask. This level of intimacy is not consistent with the rest of the boss-employee relationship. Besides, if he does know what's going on and bares his soul, he might regret it later.

Still, some bosses are not direct in their criticism. The cool, silent treatment *can* mean you're not measuring up. If the boss's mood swings are due to his irritation with *you,* there are clues. First clue: the mood swings are reserved for you, the icy treatment is not directed at everyone. Second clue: verbal criticism and general irritation regarding your work occur around the same time that you get the cold treatment. Conversely, when you do excellent work, extra work, or make unexpected contributions, the boss's behavior toward you warms up. Then you know he's reacting to you and not something in his own personal situation—and you can begin to figure out what to do about it.

19. MY BOSS IS A BLAMER

When the boss is at fault • Defusing a blamer • Is he saving his ego or his job? • Protecting yourself from a blamer

Many people cannot admit to having made a mistake, so they blame others. They are too insecure to acknowledge a slipup, believing that when something goes wrong, there's something wrong with *them.* They feel overcome with self-contempt. "I made a mistake. I always make mistakes. I'm always fouling things up. What's wrong with me?" The blamer is a person who feels so terrible about making errors that the only way he can live with having made one is to say, "It's not me, it's the other guy's fault." He makes the unbearable bearable—with blame.

If your boss is a blamer who is locked into this dynamic, arguments about the issues at hand are useless, because he's worrying about something else altogether—his worth. It's pointless to try to improve the situation by showing him that *he*—not you—caused the problem. Nor should you meekly swallow the blame he places on you.

Fortunately, there's another way to cope. You can deflect the matter of blame and move ahead to action.

I had a client who reported that her boss, a blamer, called her in one day and asked, "Where's the letterhead for account X?" My client defended herself, "You told me to wait before making one up." The boss took issue with her, "No, I told you to have it printed. And it should have been in the office by now!" My client knew that she was right, and the boss wrong. She felt unjustly accused of an error, so they got into a heated argument over who was at fault.

When my client told me what had happened, I told her she should never have gotten into the argument. What she should have done was say,

"Okay. I don't remember your telling me, but maybe you're right. In the meantime, since you need it now, why don't I get on the line and see how fast I can shove it through?" Even if the boss screamed back, "No, it's too late now!" to prove he's right (which has now become the more important issue to him), she should have set to work on the error. She should have gotten sample layouts on his desk as soon as possible with a memo saying, "Maybe we can save the day."

The technique is to put aside any question of blame in favor of action which will rectify the error. Action permits both boss and employee to come away with undamaged egos. If the blamer is reachable or teachable, you'll be giving him something to think about. When you say, "Maybe you're right," you'll be showing him that a person can matter-of-factly learn from errors without undue concern about losing respect.

If you need to defuse the blamer still more—if he still can't shift into a problem-solving gear—take things further. While still putting aside the question of who was to blame, you can acknowledge and analyze in detail the error (and, if necessary, its disastrous consequences) and then take on the responsibility for inventing improved systems to avoid a repeat of the error.

Let's say you're a managing editor, and your latest issue contained a number of factual errors in the test and picture captions because your boss told you to let the author check the facts. Now your boss denies he ever gave you this instruction. It doesn't matter. What matters is that you show your boss that you've learned how to avoid the error in the future. Say, "I agree, the mistakes are very embarrassing. I can see that authors need a backup system. I'm not taking any more chances. I'm making five procedural changes: 1) I'll have all dates, titles, names, and facts checked at the library; 2) I'd like to build a mini-library here for quick access and last-minute problems; 3) I'll lengthen deadlines to allow more time for fact-checking; 4) once a month I'll review all errors one by one with staff, to sharpen awareness; 5) I'll personally double-check the next few issues to make sure my systems are working."

It's important to discuss errors in order to understand what went wrong so that they can be avoided in the future, but this kind of boss won't let you. If you could review the situation together, calmly, that would be ideal. But, using the technique shown above—analyzing the pitfalls, proposing solutions, and keeping the question of blame out of it—you've accomplished the same end by yourself.

In addition to the ego-saving that lies behind the need to blame, there's also an important career-climbing, money-motivated, save-your-skin-at-any-cost aspect to blaming. If you're suspicious of your boss's motives—if you think he's looking for a scapegoat to make him look good; if he seems to be out to make you look bad, or even to get you fired; if he's planting the seeds of blame far and wide—you need to protect yourself. Read Chapter 7: *Protecting Yourself.*

20. I'M AFRAID TO TELL MY BOSS I MADE A MISTAKE

How to reduce your fear—and the boss's anger • Women and perfection • Lying to save your skin • Why the boss isn't interested in explanations • Putting your error in perspective

While most people will agree that it's okay to make a mistake, they don't act as if they really believe it. Many women experience utter panic, and many bosses experience utter fury, when things go wrong. In fact, this fear and anger can be so intense that it's often difficult to evaluate the seriousness of an error. My goal is to teach you how to reduce both your panic and your boss's fury by showing you how to think about and handle your errors.

Learning from errors is, as we all know, an important way of acquiring wisdom. While I'm not advocating it as the best method, it is a standard method, especially in today's workplace. Unlike the workplace of yesteryear when people trained as apprentices, and unlike school where there is a lot of teaching and reading before tests are given, many men and women have to learn on the job, under pressure, surrounded by colleagues who, for one reason or another, are not helpful.

Even if you have received some job training in college or technical school, real mastery of a job comes only with experience. In addition, there is often no orderly progression to on-the-job training—it's a catch-as-catch-can system. Thus, errors are inevitable as you gain your experience. But women have trouble understanding this, and hesitate to jump in without preparation, afraid of making a mistake or gaffe.

Men, on the other hand, seem to understand this system and are more willing to risk making mistakes in order to acquire their expertise. Of course, they are also likely to have fewer difficulties than women because of the way they are brought up—the way they are socialized and educated has prepared them for the workplace. Not only that, they get help from the people who have it to give: experienced male managers who see other men as candidates for upper-level jobs.

I think women's problems in this area stem in large part from the way our society dictates that little girls have to be perfect. The emphasis is not so much on growth and development as it is on being well-behaved and pleasing. From an early age, women's efforts are focused on avoiding the errors that bring criticism.

Your boss may not understand all this. In fact, even if he does, he probably doesn't care. He's certainly not eager to pay the cost of society's failure to educate women. All in all, he may not be very tolerant of your mistakes.

But in order to deal with your errors, *you* need to be understanding and tolerant of your disadvantage. Don't make yourself suffer for society's mistakes in not encouraging and educating you. Don't blame yourself for errors and get panicky. Rather, acquire as much experience as you can—and if you make a mistake, devise strategies to cover yourself.

Jane's Story

Jane had a long overdue bill on her desk which she was reluctant to forward to her boss for approval. The bill was higher than it should have been, because she had failed to negotiate a firm price. She kept postponing the scene she fantasized would occur when her boss saw the figures. By the time she came to discuss the problem with me, the bill had been sitting on her desk for three months. Now she would have to explain not only the high cost of the purchase, but also the length of time that she had held on to the bill.

The solution to Jane's problem would have been simple had she not compounded her error with panicked delay. What she should have done was call the supplier, try to get an adjustment of the bill and, failing that, send it along to her boss with a note informing him she thought the service was overpriced and that she had started looking for more reasonably priced suppliers for the next round. Mistakes are better tolerated when the boss sees that you understand your error and that you've taken steps to correct it in the future.

Though it was now three months later, the same solution applied. I advised Jane to find a new supplier immediately—tomorrow—and then to tell the boss she had solved the problem. She did, and he did not even raise the issue of the delay. As often happens, the delay had loomed up larger in her mind than it did in his.

When you've made the mistake of not dealing with a mistake right away, the solution is to act on it nondefensively as if the delay had never occurred. Make the right move *now*. Don't let your fear cause you to delay one more day. The sooner you deal with the mistake, the better your chances of getting away with it.

Clarice's Story

Sometimes the situation calls for an outright lie. In a meeting with the president of her company, Clarice slipped and revealed a confidence. She referred to a long-standing problem between her boss and a client. She left the meeting and called me. How could she tell her boss that she had made a mistake that could get him into trouble? Her error was enormous. She knew he'd be furious and would never trust her again with important information.

She and I agreed that her error—not having learned the importance of staying on guard and keeping business secrets—was grave, and that the price might be high. We also agreed she had a right to buy the time she needed to learn the ways of the business world, and should do what was necessary to avoid the consequences of her error. We worked out a strategy. The next day she mentioned to her boss, ''When I was in the president's office yesterday, he threw out a phrase that indicated his awareness of your problem with client X. I thought you'd better know he knows.'' She told her boss a lie to cover her mistake, but it saved her job. She used her error well. He was grateful to her for the tip, and set about preparing his own defense.

When your error is horrendous—too costly or unforgivable—get out the best way you can. If the error is tolerable, or you need help to remedy it, or your boss is likely to find out anyway, the wisest thing to do is admit it. Tell the boss the bad news in your own way before someone else does. And tell him right away. Don't count on your prayers to make the mistake go away; you'll probably just end up with two problems: the first error and the cover-up. Go in to the boss and say, ''I made a mistake. We're in trouble.'' I don't care what the error was—whether you ordered thousands of dollars worth of the wrong telephone equipment, or you missed the deadline for the most important press release of the year, or even accidentally mailed a confidential report to your boss's greatest competitor—telling the boss about it outright is the smart thing to do. He'll be reassured that you're on top of things and that you understand your error. Your intelligent grasp of the situation will help defuse his anger. Another plus: he'll feel he can trust you because you told him. If he caught you in the error or learned about it from someone else, he'd worry about your reliability.

If he is distressed at the error or even furious—a natural reaction for a lot of people—don't get defensive. Don't go into a long-winded explanation of why you made the mistake; it will probably make him angrier. This reaction is puzzling to many women. It happens because, willy-nilly, the boss is being placed by you in the position of having to get you off the hook—you want him to understand your error and forgive it. In addition to coping with the mess you made, he's got to calm you down, or listen to a self-serving apologetic explanation. He's not interested in why you made the error. Understanding why it happened is of no value to him. *You* need an understanding of the error, but he's only interested in doing something about it.

If you handle things well, he'll forget about it. He's made mistakes too. He knows you're not perfect, even if you thought you were fooling him into thinking so. And as you continue to work along with him, he'll soon be reminded of all the good, smart, competent things you've done.

You'll have to remember all these good things, too, for when a woman is fearful of admitting a mistake, it's usually because the mistake begins to loom so large in her consciousness that she forgets—and imagines others have forgotten—her contributions. Her insecurity makes her think that only her error will be remembered, and all her accomplishments will be overlooked. For the moment they may be, but people do have both memories and judgment. It may seem that anger has taken over, and indeed it may have—but not permanently, unless the error is so horrendous that you get fired. (You also might be fired because the boss wanted to get rid of you anyhow and is using the error as an excuse.)

If you're panicked about admitting a mistake, try putting yourself in touch with your accomplishments. Remind yourself of yesterday, or last week, when you bought—and at a decidedly low price—the right equipment; when your press release was printed verbatim; when you outsmarted the competition. (And don't forget, it's a good idea to drop a reminder every so often to the boss himself about these things.) If *you* can put the error into perspective, you can help him do the same.

21. MY BOSS IS TYRANNICAL AND EXPLOSIVE

How to defend your point of view without becoming defensive
• Defusing the boss's anger • What to do when he won't stop
yelling

The boss who is notorious for his office temper probably has a tremendous psychological investment in his career and his financial success. At the same time, he lacks confidence in the people he needs to rely on to achieve that success. He's constantly panicky about things not working, and he thinks that others can't grasp the importance of the issues that worry him—so he shouts or explodes. It's as if he were thinking, "Maybe if I say it loud enough, it'll get through their thick skulls." He has little faith in his employees' ability to understand, as well as little faith in his ability to make them understand. There are other reasons why people get angry, but if you assume that underneath the tyrannical boss's anger there lies a fear that things won't work, you'll probably be successful in coping with his explosive behavior.

If your boss is explosive or tyrannical, let him know that you hear him—if possible, even before he speaks (or yells!).

Let's say you're in the furniture design business. Your boss is forever screaming at you and creating a furor in the office. He yells at the drop of a hat. Sometimes he explodes just because he sees you! By now you're scared to death of him. At the least, you find being around him unpleasant, and probably go out of your way to avoid him. Try the opposite: instead of moving away, move in. Don't give him time to build up his rage against you. Be a step ahead. Raise issues yourself before he has a chance to escalate them. For example, even before he has time to think about the fall line, say to him, "My designs are sketched out in my head, and will be on paper by the fourteenth. I had lunch with three buyers this week. We all agree on trends." Be ahead, and keep ahead. Don't worry that a sudden change in your operating style will appear peculiar to the boss; it may puzzle him momentarily, but if he respects what you're saying it will calm him down.

If he explodes anyway, hold your ground. Speak firmly. When you disagree, say so. Don't be defensive or apologetic. Defensiveness implies uncertainty and a lack of confidence in your own point of view. To an explosive boss, defensiveness is particularly unnerving. He's in a rage because he thinks you don't measure up, and when you're defensive you reinforce his worst fears.

Say he shouts, "Why did you put this design through? It'll never sell. It's awful." If you answer defensively "But you gave me the go ahead! I asked you what you thought of it. I even checked it out with the fabric houses," you're defending what you did by making him partly responsible for it. Note that at the same time, you're indicating what you did might be wrong.

You can defend your point of view without being defensive, and without seeking excessive justification for your actions. Present your case objectively and confidently. "I don't agree with you. It's a with-it updating of a very successful design. I believe it will work because it's hitting the market at the right moment. I spoke to a color forecaster and a fabric designer this very week, both of whom mentioned the recent appearance of this trend. I think we're lucky that I cinched it early on."

Don't let his panic panic you. Take responsibility for your view and stand by it.

What if your boss is so angry you can't get a word in? There are ways to handle this situation once you get guilt and fear out of the way. Many women can't cope with anger; in the face of a boss's powerful rage, they're completely immobilized. They're intimidated by the boss's authority, they aren't experienced in defending themselves, and—having been devalued for so long—they feel deep down that they really must have done something wrong. Some even fear physical abuse, although that fear is generally unrealistic in the work setting.

I'd suggest trying different strategies to defuse the anger.

One simple approach—which is often effective—is to say, "I can't talk to you while you're yelling, so I'm leaving. But I would like to have a chance to discuss this problem with you."

Another is not to argue with the boss but to try to understand his criticism and repeat it back to him. Let's say he's screaming at you, "You've been doing a rotten job for us! You haven't gotten us the audience we wanted! You've been marketing the wrong programs ever since you started. You're an idiot, lady, and your days with us are numbered." Yes, some bosses talk this way. You could argue by defending your track record: "But my statistics prove I got the age level we were after." Chances are he'll return with a blast because it will seem to him that you are not even grasping the fact that he has a problem. Instead, try to understand his criticism, exaggerated though it may be, and respond to him by rephrasing it as an issue of great importance: "You're saying we haven't reached enough people and we haven't reached the right people." He'll probably continue his tirade: "What do you think I'm saying? You haven't done a thing for us." You must continue to dignify his criticism: "Okay, your audience is standing still. We have to tackle that, right now." What you're doing is validating his complaint instead of fighting it. If your statements are emphatic and not argumentative, patronizing, or sarcastic, his anger will gradually deescalate because he'll have lost his antagonist. If you're both on the same track, then there's no one left to scream at. And when he sees that you've grasped problem number one (reaching the wrong audience), he can leave problem number two behind (how to get *you* to see problem number one). He's free to work with you to define the marketing difficulties more precisely: perhaps the age of the audience he was trying to reach has shifted, or you've each relied on different and conflicting market research. Whatever it is, you can now work on solving the problem together.

By using the techniques outlined here, I'm not claiming that you'll cure people of their anger, but you will at least be able to shift it away from you—onto someone who hasn't read this book.

22. *MY BOSS IS STUPID—I'M SMARTER THAN HE IS*

What you can learn from a stupid boss • The boss's job is not like your job • What to do if he's hopeless • Going after the boss's job

Your boss may indeed have weaknesses, even gross ones. But he may also have qualities that are adequate, even central, to getting his job done. He doesn't have to be perfect any more than you do. Saying he's dumb is often more superficial and competitive than analytical or productive. Certainly you may know a lot more than your boss does about many areas, or you may think faster, but I'd be interested in hearing about what he knows that you don't know. Before writing him off, try seeing what he does have going for him.

One client accused her boss of being stupid and leaving everything up to his staff. She ran down a long list of his inadequacies from his ignorance of and disinterest in what was going on, to his general lack of culture, to his inability to think clearly or write a decent letter. When I asked whether her boss did *anything* on his own, I was surprised to hear the response: "Well, he gets the funding for the agency." In a sense, my client, and not her boss, was "stupid." My client, focusing on office procedures, had failed to credit her boss for intelligence, despite his enormous effectiveness at the important task of raising money. She was comparing him to herself, competing with him in the area she understood best.

As discussed before, women tend to focus on concrete results—reports, charts, memos—because the tangible has historically been their territory. They've traditionally been responsible for well-laid tables, dust-free houses, attractive meals—concrete, *visible* matters. But much of importance that happens in the workplace may not be visible. Women, who have a history of being excluded from the most important areas of activity, have to learn that in reality these activities are just as concrete and certainly as valuable as what the women themselves are doing.

The best strategy for dealing with a boss you think of as stupid is to cultivate some perspective about his job. Besides thinking of what he does poorly, think of what he does well. And bear in mind that what you consider stupid may be the result of his expending his efforts on just what *his* bosses expect of him. It's important to try to get perspective on him and his job, because if you don't respect him, he's going to sense your disdain, and your relationship is bound to deteriorate.

Now suppose a boss really *is* totally inept. He's making bad moves all the time at every level. He doesn't have knowledge and he doesn't have judgment. I'd say you have a rare opportunity for advancement. Take advantage of it. Maybe management sees the same defects in your boss as you do. If not, subtly encourage them to do so. (You don't always have to rescue your boss.) Let management see *your* intelligence. Use it to become visible as the superior candidate for the next promotional opportunity—possibly your (ex-)boss's job.

23. *I DO ALL THE WORK AND MY BOSS TAKES ALL THE CREDIT*

Maneuvering around the boss-takes-the-credit system • Taking advantage of the system • Getting the credit due you • Publicizing yourself

Right or wrong, that's the custom. It's built into the pyramidal structure of the workplace, where the name of the game is looking good. Most people in business life will take their ideas from wherever they can, without crediting their sources. But, custom aside, the boss does orchestrate his department's operations and is entitled, as the final decision-maker, to take credit for whatever is produced. Still, the system can provide *you* with the same advantages it provides your boss. If he can take credit for work done by people under him, why can't you take credit for the projects *you* orchestrate?

Some bosses, of course, give more credit than others, or give it at certain times. Their generosity often has to do with how secure they are, both professionally and personally. If a boss is in a secure position and things are going well for him, he's more likely to let others know you're valuable—or at least to take the credit for having found you—than he is if his own situation is precarious. And if he feels you are loyally helping him to build *his* image and not competing for credit, he's likely to be more generous. In addition, some bosses appreciate the practical wisdom of giving credit. They know how to give enough to encourage and motivate people, yet also take enough to get rewards for themselves.

But if you have the kind of boss who goes overboard with taking credit for your work, don't despair. Look for ways to hold your own. One of my clients, a stage manager, was distressed to discover that the producer of a show she'd worked on had, in a fit of pique, left her title off the show's program. That credit was critical for her future job hunts. I suggested that she go to a printer and have a new program made up for her own use—one that would accurately reflect her involvement in the production. The new program would be exactly like the old one, except that it would bear one additional line: "Mary Jones . . . stage manager." My client's reaction to my suggestion was, at first, horror. She felt she'd be doing something virtually illegal. But her initial reaction was soon replaced with delight when I persuaded her that her program would be the accurate one, and that no one, including the producer, was likely to call her to task for telling the truth—a truth that could easily be verified by all who had worked on the show.

In general, if you take time to develop relationships with people in your company and profession, you'll have many opportunities to let them know what you're doing. Don't use your contact with other people to accuse your boss, or to brag. Just let significant parties know in a subtle way, from time to time, what you've done. Say, "I was too busy yesterday to call you. I had my hands full—when Bill edited out one line of the speech I wrote for his regional meeting, I had to rewrite the whole thing to make it work." Or, "When I created the concept, I had no idea of the impact it would have—at the time it seemed like just another spin-off of the theme I'd presented last year." Self-publicizing is an essential part of getting the credit due you.

24. MY BOSS HAS FAVORITES

The marital model in the workplace • Women and competition
• When you're losing to the competition • If you *are* the favorite
• Alliances change • When to consider leaving

"I've been upstaged by a newly hired colleague. I don't have a chance." Women are particularly vulnerable to the feeling of being displaced. They grow anxious in office situations in which they perceive that they aren't their boss's exclusive favorite. The boss probably *will* have a favorite, and that's a good thing to be—but if you're not it, don't overreact. The danger lies in feeling you're nothing, and/or in making harsh judgments about the boss's "unfairness." (What you call unfairness others might call motivating high-potential candidates.)

I believe the anxiety women feel when they aren't the boss's favorite, or when they are replaced as his favorite, has to do primarily with women's limited experience of the workplace. On the job, they still rely on attitudes developed in other spheres of life. For example, they use a marital model. They imagine that there's room for only one woman in the boss's work life because, in our monogamous society, there's room for only one (legal) wife. While women know intellectually that the workplace isn't like the home, that there's a need for many people in many capacities, they react to competition with their emotions rather than with their rationality. They fall into the either/or trap. They feel, ''Either I'm number one or I'm nothing, I'm nowhere.''

Further, they imagine they are dependent on one man, one situation, one job. If they lose out to a competitor, they think their very lives are going down the drain because they'll never again have the opportunity for advancement they just lost.

If you feel any of these things when your boss has a favorite, chances are you're relying on a marital model instead of a workplace model. Or you're reacting the way a woman does in a courtship or sexual relationship. Often when we meet an attractive man, we're seized with the feeling that if this doesn't work, we've had it. We believe each time, ''It's my last chance.'' Even experience with several men doesn't change the belief that every man is the last man. But in the workplace, there's a lot of room for a lot of people. Try using a friendship model instead of a courtship or marital model; we all have a number of friends, chosen to satisfy our different interests and needs. A boss chooses staff as we choose friends—and he can have many good and important relationships.

Our childhood affects the picture, too. Children are inadequate and dependent, and the more that fact was driven home to you then, the more you'll feel it now. But the more, in childhood, you were given a realistic view of your own ability to grow, the more likely you are to have a balanced perspective now. It's only when we believe we're permanently dependent (whether on a parent or on a man) that we feel desperate about being displaced. If this is your problem, you'll have to develop perspective for yourself—now. Remember that as an adult, although you may be handicapped by your past and by inexperience, you are able to make any number of independent moves.

Once you understand why you feel the way you do, you can start working on the problem. Above all, don't withdraw as if you've been defeated. Work on your relationship with your boss. Keep the importance, the value, of your particular contributions before him. Don't stop functioning when you feel you're in competition and you're losing. Stop worrying about the competition, and start producing! Keep in mind that, most of the time, even when a boss does have a new favorite, this doesn't mean you're being replaced—just repositioned.

It's important that you don't see the boss and his favorite as constituting an exclusive in-group, with you permanently on the outside. Entry—or reentry—is always possible. New teams are always forming. If you are emotionally locked into the romantic concept of the twosome, you will have difficulty with the all-important task of teaming.

If you are the boss's favorite, don't rely overmuch on 'his state of grace. If you think of the two of you as a permanent duo, you're heading for trouble. Remember, bosses get fired, people resign, relationships shift and develop and change. *In the workplace, feelings and loyalties are not forever.*

Sometimes, a new favorite *does* mean you're being replaced. Chances are it's not because someone more interesting or more valuable came along, however, but because there was a gap, a preexisting problem created by the failure of the relationship between you and your boss. If your new status is measurably down-graded or unworkable, learn the lesson and consider bailing out. You might try to repair the damage, but since you've been replaced, your time and energy may be better spent elsewhere.

25. MY BOSS HAS A FAVORITE—HIS BEDMATE

Why women tend to slip back into a subordinate role • The boss's wife • How to handle work you don't want to do • How to keep your authority • The secretary/bedmate • Winning through teaming

A woman's feelings of vulnerability and anxiety are multiplied when the boss's favorite is someone with whom he has an intimate relationship, and in such cases some of these concerns are valid. The wife or playmate does have a powerful position from which she can influence the boss against you. But that doesn't mean the situation is impossible, even though it may seem so.

Elizabeth's Story

"My boss's wife tries to run everything, including me. How can I possibly stand up to her?"

Elizabeth, a professional fund-raiser, had been hired to set up a fund-raising department by the executive director of a small but growing non-profit agency. She had been on the job for only a week when the boss's wife, Hazel, a nonprofessional who had been helping her husband on a volunteer basis, said, "I want to show you how the records are kept." Until that time, Hazel had handled the records. Elizabeth sensed that Hazel was trying to push off this unpleasant detail work on her. Because Elizabeth's department was new, she had no staff to handle this duty. She was afraid if she did the work herself, she'd get mired in routine details and would not be able to concentrate on the much more advanced job for which she had been hired. But how could she say no to the boss's wife? Wouldn't that alienate her and, through her, the boss himself? How could Elizabeth refuse to do the very work that someone as important as the boss's wife had been doing all along?

Elizabeth panicked. She couldn't see a way to refuse the assignment, even though she was a seasoned professional with a position and responsibilities well above the level of work her boss's wife was trying to foist on her.

Elizabeth felt powerless because she saw Hazel and her husband as one and the same person, with the same status and the same authority— just the way Hazel herself saw things, as a matter of fact. Indeed, in our society we are accustomed to identifying women with their husband's power and position; marriage, for some women, is a way to get clout by association.

Although the wife's relationship to her husband does give her many advantages (which you do well to bear in mind), she does not have the same authority in the workplace as she would at home. While the domestic organization chart automatically positions the wife as second-in-command, the business organization chart positions you according to your job title.

When a wife or playmate decides her privileged position allows her to act as your boss, you have to reject her logic. While you must acknowledge her privilege (in Elizabeth's case, she went along with the wife's desire to get rid of the record work), don't demote yourself. Simply respond as the professional you are. Take over the work, but don't take on the actual detail yourself: *take it under your supervision.*

I advised Elizabeth to say, "You don't want to maintain those records. That's understandable—it's probably quite tedious. I'll speak to Jeff and see what can be worked out. Maybe his secretary can do it, or perhaps I will hire a part-timer. Do you have any suggestions?"

If, in a situation like this, the boss's wife persists in trying to get you to do the actual work, reject her suggestion by deliberately misinterpreting it. Say, "I have to get budget approval for hiring some clerical help before I undertake that. I have no clerical staff." You're not being unsympathetic, but you're not even considering doing the work yourself. This "misinterpretation" will serve you better than the direct refusal. You're often accepted as you present yourself—in this case, as a manager, not a clerk. The stronger the image you present, the less likely it is to be questioned. This approach worked for Elizabeth, who was able to establish her level of responsibilities on the new job right away.

In all these situations, the solution depends on your being in touch with your own value as a professional. Even when your job title says that you are more important in the hierarchy, it's difficult to position yourself as more important than the boss's favorite. Women are trained to be subordinate in our culture, and are too quick to accept a subordinate position. You have to keep hold of the fact that you've earned your position with your professional accomplishments. You have to feel your worth at the level of skill you've acquired. If you don't, you'll waste your boss's money puttering around with less important work than you're being paid to do. What you should be doing is generating enough activity to contribute to the growth of the department and to justify moving up and bringing in help under you.

Belinda's Story

Related to the problem of the boss's wife is that of the ambitious playmate who has a less important position and who resents your professional success. She may start undermining your activities and challenging your authority.

Belinda's boss was sleeping with his secretary, Stacey, a highly competitive young woman who used her personal advantage to create disputes and to upstage women with more status in the hierarchy. She ignored Belinda's business requests and even blocked meetings between Belinda and her boss. The boss seemed always to acquiesce to his secretary's demands and to take Stacey's side when Belinda complained. When there was conflict or something went wrong, Belinda got blamed. Stacey was feeding the boss a steady flow of distorted information between the bedsheets, and it wasn't long before he began peeling off some of Belinda's job functions and assigning them to the secretary.

By the time she came to me, Belinda thought the situation was quite hopeless and had decided to look for another job. She felt she couldn't compete with Stacey, who, as far as Belinda could see, had all the advantages.

The solution I proposed was: join the duo and make it a team. Look for the playmate's most competent work skills and propose assignments for her at the highest level possible. Beat the boss to it. Before he promotes her, you propose her promotion. While others may talk about her as a ''body,'' you need to see what she's really made of. She's as likely to have potential as any other woman in the workplace. Don't ignore her value and join the sexists who see a woman who's having an affair with the boss in the worst possible light.

Belinda gave it a try and was discouraged when Stacey's competitiveness didn't dissolve on the first try. But Belinda stuck to it, and continued to treat her as a colleague, suggesting both to the boss and to Stacey that Stacey take on more and more responsibility. After a while, Stacey began to stop seeing Belinda as a threat, and eventually even saw her as an ally. The flow of information to Belinda's boss changed dramatically. Everyone was happier, and the department's output both improved and increased.

Some of the responsibilities Belinda suggested Stacey take over were part of her own job, but instead of worrying about losing ground, Belinda took advantage of the free time she'd gained to plunge into more advanced work herself. By acting positively and not wilting under the threat of unfair competition, she was able to turn a very unpleasant situation into a productive working arrangement that benefited everyone—the boss, Stacey, the department, and not least, Belinda herself.

26. MY BOSS MAKES SEXUAL OVERTURES

The low-risk way to turn down a pass • Reducing the problem of sexual harassment • The she-slept-her-way-to-the-top slander • The dress-for-respect controversy

In the past, a woman's status and, indeed, her economic security depended on her attractiveness to men. A flirtatious overture or even a sexual ''pass'' made by a boss might have been disturbing, but it nonetheless was tolerated, even hoped for. It was flattering. The woman worker felt attractive and valued. In those days, women had little else beyond their attractiveness to make them feel exceptional or highly valued. Nowadays, however, most of us have found new ways beyond being the recipient of men's passes to achieve status, and consequently we feel quite differently about flirtatious or sexual overtures. Now such passes are often interpreted as disrespectful. They undermine our monumental struggles to overcome handicaps in the office. We're angry and insulted, and we're often tempted to let our feelings be known.

That's okay. Letting people know what you feel is important. But *how* you let them know is equally important.

If you turn down a boss's pass incautiously—if you insult him, or bluntly criticize his behavior—you may have gone too far. It's not appropriate to criticize his behavior, to tell him how to be. It is appropriate to tell him who *you* are. Reject the pass, not the person. Say, "I enjoy your company and our business relationship, but I don't want to get involved with a married man. That's not what I'd like for myself." Put your response on this personal note, instead of abusing the boss or pointing out to him the insults you perceive in his approaching you. Or else try to turn away the overture by reminding him of your value in business, even if he's forgotten it. One client of mine told a Don Juan boss, "On a personal level, you can get all the women you want. But a good assistant is hard to come by." He laughed, enjoying the flattery, while accepting her reminder that she was wisely protecting both of their long-range interests by refusing him.

Can you get fired if you refuse a boss's pass? You might. Some women are hired for a dual function. The boss hopes to obtain not only an assistant but also a sexual companion. If the woman is cooperative, he can have his sex paid for by the company. He can offer his employee a salary increase for her sexual services without its costing him a personal dime. In such circumstances, excellent performance at work and in bed are part of the job requirement, and if you won't do the job, you get fired. In most cases, however, you are more likely to be fired *only* if your rejection is moralizing or hostile. So don't slap his hand. Your mission is not to punish him or to change him, but to take care of yourself.

Nevertheless, there's no surefire way to hold on to your job when the powerful boss is pressuring you sexually. Even complying with his demands doesn't guarantee you'll keep your job; there's risk in complying with sexual overtures. If you sleep with the boss because you're attracted to him or because you think it will bring you business advantages, you might end up marrying him, or getting the promotion, or both, but you also might end up getting fired. Sleeping with him can be as dangerous to your job as refusing him. If all doesn't go well in the sex/love department, there'll be trouble during the cooling-off period. If *he* backs out, the odds are you will resent him—and there's also a chance he'll feel guilty. If *you* back out, he'll be furious. And, being the boss, he doesn't have to deal with resentment, guilt, or anger. He can fire you instead.

While I don't believe women can easily sleep their way to the top—these days sex is not so well-paid—I do think the competent woman who sleeps with her boss might keep her job. She might even keep both her sexual relationship *and* her job. But the higher you go, the more the deciding factor is business ability. The boss/lover doesn't take too many dollar risks on someone who is incompetent on the job, whatever her other qualifications may be.

The phrase, ''She slept her way to the top,'' is male chauvinist slander, whether it's said by a man or a woman. The fact that a woman sleeps with her boss doesn't mean she doesn't have ability, any more than it means he doesn't.

So weigh it up. But remember, the odds are you'll go further on competence than on sex—and have less risk and less necessity for compromises you'd rather not make.

There's another issue that's important to consider when discussing the boss who makes sexual overtures, and that is: who is responsible for the overture? Often women who complain of sexual harassment on the job are accused by their peers of bringing it on themselves. ''You asked for it,'' they are told emphatically, ''by the way you act and dress.'' But I don't accept this view. A man's behavior toward a woman is determined by his own history and personality rather than by a woman's style of dress or manners. Her decolletage doesn't control his behavior; he does. Otherwise how explain the difference between one man's macho wisecracks and another man's respectful invitations?

But while you are not responsible for a man's attitude toward you, it is to your advantage to manipulate it. Dress for professional respect and reduce the problem of the pass. You may lose attention on a sexual level, but your professional image will be the gainer.

One pitfall: consciously or unconsciously, you may want both to be seen as sexy and to be respected as a professional. You may be sending out conflicting signals: ''I'd like it if you were interested in me as a female,'' *and,* ''Don't be!'' The clearer you are about what you want, and the more consistent you are in communicating it, the better your chance of getting it.

27. MY BOSS IS A CHAUVINIST SLOB

How to solve the problem without moralizing • When the boss
constantly makes chauvinist remarks about women • How to take
care of yourself—and womankind—without getting into a war

*"He has no respect for women; he's constantly making derogatory
remarks. It's infuriating and I don't know how to respond."* Male chauvinism—allegiance to the idea of the superiority of the male sex—takes many
forms, from the refusal to consider women for managerial positions to the
crude wisecrack to the automatic macho pass. In this section, I'd like to discuss the more subtle, everyday kinds of expressions of chauvinism that
women at work so often encounter. My aim is to help you decide when and
whether to overlook slurs—when and how to respond to chauvinistic insults. The difficulties of handling this touchy situation are compounded
when the put-down comes from the boss.

In each case you must decide on your goal: is it to raise your boss's consciousness, or to succeed in your job? Sometimes you can do both, and
sometimes you have to choose. If you allow your anger about chauvinistic
remarks or acts to dominate your reactions, you may indeed be able to silence and apparently "reform" the chronic chauvinist. But you also are
taking a risk. If you splatter his ego all over the place, he may take revenge.
This isn't to say he hasn't splattered yours, or doesn't deserve to get his—
but it's to your advantage to think through your goals first.

Mary and Anne's Story

"Look," my client Anne told me, "I was furious when one of the salesmen
patted my secretary Mary on the butt, and my boss, who's a slob, whispered to me, 'With her face, she should be grateful.' I blew!"

But Mary handled it perfectly. She simply said, without a smile, "Hey,
cut it out!" She avoided the reaction of a more compliant woman, who
would have laughed off the incident for fear of hurting the man's feelings or
crushing his ego. If Mary had responded with an affable giggle, she might
well have hurt herself instead. If you permit a gesture inappropriate to a
work relationship, you may be redefining that relationship. A giggle in response to a colleague's insulting way of seeing you can be a statement of

acceptance, of acquiescence. You wish he'd treat you as a fellow worker, yet you invite him—with your amiable response—to continue to view you just as a female sex object. Mary knew better. She avoided acquiesence, but at the same time she didn't lecture, moralize, or retaliate with an insult. She was self-respecting. She established her position without initiating a counteroffensive.

Anne, on the other hand, got into an angry exchange with her boss, saying, "I find that insulting. That's a chauvinistic crack if ever I heard one." He agreed and walked off laughing. She was fuming. I believe she would have done better to express her own view without judging his. She might have reacted to his ugly statement by saying, "*I* think Mary is a very attractive and together woman—I like her a lot," or, "Many men might feel lucky to have her around." Such statements communicate your refusal to join in the demeaning of a woman—and therefore all women, including yourself.

This kind of nonaggressive, on-the-spot handling doesn't come easily, but keep trying. It's important to be able to express your point of view in a dignified way without alienating the men in your office—and to do it without getting into an ideological debate. The office is not the place to iron out political issues.

There may be times when you can educate a chauvinistic boss. If your relationship with him is solid enough, if he's educable, and if he's interested, you might take a stab at explaining how women feel and why. Explain that many women have heard too much about their appearance and too little about their professional ability. Their concern at work is to know they're valued as pros—their careers depend on it.

If you can explain this with empathy for your boss's lack of understanding, you might make progress. But don't count on overnight change, or even any change at all. Remember, a man sees flirtation as flattering: "What's wrong with being a sex object? I'd like to be one myself." Since men were never seen as important only for sex and sympathy, they don't understand the price women have had to pay as a result of such views. If you're going to try to educate a boss through discussion, think out your approach, and be aware that no matter how you launch into the discussion, you risk being labeled as oversensitive, touchy, and fanatical, and you risk being baited and teased. Practice these discussions with a lot of men outside the workplace until you've learned how to achieve a respectful response.

Chapter Three

MOVING UP

CONTENTS

Introduction

INTRODUCTION

To try to move up, or not—that is the question for many women in the workplace today. Would staying in your present job get you what you want? Would it be comfortable and satisfying? Or should you step forth and try for a higher-level job? Would that be the more rewarding alternative for you? The choice is yours.

Stay or step. It's a relatively new question for women to face, so before you make your decision, you might ask yourself the following key questions. Undoubtedly others will come to mind.

1. Does the work at your present job level provide you with opportunities for growth and learning? Or would you have to look elsewhere—to levels above your present one, either inside or outside your company—in order to have these opportunities?

2. What is the "boredom quotient" in the tasks connected with the job you are now doing? Are you likely to become bored with what you're doing in the next five—or fifteen—years?

3. Does your present job level involve you with people you like?

4. Does your present job level provide you with access to and participation in the social and intellectual circles you would like to be part of outside the company? (In the past, the life-style of most women depended completely on their husbands' or their fathers' level of achievement. Now, you have a choice in the matter.)

5. Look around you. Are your day-to-day activities in your present job more or less interesting to you compared with those involved with higher-level jobs in your company?

6. With anticipation of the raises in salary that might normally go with your present job, do you expect to be able to provide for your future financial needs by yourself (as well as those of your dependents, if you have any)? Think about this, dispassionately, whether you are presently married—or sharing expenses with someone else—or not.

7. Would moving up give you the opportunities for independence that you would like—inside as well as outside the company? How much inde-

pendence do you have inside—to make decisions, act on your own, run
your department or section? Does your job, and the particular company you
work for, influence adversely your independence on the outside—such as
being able to join organizations you might wish to belong to, engage in political activity, take vacations, enjoy a social life, and so on?

8. Is your present job meaningful to you? Do you feel that the work you
are now doing is making a contribution that you think is worthwhile?

Caution: in order to judge the pros and cons properly, you should think in
terms of the upper-level job *goal* you might want—not the job directly above
your present one, or the one above that. Sometimes we have to go through several levels of less-satisfying jobs in order to attain the one we hope for.

And another caution: try not to join the fantasy "big careers" band-
wagon or play the status game, thus giving in to the pressures of what's
supposed to be "in" these days. Be sure that you are not motivated by the
need to look important in other people's eyes. I suspect that you will be
more satisfied in the long run if you search for the job level or career that
corresponds to your interests and your values.

If the balance weighs in favor of staying where you are, thank your
good fortune. You are where you want to be.

But, if the balance shows in favor of moving up—then get going.

There are a number of women who want very much to move up, but
they back away because they are frightened to do so, or they don't know
how, or, sometimes, they've tried and been knocked down. This chapter is
designed to help you overcome these reservations—if you have them—by
providing you with a close-up view of the problems and situations you
might encounter, as well as with some tried-and-true tools that you might
use to move up successfully.

1. I'M THE BEST IN MY DEPARTMENT, BUT I DON'T GET PROMOTED

Why promotions are not given as rewards for good work • How to
figure out what *will* get you a promotion • How to unearth the
sometimes hidden requirements for the next job up • Networking

The idea that a promotion is given as a reward for working long and
hard and well at your present job is one of the greatest illusions women

have about how the workplace operates. Promotions are not given as rewards. The fact is, although you do have to do good work in order to get promoted, you won't get promoted *just* for doing good work. Why not? Because—and understanding this is a key to moving up—jobs at different levels call for very different qualities and skills.

In order to get promoted, you have to convince your boss that you have the higher-level capabilities he's looking for. If he isn't sure you have them, you won't get the job. Bosses generally won't take a chance on an unproven quantity. They can't afford to: the pressures are too great, and the risks too large. That's why the best worker at one level won't automatically get advanced to the next level. And that's also why so many of the moving-up strategies in this book deal, in one way or another, with proving you are a next-level person.

If you want to move up, you have to analyze the job for which you are shooting. Be a detective. Look for the key qualities needed in that spot. Study the people who are in that job already. I find that a good way to put your finger on the critical requirement for the next level is to look at what the people at that level are doing, and then figure out how it differs from what you are doing. Do they have any special talents or skills? Do they have to be able to get along with clients? How articulate are they? Do they give speeches? Do they have to be aggressive? Do they have to be administrators? Planners? Persuaders? Deal-makers? Do they have the ability to make the right contacts? What about their personality and style? Are they low-key and amiable? Tough-minded? Precise? Are they socially adept? Do they know how to handle themselves in high-level places?

Don't look only for admirable qualities and technical skills. Some companies want people at higher levels who are insensitive or ruthless. Or they might want someone who is willing to be less than straightforward when dealing, say, with government or labor or customers.

Once you've located the key qualities and/or skills that are required at the next level, you have to decide whether they are the ones that *you* want to develop, that you will feel comfortable with. Sometimes the keys to the next job up aren't immediately obvious.

Jenny's Story

Jenny, a speech therapist, was a supervisor in an agency that worked with the handicapped. Her next step up was the position of program administrator, but she was passed over for promotion. When she first brought her problem to me, it seemed quite mystifying; she was clearly so quick and bright and confident. Indeed, she was so impressive that it seemed that her assessment of the situation was probably correct: she said she was not only the best in the department at her level, but also more competent than the current program administrator, her boss. Nevertheless, I asked her the all-important, get-to-the-heart-of-the-problem question: "Are there any activities that the program administrator is involved in that you are not?" Her answer was emphatic: "No, I do *everything.*"

Her relationships were good. Her work was good. It seemed there must be some important quality or ability that higher-level people had that she didn't have. I rephrased my question: "What does your boss do that you don't do?" "That's easy," she laughed. "Waste time. He sits around, talking about nothing. He's more involved with baseball, boats, and cars than with work. He's on the phone all day long talking to his pals about all this dumb stuff." I had a hunch that this was the clue I needed. "Who are his friends?" His friends, she answered, were all over the place—inside the agency, outside, in other agencies, in the government, at the foundations they worked with. All over. Because I was thinking in terms of key job functions, I was quite sure we had found the answer.

The program administrator was responsible for getting the funding for the projects in his area; therefore, good connections were vital to his job. And indeed, it developed that he was more than just a sociable fellow who liked to yak about baseball. He had built a web of excellent relationships throughout the field. Like the client in Chapter 2 who thought her boss was stupid, Jenny missed the point. Jenny did so much of her boss's job better than he did—including writing proposals for grants—that she failed to see that his important contacts were crucial. Through these relationships, he was in constant touch with what was going on in the field. He knew what kind of projects were getting money, and he knew which agencies or foundations were receptive to what types of projects. Once he had gotten his proposals to the right place, he had friends who saw that each one received the right kind of attention. As a result, he got a very high proportion of his projects funded.

Jenny, on the other hand, didn't have many personal contacts outside her immediate department. She was, in fact, quite isolated. She wouldn't have been able to handle the job of the program administrator because she didn't have the kind of network that was essential to securing funds for department projects.

Now we knew what Jenny had to work on: she had to build up her own web of personal and business relationships. She had to join professional organizations and take an active role in them. At work, she had to regard every phone conversation and every meeting during the course of her day as a chance to develop a contact. She had to slow down her pace, stop trying to get so much done, and take the time to talk with people so that important relationships could grow.

This was not an easy assignment for Jenny. She felt uncomfortable making overtures and courting people. She hated picking up the phone to call someone; she disliked walking over to a colleague she didn't know well at a meeting. Taking the first step felt all wrong to her, as it does to many women. We are taught to play a waiting game; taking the initiative in a relationship feels aggressive, unfeminine, and inappropriate to us. Jenny had to challenge her feeling that taking the first step would be met with a negative reaction. She had to take a chance with more aggressive behavior in the hope that it would win respect—which it usually does. After repeated experience with reaching out, she came to realize that people responded much more favorably to her overtures than she had ever expected.

Now, she had a circle of important business connections. She was able to introduce her boss to people who were important to him and, through her network, she began to gather and pass along helpful new information to him. Six months after she began to enlarge her circle and develop solid contacts, he recommended her for a promotion.

Again and again in this chapter you will read stories, like Jenny's, that show how a client analyzed a job at the next level, decided what was required by the job *and* by the company, assessed her own qualifications and began to do something about her deficits. Although it can be quite a puzzle at first, you will, as you see how others have done it, learn how to go through this process yourself.

2. HOW CAN I PROVE I'M A NEXT-LEVEL PERSON?

How to get hold of the assignments that show off your abilities
• Seizing the initiative • Teaming with the boss • Watch out for
stepping on toes • The importance of breaking the "rules"—and
how to get away with it • Why women find it hard to jump a job
description

If you believe that you have the qualities the higher-level job you're after demands, you now have to make sure your boss knows it also. Look for
ways to demonstrate these capabilities. Prove to him through your actions
that *you* are the right person for *that* job.

Seek out the kind of work that will show off the particular talents
needed for the job you are after. If you are lucky, your present assignment
will give you that chance and you will be able, as you go about your daily
routine, to look like more of a salesperson, or a negotiator, or whatever it is
you need to be for the next job up. Most likely, however, to prove your
next-level capabilities, you will have to jump beyond your present job description and take on higher-level work.

Here's how to do it.

• *Take the next step in every function you perform.* If you're researching, start writing up the research into reports. If you're in personnel
and your job is to greet people, do a preliminary screening, select those
who should be sent in to the interviewer, and politely send the others on
their way. If you're already screening people, move yourself up to interviewing and proposing candidates.

• *Look for gaps.* Any unfilled slot—where someone has been promoted
or fired or transferred, or is out sick or on leave or on vacation—gives you a
great opportunity to find work that isn't being done. If it's work that might
make you look good to management, go to it. Look for gaps above you,
next to you, and in other departments.

• *Grab at the chance to handle things as they arise.* If something needs
doing, do it. For example, if your boss comes in late in the morning, don't
store up the work for him—do it yourself. Take initiative. But if your boss
has a say in your promotion, be careful not to threaten him when you start
jumping your job description into his territory. He may be impressed by
your dynamic new image, but if it outshines his, you may get fired before
you get promoted. Nevertheless, if you are working well with your boss,

and you are not competitive with him and don't grab credit, he'll probably welcome your help. Let him know you're an ally. Keep him informed of what you are doing. Cover for him, and let him know that you are. Don't go too far on your own initiative before checking with him. And don't ask for work that serves only *your* best interest; make sure it serves his interest as well.

• *Learn to recognize opportunities.* Often I find a client will have gotten the go-ahead on new work but can't quite believe it because it hasn't come in the form of a detailed, official instruction. Start to move on casual directions from your boss; don't wait for further clarification or for specific, spelled-out directions.

• *Get hold of work that your boss or co-workers can't or won't do.* Offer to help out when someone has a project he or she doesn't like doing or when someone is overloaded or just plain lazy. If someone is neglecting work or doing it poorly, simply take it on yourself. Although some of your co-workers may become resentful if you threaten their territory, and some may be envious when they see you pulling ahead, the important person—the boss whose sponsorship you need—will see you in a new light.

Often, you can pick up a clue from someone's offhand complaint. I'm sure you've heard your boss say, "Oh, if I only had time, I'd get that done." Next time, listen carefully and evaluate his comment. Does he really mean it? Is the project important? Will it show off the abilities you want to highlight? If the answer to these questions is yes, then start to make it happen. But be cautious: before you spend too much time on it, check it out with him. After you've completed part of the task, show him your work. Display your initiative and at the same time give him a chance to halt the progress. Say "I've drawn up a list of such-and-such. I'm doing this-and-that." Then if he has any objections to your doing this work, you can drop it without having spent too much time on it. If his reaction is positive, you've gotten hold of some functions that will show off your next-level abilities.

• *Apprentice yourself.* Approach someone on a higher level who is doing the kind of work you want to do and ask to take on some of their lower-level work. Be very open about your goal, so that you don't seem pushy, or look like you are trying to put something over on them. Make a speech that is clear and definite, not mousy or apologetic: "I want to get going in the field. I know it's going to take me years to get the kind of skill you have, but I want to get cracking. Do you have any work that I could help you with?" Because people often forget that it took them years to build up their expertise, you can remove any possible threat by reminding them that you are a beginner and that they are light-years ahead of you. Caution: if you're trying to jump your job description, don't walk in to your boss, or in to anyone for that matter, with a blanket offer of help. You don't want to get buried in work that's not going to advance your career. Ask only for work that will show off the qualities needed to convince your boss to promote you.

• *Create new work by coming up with innovative ideas.* Although this may be the most uncommon way to jump your job description—because it's so hard to come up with good new ideas, let alone get approval for them—it can be a very effective way to show your higher-level abilities. Keep in mind the two keys to success for getting acceptance of new ideas: the new idea has to address problems that have high priority from *management's* point of view, and it has to make sense in terms of available resources and budget.

When I was the director of volunteers in a home and hospital for the aged during the turbulent sixties, I created a new program—as mentioned in Chapter 2—that solved a major problem for that institution. The hospital was an opulent complex of buildings of stainless steel, glass, and marble that rose up from the middle of a slum. The neighborhood kids found us a natural target. They attacked the hospital, throwing rocks, breaking windows, assaulting patients and staff on the street. It was a dangerous situation.

Although the problem was outside my responsibility and my department, I was looking for opportunities to go beyond my job description. I was aware that I had a tendency to rely on ''important'' people to solve knotty problems, and I was making a conscious effort to wrench myself from that classic feminine mold. I trained myself to think of myself as *the* problem-solver in my life. When presented with a problem, I made myself tackle it rather than look around for the smart person who could solve it for me. While no one in the country had been able to come up with solutions to the turmoil that was sweeping our cities, I isolated the problem in my mind to: ''What is going on with these kids on our street?'' My guess was that they had been fooled by the seeming wealth of the physical plant and had no idea that if any group in society was worse off than the kids themselves, it was the residents of that hospital. They were not only poor and on welfare, but they were helpless and sick, and, because of their advanced age, had little hope of recovery. My feeling was that if the kids understood who they were attacking, they would see that their anger had been misdirected.

My idea was that we try to bring these youngsters into the hospital as volunteers, and, with some maneuvering, I convinced administration to go along with my efforts. To get the kids interested and involved, I toured them through the buildings and showed them how much help these old and fragile people needed. The youngsters responded with real compassion, pitching in as wheelchair-pushers, recreational aides, and even as assistants to the security guards to prevent the very crimes that they themselves had been committing. From that point on, the whole atmosphere of the neighborhood changed.

The program was a success on several levels. It defused a dangerous situation. It benefited both the kids and the patients—the old people enjoyed contact with all that youthful energy, and the youths felt important, useful, and appreciated. The program and the agency got good press coverage, our relations with the community improved substantially, and, because I had dealt with the kinds of delicate sociopolitical problems that are central concerns of top management, I began to look like a candidate for higher-level responsibility. Indeed, soon after, I was offered—and I accepted—one of the top jobs in the field.

Women often find it difficult to take over work that hasn't been specifically assigned to them, and they have even more reservations if it's work that someone else is already doing. We tend to take job descriptions literally. We believe the company when it says, in effect, "These are your responsibilities and here are your boundaries. Do what we tell you to do, and do it well; don't overstep your bounds, and you will be rewarded with a raise and, eventually, a promotion." We're not aware that there is quite a different message given to movers and shakers. This unspoken rule says, "Leap to the task at hand and do what has to be done, even if you have to trample boundaries. Do it artfully and you'll be rewarded. You'll be given—formally—what you've already taken, plus a title that suitably reflects your stolen empire."

These two contrasting sets of rules coexist because companies want two very different kinds of workers: docile, obedient people who stick to the job no matter how monotonous; and enterprising, aggressive people who are willing to respond to the needs of the company, whatever they might be. The routine following of orders is valued only in lower-level people. The higher you look in the business structure, the fewer people you will find who are bound by job descriptions. Men, more than women, seem to understand this unspoken rule of breaking the rules. Not every man, by any means, but those who get this message are generally found in that group favored in our society by history and tradition: upper-class Caucasians. From the moment they are born, they are seen as candidates for management. They are expected to be leaders, and they are trained for that role. Teachers, parents, and the culture tacitly encourage these boys to be aggressive, to forge ahead, to develop their own goals. The whole world is their territory, as it was and is for their fathers. A man with this background would naturally see a job description not as a box to which he's confined, but as a launching platform from which to propel himself into his (high-level) future.

Nothing in women's training prepares us for jumping a job description, for leaping over boundaries. On the contrary, enterprise and aggressiveness are actively discouraged in little girls, while docility and dependence are encouraged. Most women, even today, are brought up to be homemakers. They live in a culture that nourishes attitudes, interests, and skills that draw them toward the housewife role. And housewives *can't* jump their job description: in the home there are no next levels up. No wonder women in the workplace see the job description as confining, as a box (like the home) to which they are restricted. But, clearly, women who want to achieve at the level that men do, have to be able to break out of the perimeters of their jobs and snare higher-level work.

3. I TOOK INITIATIVE AND IT GOT ME INTO A LOT OF TROUBLE

"They tell me to be aggressive and then they resent it" • The cardinal rules of jumping your job description • Defusing a boss who's threatened by you • Shedding work • What do bosses really want? • Putting the boss in a parental role • How and when to be aggressive • The diplomatic way to take initiative

Both Dorothy and Maggie, whose stories follow, jumped beyond their job descriptions and, as often happens, ran head-on into big trouble with their bosses. It's a risk that's inherent in taking over new work, but if done artfully, the danger of stepping into unassigned territory can be minimized. There's a right and a wrong way to take initiative.

Dorothy's Story

"I showed initiative, I took over new work, and I got slapped down hard. My boss doesn't like aggressive women."

Dorothy was a bright, energetic thirty-year-old woman, full of drive, with a successful career as a teacher behind her. When she switched fields she started at the bottom—as secretary to the president of a small package-goods company. She was eager to advance her new career in business, so she took every possible opportunity to prove her managerial ability. Soon she had involved herself in all aspects of running the office. When the executive offices were relocated to a nearby suburb, she immersed herself in the challenges of this large project, running the entire move.

Up until this point, Hugo, her boss, had appreciated her efforts and had even encouraged her. But now, he clipped her wings. He took away her newly acquired activities and told her that her main responsibility was the secretarial work she had been hired to do in the first place. Dorothy was furious. She did the secretarial tasks, but she bitterly resented it, especially when Hugo asked her to do personal things like typing letters to the members of his golf club committee. He saw it as part of her job, and she saw it as doing his personal work at the expense of the more important work she wanted to do. They were soon locked in a classic office war. Each assignment became a battle over her job description. He would send her to the coffee shop for doughnuts and coffee, and she'd fight back the only way she felt she could—indirectly—with cool responses, annoyed looks, and irritable behavior. Dorothy was full of fury over the injustice of the situation. While she was trying to make her point that she was ready for better things and that she resented being held down to the level of simpler tasks and personal errands, Hugo was getting resentful of her resistance to doing his work.

It seemed to Dorothy that Hugo did not like aggressive women. But it seemed to me that her problem was due to her losing sight of the cardinal rules of jumping your job description: 1) make sure the work you grab is more valuable to your boss than the work you abandon, and 2) make sure the abandoned work is covered—at least on the surface. Dorothy had inadvertently set up a competition between her need and that of her boss. Her need was to do interesting work and to get ahead, but his need was to have a helper so he could function effectively.

If your boss sees your initiative as purely self-serving, he will, of course, chop you back. He might accept your ambitions, even encourage them, but not at the cost of undermining his own work. However, if you are helping him while helping yourself, he won't object.

Dorothy had virtually stopped doing the job for which she had been hired, leaving her boss without any way to cope with his minute-by-minute needs. He hadn't pushed her back down because she was aggressive and took initiative, but because she had dropped the work *he* wanted her to do.

She was caught in a problem women often face. While it's true that she moved fast and was insensitive to her boss's needs, if she had been a man she might have gotten away with it. A man's movement upward is acknowledged more readily than a woman's; after a man has proven his higher-level abilities, he is more likely than a woman to be promoted and a replacement brought in to relieve him of the lower-level work. Women who show next-level initiative are expected to do the new work in addition to the old. Like the husband who says to his wife, "Sure you can get a job, as long as you have dinner on the table when I get home," the male boss says, "Sure you can do higher-level work, as long as you get everything else done." They deliver the problem, unfair as it may be, back to the woman.

Now that Dorothy realized her error, we decided she should try to jump beyond her job description again, to see if this time she could take initiative without getting into trouble. But before she could even attempt a new moving-up strategy, she had to get out of the mess she was in. She had to reestablish her image as cooperative, as being on Hugo's side. Once she stopped competing—stopped asserting her needs at the expense of his— Hugo began to see her once again as someone he could count on to be helpful to him. She was surprised, as most people are, at how quickly their good relationship was reestablished once she eliminated the behavior patterns that had angered him. When a new opportunity arose for her to take initiative, he didn't resist. Just as he hadn't fought her initiative on the first round—until his work was abandoned—he didn't fight her now.

Hugo was scheduled to appear on a cable TV program on product development and trends, but he was swamped with vital, year-end work. Dorothy proposed that she appear for him. She pointed out that, since she had taught for years, she was experienced and comfortable in front of an audience. And she reminded him of her curious nature that had gotten her involved in reading and discussing the technical side of the business: "You know I understand the subject; we've had many discussions over the past year." To Hugo, Dorothy's offer was an opportunity to get rid of a relatively unimportant though necessary obligation and he saw her now, as he had been seeing her in the last few weeks, as nothing but helpful. Indeed, it was such a relief to him that he began to send her to make other appearances in his place.

Throughout this period, Dorothy was very careful. No matter how hard it was to accomplish, she made sure she got the important secretarial work done. Then, at the first opportunity, she began delegating some of her more routine work to the receptionist. The receptionist was happy to be doing what to her was more interesting, higher-level work; Dorothy was happy to be doing *her* more important work; and Hugo was free to concentrate on *his* more important work.

Maggie's Story

"I did what you said: I dreamed up a project, got it going, and now my boss is threatened and he's taking it away from me."

Many women race forward, contributing ideas and taking initiative in good faith. When their ideas and efforts are rejected, they are mystified and demoralized.

Maggie, an assistant in the promotion department of a marketing organization, worked on preparing audiovisual presentations for salesmen to use with their customers. She developed a new theme for a sales presentation, something that was quite beyond the scope of her assigned responsibilities. Her boss, Joe, gave her the go-ahead, and she then discussed her new idea with the director of sales. He was enthusiastic and asked her to present her idea to his regional managers. He wanted her to have their reaction before she set about creating the actual script and visuals. The meeting was successful; Maggie gave and got lots of good ideas. But no sooner had she launched the project than Joe suddenly took it back because, he said, "It was too big and important" for her; it required a more experienced person. Maggie was stunned. Her idea had gained acceptance throughout the company, and she had no doubt that she could produce an impressive product. She argued with Joe, but to no avail. She was off the project.

What had gone wrong? "The problems began when the regional sales managers came in last Wednesday. My relationship with Joe was fine until that week. We even had lunch on Monday. On Wednesday, just before the meeting with the regional managers, I popped my head in his office and said, 'I'm on my way to the meeting with the regional sales managers; I think you'd probably like to come.' He replied, 'I'm too busy.' Then after the meeting, he made sarcastic remarks, as if he'd never been invited at all.''

Maggie was puzzled. Joe *had* been invited. She knew he had received notices of the meeting, and that the arrangements had come up in several conversations. As she told her story, I began to realize that, from Joe's point of view, he had not been invited—because he had not been invited to make the presentation. *He,* not Maggie, was the one who represented his department. For Joe to attend that meeting without participating would have been humiliating. Joe felt shoved aside. He was angry and mortified. "I'm too busy" meant "I'm not going to any damn meeting where you are the whole show and I've been squeezed out.''

Maggie had moved into the limelight too fast. Flattered and excited by the generally enthusiastic response to her idea, she had dashed ahead without looking around. It never occurred to her to take care of her boss's feelings. The attention was focused on her; she was on center stage. She was like a child whose efforts are being praised. When the child's mother says, "Oh, that's beautiful; what a good artist you are!" the child doesn't think to turn around and encourage his mother. His mother's needs are beyond his notice. Just so with Maggie—she had seen herself in this childlike way, and hadn't recognized her boss's need for attention and praise. She could have handled the situation more diplomatically. When she was invited to discuss her ideas with the regional managers, she could have said to the director of sales: "I'll work out the presentation with Joe." Then she could have consulted with Joe on how they might prepare for the meeting and present their ideas.

Though women often play the parent at work, and certainly in their personal lives—being overly considerate of other people's feelings, while erasing their own—Maggie's oversight came from her habit of putting bosses in a parental role. She was unaccustomed to seeing herself as an equal, as a colleague.

The damage done, the best Maggie could do at this point was to retreat and, like Dorothy, work at restoring her image. She had to consider how she appeared to Joe and correct his mistaken view of her as grabby and competitive. Instead of fighting to get the project back, she cooperated with Joe by agreeing, "The project has grown. I can understand that you want to handle it. If there's anything you want me to do, I'll get right on it." When he was safely restored to his leadership position and confident she wasn't trying to exclude him, she could think about presenting a new idea—and this time she'd keep Joe a part of it.

Both Maggie and Dorothy took the kind of initiative that could get them promotions, but both went too far, too fast. Maggie, in forging ahead, disregarded her boss's feelings, just as Dorothy, in taking on important activities, neglected her boss's work.

Although in this book I advise women to jump their job description and be aggressive in that way, here I have to say when you leap ahead, remember you are not going solo. The people who have the power to stop your progress should see you as working with them and for them.

Moral: be sure that jumping your job description works for both you and your boss, so that he doesn't see your initiative as purely self-serving. Make sure your initiative works to his benefit as well as yours. When things are going well with your new functions and your boss sees you as valuable at the higher level, you can begin to negotiate for a new job—and for a replacement in the old.

4. MY BOSS IS SO DEPENDENT ON ME HE WON'T RECOMMEND ME FOR A TRANSFER

How to use your boss's weakness to your advantage • Why women endow bosses with more power than they really have • Avoiding the trap of overwork as you move up

Lynn's Story

Lynn, who had worked for four years as a paralegal aide in the governmental affairs department of a large corporation, found herself caught in a classic trap. She had done all the right things to move up—she had taken initiative, started doing higher-level work, shown leadership, been aggressive—but she couldn't get promoted. The reason was clear. The more she did to get promoted, the more valuable she became, and the more valuable she became, the more her boss, the vice president in charge of legal affairs for the corporation, depended on her. Lynn was stymied. There was no place for her to go in her department, since the jobs above her required legal degrees, and her boss would not transfer her to another department where there was a good job open because he was so dependent on her. As she put it, "He'll never let me leave. He'd be lost without me." He gave her titles, money, anything to keep her happy where she was—along with a lot of excuses to avoid transferring her.

Lynn felt helpless and defeated. "If that's the way he wants it, what else can I do? I've got to go along with him, or leave." She couldn't see a way to get what she wanted because it was in direct conflict with what he wanted. She felt she had no leverage because, as many women do, she had endowed her boss with all the power in the situation.

True, her boss had formal decision-making power. But more important, he had—with Lynn—enormous psychological power. She was caught in the belief that when her needs were inconvenient to someone else, she would have to defer. She had learned over and over as a child that her needs were not important. "Don't bother me. I'm busy. Go outside and play." Her parents taught her in a thousand ways that she was unimportant as a person. And school, church, television commercials, films, newspapers, books—the world—all reinforced the sexist message of her insignificance as a female. Society had done its job. By the time she got to work, she was the perfect, undemanding employee. On the job, her feelings of unimportance were exacerbated by the hierarchichal structure of the workplace and all its trimmings. Bosses, with their big desks, big offices, and big cars seek to impress the world with their importance—and the employee's unimportance.

No wonder Lynn's boss had psychological power over her: the whole world had colluded to impress upon her her insignificance. She couldn't possibly see herself as equal to him. So Lynn and her boss played out their symbiotic roles: she made him a king by being his subject, he made her his subject by being king.

Because Lynn did not perceive her own strength in the situation, she believed her boss had to solve the problem. All she could do was wait, hoping for a miracle. In a bad job, as in a bad marriage, the woman who feels unable to change things dreams of the powerful man who can. But Lynn's boss had no reason to help her. Why should he save Lynn if he'd drown in the process? If Lynn wanted to get ahead, she had to rescue herself *and* her boss. She had to come up with ideas that would take care of his needs as well as hers.

Thinking in these terms gave us the solution: why not begin to build a department of her own? Lynn grabbed the idea and ran with it. She showed her boss how, with the help of an assistant, she could supervise her old job and, at the same time, do the new job in the other department. This would solve her boss's difficulty with her transfer—he'd still have her as part of his team—and would also solve her own problem of getting into a department with more promise.

It was important that Lynn take a strong position when presenting her plan. Her boss had to know that she was dead set on moving ahead. When he felt the strength of her new resolve, his dependency would start working for her. He'd sense he didn't have much choice: he had to restructure his division to allow this unorthodox crossing of departmental boundaries or he would risk losing Lynn altogether.

Lynn used her boss's weakness to take a giant leap forward. Once she realized the strength of her position, she was able to get much more—a new, higher-level job in a department with more opportunity, plus the parts of her old job that gave her power within the division, and in addition the beginning of her own staff to handle the less-interesting work.

If you are in this situation, don't complain about your boss's dependence on you; use it. A boss might come to rely on you for any number of reasons. In Lynn's case, her boss needed her knowledge and judgment. A compliant boss can be dependent on your assertiveness. If your boss is afraid to initiate contact with people, he can become dependent on your ability to call strangers. If he's not creative, he may rely on you for ideas. And the more he relies on you, the stronger your position becomes.

Caution: Lynn, in her eagerness to convince her boss to go along with her plan, nearly gave away more than she had to. She almost made the fatal error of telling him that she could handle both jobs herself. While sometimes it is wise to take on extra work to prove yourself, this was not Lynn's problem; she had more than proven herself already. If she had taken on *both* jobs, she would have entrapped herself in overwork, something women often do. She would have been so buried in details that she wouldn't have had the time or the energy to focus on the more important aspects of either job. Don't, in a negotiation, give more than you have to.

5. I WAS PASSED OVER FOR A PROMOTION BECAUSE I DON'T HAVE THE RIGHT CREDENTIALS

The truth about credentials • How to evaluate management's reasons for not promoting you—and what to do about them

Be suspicious. If management tells you that you didn't get promoted because you don't have the right credentials, and you can do all or most of the job you're after, they are probably not telling the truth. Companies are not as enamored of credentials as they sometimes appear to be, even though they may include specific educational requirements in job descriptions. Good managers know that the practical wisdom gained from being steeped in a company and in a job, day in and day out, will usually far surpass what is learned in any school, no matter how prestigious. If you are in this situation, the lack of a credential is not enough reason to turn you down.

Management uses a lot of excuses like this for not giving promotions, ranging from "You're too young" to "You need such-and-such experience" to "There's no room for another person at that level." They could be valid reasons, of course, but when I hear them, I'm suspicious, because they have one thing in common: they have nothing to do with your actual ability to do the job. And that's the tip-off. They are probably cover-ups.

Why wouldn't management tell you the truth so you could go to work on the problem? Usually it's something that, in their view, is better left unsaid. A smart manager, for example, will not give you a reason that will get him into legal trouble (you're a woman, you're too old, you're the wrong color). And he won't give you reasons that are debatable—that are a matter of opinion—because he doesn't want the bother of arguing with you about it. He's made up his mind; it would be a waste of time to discuss it. And, finally, he won't give you a reason that might offend you (in his view, your clothes don't have the right look for the next level, or you're indecisive, or you're too fat, or you're too quiet, or you don't catch on fast enough). He doesn't want a grumbling, grudging, uncooperative worker on his hands. He doesn't want to start a war with you, and, while he may not want to promote you, he may not want to lose you, either.

Management's way around all these problems is to find an explanation that puts the blame for your failure to get promoted squarely on the "facts," as if they had no choice but to rule you out. It's very clever: you feel inadequate, but not aggrieved, and management isn't to blame.

If you are passed over for a promotion and are given an explanation that doesn't make much sense in terms of your ability to do the job, it probably is an excuse. Something else is holding you back. If you want to move up in the workplace, it's to your advantage to try to figure out their real reason for not promoting you.

Sometimes you can change the "defect" or deficit, and in other instances you will need to work on your image. If you are considering fighting company policy, read the discussions of the risks and rewards of such a fight. (See pp. 113–117.)

6. I CAN'T GET ANYWHERE IN MY COMPANY—THEY STILL SEE ME THE SAME OLD WAY

The importance of style • The importance of enthusiasm and selling yourself • The importance of resisting the force of authority and using your own judgment • Diagnosing the qualities you'll need to get ahead • How you are perceived: a checklist • Breaking out of the mold

"Everyone thinks of me the way I was when I first came here—they won't promote me because they don't acknowledge my development." What I usually find in this situation is that, while a woman may indeed have grown and developed, her manner doesn't reflect these changes. She hasn't developed a new style; she doesn't project her new qualities in a pronounced enough way. Women, unlike men, have to flaunt their growth and development or it won't be noticed. We are seen through the distorting lens of ancient stereotypes as compliant, emotional, girlish, and with a low horizon of development. We're not expected to change. While management is on the lookout for men who are going to rise above the crowd into leadership positions, they hardly even glance at women. If a woman wants to be seen as a potential leader, she has to highlight her leadership qualities dramatically to get past the prejudice.

Of course, there is a chance that you're seen in "the same old way" because you really have *not* changed. Or perhaps you haven't changed in some way that is essential for success at the next level. Your development may not correspond to management's needs.

Leila's Story

Leila was on the verge of resigning after eleven years as a writer in an advertising agency. She worked exceptionally well with the people around her, her commercials were successful, and she had, over the years, developed a reputation as a first-rate creative writer. Yet she was turned down for a promotion to group head because, as she saw it, the company didn't acknowledge the reality of her development over the years.

I was puzzled. I wondered why the company would not have seen her development. Was that really the reason she had been passed over? Or was it that she had not grown in some way that they saw as important? To find out, I asked her two questions: how did the company see her? And what kind of person *did* the company promote?

Leila thought they saw her as very capable, businesslike, but perhaps a bit plodding. A good, steady workhorse.

She then described Bill, who had been rapidly promoted from copywriter to group head. He had good concepts, she said, but there was nothing special about his writing. Was there *anything* special about him? "His enthusiasm," she answered. "He gets everyone revved up about his ideas." Of course! This was the clue we needed. Bill was a super salesman: the excitement he generated bred confidence in his work and sold his product—his ideas. Leila delivered first-rate work but didn't know how to sell it. She was essentially in a sales-oriented business, but she had neglected to develop the sales-oriented side of her presentations. That might be the growth quality the company was looking for. A group head has to generate good ideas, but beyond that, a group head also has to be able to get people enthusiastic about them—the creative director, the company's account executives, and finally, the client. It's just not a job for a good, steady workhorse.

Why was Leila so restrained? Why didn't she radiate enthusiasm and excitement about her ideas? Leila was, in fact, excited about her ideas, but she had been conditioned, like many of us, to control her excitement in a business environment. As a child, she had learned that grown-up work was a serious matter. As an adult, she had heard women criticized for not being serious about work.

By the time Leila got her first job, she was thoroughly convinced that seriousness is the order of the day in the business world. Her first boss inadvertently reinforced that notion. She would bring her ideas to him, full of enthusiasm, and he, playing devil's advocate, would challenge every aspect of her presentations. His intentions were constructive, but she heard his every question and remark in the context of her upbringing and cultural conditioning. She thought he was saying: ''Cut out the fun (the excitement) and be more businesslike.'' Feeling criticized, she began to repress her excitement. She tried to forestall his questions by covering all possible objections before they were raised. She would say, ''I know you're worried about such-and-such so I did this-and-that,'' or, ''I thought of this idea but it wouldn't work because . . .'' and ''We could have done it in blue, but blue doesn't really come off, and we couldn't use green because of whatever, and purple would etc.'' By the time she got to the idea, she undoubtedly had her boss thoroughly befuddled and bored. She had completely overlooked the need to stage her presentations in order to sell them. She had become lost in a sea of tangled qualifiers.

Leila had tried so hard to do it right, to follow what she imagined were her boss's instructions, that her own independent judgment had gotten lost in the process. She had failed to step back and make her own decisions about the appropriate tone and mood needed to gain acceptance for her ideas.

Losing touch with your own thinking and surrendering your judgment to the force of ''authorities'' is a problem that many people face. It generally starts when children are pressured and manipulated into doing what they're told and are not encouraged by the adults around them to exercise their own judgment or to influence decisions.

It's a problem for both men and women, but boys can usually move more easily to independent thought. They perceive early on that the women who raise and teach them are considered, in many ways, their inferiors. This can breed arrogance and chauvinism, but it also leads to a disposition to believe in and to exercise their own judgment. Moreover, it helps to build up their confidence vis-à-vis the adult world. A boy still has to face the challenges of one day measuring up to his father, but at least he has the advantage of having pitted his child's perceptions against those of an adult and has discovered his power to exercise judgment and make decisions. He's becoming an autonomous person.

Girls have no such advantage. Any thought that they are superior to their mothers is ultimately negated by their identification with all women—the inferior sex. The importance of their own independent thinking and judgment is never established. They never learn to make decisions based on their own evaluation. They remain followers of directions, trying to please by doing things "right."

And so it was with Leila. She hadn't brought her own judgment to bear on analyzing the real needs of the situation. Now, however, she understood the source of her follow-the-leader mentality, and with this insight was able to extricate herself from it. She could now look objectively at what the company needed in a group head. She realized she had to develop a new style.

She changed her presentations. She introduced each idea with the excitement she'd felt when she had first thought of it. Only after she had stirred up her colleagues' enthusiasm would she raise questions, objections, and possible problems. She still covered all bases, and showed that she had thought the matter through, but by doing so *after* she got people interested she reinforced rather than undermined her sales pitch.

Leila backed up the impact of her stronger, more dramatic presentations with a new, more lively appearance. Her aim was to overcome the long-standing impression that she was plodding and overly serious, so she wore more vivid clothes and brightened up her makeup; she frizzed her hair into the latest style and put more energy into her walk and her body movements.

A few weeks after she changed her image, the validity of our analysis was confirmed. She was asked to attend a client meeting for the first time in her career, an assignment that in her agency was usually reserved for people at the next level. And after the meeting her boss gave her the plum job of showing the out-of-town clients around the city—and thus, a chance to establish important business relationships. Clearly, her boss had begun to see her as a next-level person.

Leila had been passed over for promotion because, in terms of what was needed for success at the next level, she had not grown. She was seen in "the same old way" because she hadn't developed the qualities essential to moving up in her industry.

If you feel you are seen in "the same old way," ask yourself these questions:

1. How does the company view you?
2. Do they see that you have the qualities that are needed at the next level? Look at the people who were promoted in your company. What skills or qualities do they have that are essential to the next job up?

3. What might the company see as your weakness? Are you too intellectual? Too competitive? Not competitive enough? Are you seen as too emotional? Too cold and remote? Are you inflexible? Perfectionistic? Are you sloppy? Bad at detail? Do you lack an authoritative image? Are you too angry? Do you have trouble supervising? Make a list of your possible weaknesses and analyze them. Do any of them present major handicaps at the next level? Try to correlate your possible flaw with the qualities you've determined are necessary for success at higher levels.

4. Once you've determined what characteristic might be holding you back, make your decision. Do you value the quality, or do you want to change? If you want to change, you now have the key: you know what kind of behavior is valued by your company at the next level.

In my experience, these insights are enough to enable many women to start practicing a new style. In addition, you may want to explore the many resources that exist these days to help you develop your style and skills, from feminist consciousness-raising groups, to training courses in a whole variety of areas—including assertiveness, management, sales, public speaking, and writing—to psychotherapy, to the tips and case histories in this book.

7. MY COMPANY DOESN'T PROMOTE SECRETARIES

Why it's so hard to break out of the secretarial trap • How to get onto a professional or managerial track • Acting and dressing the part • How to use a secretary's position as training for a profession • The fairy-tale fantasy that may stand in your way • When and whether to let your boss know about your ambitions

"How can I get out of this secretarial trap?" implored one of my clients, a highly competent and intelligent executive secretary. "I told my boss, a brand manager, that I really wanted to move up, that I would like the opportunity to learn more. He knows I'm very capable, but he never did anything about it."

"You may be an excellent secretary," I allowed, "but what have you done to make your boss see you as a potentially top-notch brand manager?"

My client's request for a promotion had gone unheeded because a boss sees a secretary as a collection of skills that, though they may be highly developed and valued, have no relation to his field. While you may see the logic behind your request, to him, making a secretary into a junior brand manager would be like making a waiter into a pharmacist, or a pharmacist into a longshoreman. You are literally asking him to change your career. That's one reason it's so hard for a secretary, even a good one, to get promoted out of a secretarial spot. It's more than most bosses want to get involved in.

Not only do bosses see secretaries as belonging to a different and unrelated field, but most bosses share the bias of our culture: women, like minority group members and blue-collar workers, are not expected to develop and grow. They are seen as what they are—permanently. Once a secretary (or machinist or truck driver), always a secretary (or machinist or truck driver). At best, the career path for a secretary typically leads to a supersecretary's position like office manager or administrative assistant or supervisor of the secretarial pool.

In a better world, one in which women were not seen in such a rigid way, a secretary's job would be considered an entry-level position that could lead to a whole variety of other possibilities within the company. This would make good sense all around: management would have a new source of talent, pretested on the job, and a secretary, like all management trainees, would be using her on-the-job learning to prepare herself for moving up. And knowing she had a chance to move ahead, she would have chosen the industry carefully, in line with her long-term career goals.

But that's not the way our world is. So if you want to move onto another track and you don't want to go back to school to get new professional credentials, your solution is to carve out a new career with the credentials you have—your secretarial skills. In fact, that's exactly how I began. I decided on a long-term career goal and then got started toward that goal by getting a job as a secretary.

I was thirty-seven years old when I went to work for the first time in a serious way. Years before, I had had some not so serious pickup jobs, in the way women did back then (and sometimes still do), earning just enough money to get by until my real job—marriage—began. But now I had to go to work to support myself and my child. I didn't have a profession or a college degree, and I didn't know what careers were possible, or even what jobs existed out there. I couldn't afford the time or the money to go back to school; in fact, I needed a job badly. But I avoided one major mistake. Instead of just grabbing a job—any job—I borrowed money and took a few weeks to figure out what direction I wanted to go in. It was the best thing I could have done. I looked into several possibilities, then one day stumbled across the title "Hospital Director of Volunteer Services." I thought it might be right for me for many reasons, not the least of which was that it was a helping profession that didn't have rigid degree requirements. The idea of aiming to be a director made sense to me because I expected to be working for a long time. I'd need a challenging job, interesting work, and enough money to feed, clothe, and send my child—who was then only four years old—through school.

Until I was responsible for supporting a family, I hadn't thought much about my career future or about how much money I could earn over the long haul, and I certainly hadn't thought about the fact that as time went on I would develop and grow and want more challenges. But now I had to think like a man: that is, I had to think—career-wise—about where I would be in five years, ten years, twenty years. I knew that every decision I made now would affect my future earnings and my future interests.

I had figured out that I wanted to be a director of volunteer services, but obviously I couldn't start out as a director—I didn't have the experience, and I didn't even really know what the job involved. So I went for the secretary's job, after all. I brushed up on my typing, invented a shorthand (I eliminated vowels and used symbols for common words—I wrt fst), and got a job as secretary to someone who had the title I was aiming for. In a sense, you might say I went to work for the person I wanted to become. And I made it clear to everyone from the start that I was there to learn how to be a director of volunteers. I told my boss, but more importantly, I showed it through my interest in the work, through my level of commitment, and, in general, through my demeanor.

While I was a secretary, I considered myself a management trainee. I never got bored because I was constantly busy mastering new skills. I learned the ABCs of running a hospital volunteer department; I taught myself how to write good letters and memos (by drafting them as I saw the need, and giving them to my boss for correction and signature); I mastered public speaking (by participating in orientation seminars for new volunteers); I practiced managerial style (by observing how my boss related to volunteers, to the staff under her, to her boss, and to other directors in the hospital, and by "supervising" volunteers when my boss was out of the office).

I knew that to get promoted I had to show that I not only had secretarial skills, but that I had the skills that were relevant to the position of director of volunteers. I had told my boss that I was there to learn that job, but I didn't sit and wait for her to teach me. I looked for opportunities to do some of my boss's work. The best way to do that, I found, was to see that she benefited from my taking over some of her activities. For example, she liked work that took her out of the office, so I did more and more of the inside jobs and left her free to move around the hospital and the community.

Another part of my plan was to dress at the higher level. Even as a secretary, I wore the "uniform" of directors in that industry—simple, somewhat prim clothing that was refined and "ladylike," but not too jazzy. The accepted style was similar to that worn by the wealthy and influential volunteers themselves, all of whom looked like they were dressed for the day: morning work at the hospital, then off to lunch and a matinee.

My strategy paid off. In four years I was able to negotiate three new job titles for myself: assistant to the director, assistant director, and associate director. As an assistant director, I was eligible to join the Association of Hospital Volunteer Directors. Through this membership, my name was printed and distributed in a professional directory, giving me the visibility that led to my being approached by several hospital administrators looking for a director of volunteer services. These offers gave me the impetus to apply for that same position at another agency, one at which I wanted to work. I got the job.

It took me four years to get from secretary to where I wanted to be. I might have done it faster but, although I had learned the technical side of running the department relatively quickly, I had had a lot to learn about managerial presence and style, and I had needed the time to gain self-confidence.

By establishing a long-term goal at the outset, before I even took a secretary's job, I was always a step ahead of my title. It was clear to my boss that I was a serious candidate for each of the promotions and that I wasn't just trying to escape from the boredom of my job. I wasn't focused on getting out of being a secretary, but on getting *into* a profession, and that fact influenced my whole attitude and approach to the work—as well as the attitude of everyone, and particularly my boss, toward me.

I can hear the objections now: is all that planning really necessary? What about the secretaries who have moved up without any plan at all? How did they do it? I'm convinced that these women were lucky enough both to land in a field that was compatible with their interest and capabilities, and to know how to show their interest and capabilities.

The secretary who hasn't had that kind of luck has to take the reins in her own hands. She has to make her future happen. She can't afford to succumb to the fairy-tale fantasy that stands in the way—the one where the hero (the powerful boss) discovers you sitting shyly at your typewriter, magically sees your true executive ability, promotes you, and carries you off into the executive suite.

Women who, early on, are discouraged from being self-reliant, from taking their fate into their own hands, find it hard to give up this dream of rescue. Unable to count on themselves, it is their only hope for a better life.

The decision to give up the fantasy is a decision to rely on yourself. The real magic lies in the discovery of your own ability. When you are doing everything you can to show your boss you have the qualities needed to succeed in your newly chosen profession, you will be noticed. I invariably find that when a boss ''discovers'' a secretary's talent and promotes her, she has been, consciously or not, displaying abilities that could get the new job done.

How to Launch Your New Career

Decide first on your specific long-term career goal. There are many good books and workshops that can help you with this decision. It's important that you settle on a concrete job title like fund raiser, executive recruiter, brand manager. Don't stop at a description of the conditions of the career you want, such as ''challenging'' or ''interesting work'' or ''a career with an opportunity to advance.''

Analyze the skills required by the new profession so you can begin to display them in your work as a secretary.

In order to get on-the-job training, you will probably have to change jobs and work for someone from whom you can learn—someone who is doing the kind of work you are shooting for. When you change jobs, you should try to bypass the entry-level secretarial position and move into your new situation at the highest possible level; however, if you can't, you can use your secretarial skills to get your foot in the door of a higher-level job.

If you are applying for a secretarial job, should you tell your prospective employer about your long-range career plans? Is it wise? This is one of those questions to which there is no one right answer. So much depends on the individual employer, the policies of the company, and what the needs of the industry itself are. Nevertheless, since good secretaries are hard to come by, the odds are that the interviewer is hoping to find someone who wants to remain a secretary forever. Also, during the interview stage, remember that your prospective employer is focused only on getting a secretary. He's not thinking about you and helping *your* career. If he thinks you feel the job is only a stepping-stone, he might reject you. After you have been on the job for a while and have demonstrated what you have to offer at a more advanced level, you can unveil your ambition. Even though the boss has something to lose, you've shown him that he also has something to gain. At this point, he'll be a lot more willing to encourage your career change.

If you have decided to play the odds and keep your ambitions quiet, when the interviewer asks: "What are your career goals?" you can answer: "I do like being a secretary. I'm a good secretary and I enjoy secretarial work, but I'm always happy to accept challenges."

Once you've landed the right job, your next step is to give your new boss evidence that you have the talent and interest required to advance to a new profession. Demonstrate your knowledge and grasp of the field. Bring to your boss up-to-date information that he isn't aware of—facts, news stories, business gossip. Keep proving to him that you are involved with the content of the work and *not* the housekeeping. Do your secretarial work with your left hand and don't, whatever you do, involve your boss in it. Don't come in with questions like: "This photocopy of your memo isn't perfect. Is it okay to send?" Learn your boss's standards and figure out the answers yourself. Comment, instead, on the substance of the memo: "When I was looking at so-and-so's catalogue, I saw a record cover similar to the one you described in your letter. Here's a copy of it." Display a whole new persona. Become whatever it is you want to be—a brand manager, or a sales manager, or a systems analyst, or whatever—in your head and in your heart.

Pay attention to surface detail. It can be important to look and act like you fit in with the people in your new profession.

After you've shown your interest and ability, you can broach the subject of your career plan with your boss. When you raise the issue, be sure to underline the fact that your decision to become, say, a brand manager was very deliberate, the result of a thoughtful investigation of various possibilities. He'll be impressed—like a man who knows you chose to be with him because he's special, not because you're desperate to be with someone, anyone. If your boss thinks you are desperate for a better job, any job, he won't see you as a credible candidate for this particular career.

Convey your purposefulness by saying something like: "I've done my homework. I've analyzed a number of possible careers for myself and I've done a profile of my aptitudes and interests. I think my strengths and background qualify me for this field.'' Then spell out those specific strengths so he can see the correlation.

No matter how the company views secretaries, you will be seen in a new light. You've shifted your image from that of professional secretary to that of the new professional you plan to be.

8. MY COMPANY DOESN'T PROMOTE FROM WITHIN

How to get around ''company policy'' • The qualities management looks for • Why it's so hard for women to take the lead—and what you can do about it • How to win authority • The fear of taking charge

Why would a company bring in new managers from the outside when there are good people inside? Why would a company not promote from within? To the bypassed employees, it appears to be company policy. They say it categorically—''My company doesn't promote from within''—as if it's a hard and fast rule. While it is true that some companies tend to bring in more people from the outside than others, I've never heard of a company that had a policy of totally blocking the advancement of the kind of people who could serve its needs.

Don't take the rumored ''policy'' too literally. If someone is brought in to fill the job you'd hoped for, it's probably not policy; it's a decision against you personally. Management, for some reason, is convinced that they really could do better through an outside search. In their eyes, you don't measure up.

The reason could be anything. Maybe you haven't shown the skills or qualities they feel are needed at the next level—the ability to negotiate, for example, or to speak on your feet, or to hold people to deadlines. Perhaps they think you don't have enough talent. Or maybe they think you are not enough of a ''company man,'' that you are not sympathetic enough to management's point of view. They may feel you are too high-minded to be let in on certain company practices. Perhaps you don't cut enough corners. If you want to get promoted, you will have to figure what the reason is.

Sally's Story

Sally, a sales representative for a fabric company, was ready to resign when, for the second time in four years, a new area manager from another company was brought in over her. She wanted to quit: "I can't go any further there. They always bring in higher-level managers from outside." I questioned her on that point because I was sure that there was *someone* inside the company who had moved up—there always is. If we could find out what made this person the exception, we could learn a lot about what the company was looking for at higher levels.

She finally thought of Tom, who had been promoted to area manager two years earlier. She even knew why. It was common knowledge: he had control over his accounts. He was authoritative and persuasive: if the size or style of his clients' orders were not in what he considered their own best interests, he was generally able to convince them to go along with his recommendation. Conversely, when the client demanded services or delivery of goods that were not in keeping with Tom's or his company's best interests, he was able to swing them around to his point of view. Moreover, if his boss tried to move in on his account, Tom would be receptive and respectful of any suggestions, but he didn't let the boss take over, any more than he let the client take over.

Tom's big stock-in-trade, as Sally now realized, was that he took a strong leadership role. He did this with his accounts, his clients, and even, in a way, his own boss.

What about Sally? How did she handle her accounts? She had an excellent working relationship with her clients, she assured me. They really liked and respected her. I kept probing. What happens if something goes wrong? "Well, if there's any trouble on an account," she answered, "the client generally goes to John, my boss, and he deals with it." *This* was the clue I was looking for. Her boss was seen as the real authority, not Sally. Why? Because, as we discovered, Sally failed to take the lead role in a number of subtle ways. For example, John always went along with her to client meetings, and while Sally would present their new designs herself, if the client objected to anything, she would defer to John. He would step in and defend or modify the item as *he* saw fit. Moreover, if the client called her with anything that was out of the ordinary, she would say, "I'd like to talk it over with John," thus emphasizing her "helpmate" status. Contrast this with the authoritative image she would have created had she covered herself by saying, "I'll get back to you. I'd like to give it more thought."

Why didn't Sally take a lead role? Because, she said, "When a guy is there, I step down. I take second place." It was automatic. Instead of responding to the needs of the situation, she unthinkingly moved into a subordinate position whenever a man came on the scene. She deferred even when it involved an area where she had been put in charge—her own accounts.

Sally had a classic leadership block. Somewhere in the inner recesses of her mind, she believed that if she challenged custom and took the lead over a man, he would feel diminished. If she were the leader, he'd be the follower. The consequences of placing him in this weak and womanly position were too frightening. She would feel guilty, she would fear his anger, and she would risk losing him. He was someone she could count on, someone who would handle the rough stuff for her. Men don't rescue strong women—if you show your strength, you are on your own. It was far less painful for Sally to step back into second place than to chance having to stand alone.

With this insight, Sally was able to start challenging her ingrained reactions to defer. She began to experiment with taking command of her accounts, and she began to see, firsthand, that taking the lead in the business world could inspire respect. She started handling problems as they arose with the client, without consulting John. She took an active role in the development of the products she presented to her clients, researching every detail and thinking through what direction was best for the client. Now, at the presentation meeting, she was in a good position to move in and defend the proposed products confidently and convincingly.

No one seemed surprised at her new, more commanding role. In fact, John even complimented her on her handling of the meetings.

It wasn't all smooth sailing, however. Sally, emboldened by the good reception she had gotten by taking charge, suggested to John that she could handle the client meetings by herself. He balked. He didn't think she was ready. At this, all of Sally's old anxieties swept over her and she collapsed right back into her "follower" role. One refusal had erased all she had just learned: she'd forgotten that everyone had reacted very positively to her stepping out front and taking the lead. One setback and she viewed things with the kind of selective perception that I often find in my clients when they get scared. They see only those facts that substantiate their worst fears, and thus they convince themselves to take the "safe" course.

But when you are working with a strategy—a course of action based on your analysis of a situation—you can't abandon it with the first problem. Was your analysis wrong? Or is there another explanation for the new difficulty? Sally's basic strategy was to display leadership qualities, and the preponderance of evidence indicated that it was working well. True, John was reluctant to let her take over the client meetings—but maybe he needed more time to be convinced of her ability; or maybe he needed to hold on to the symbols of his superior position; or maybe he had nothing else to do. There were many possible reasons. Now, Sally decided to cover all bases and see if she could overcome his objections to giving her a more important role.

Sally reminded John that his most successful colleague was the one who gave the people under him the most autonomy. She argued that by relying on the old pros (like Sally) to carry on the day-to-day client work, he would be able to concentrate on training and developing the newer people on the staff to make them more productive. Sally played on her boss's ambitions. She persuaded him that it would be better for him—and his career—if she took over the routine client meetings.

Clearly, Sally had started on the path of gaining control over her accounts by establishing authority with her clients—handling their problems herself and running her own meetings. She was overcoming the key barrier to her promotion, and indeed, a few months later, she got the area manager's job she had been working toward.

If you've been passed over because your company brings in new people from the outside, your best bet is to search out the rare bird who has gotten promoted. Try to determine what it is about this person that made him or her the exception. Then decide if these key qualities are acceptable to you. Often you will find that what management wants you to be is what you yourself want to be—more assertive, more of a leader, a more confident decision-maker, able to influence people, more astute politically, having a wider range of skills. If that's what they want, and that's what you want, then go to it. Develop the desired qualities and prove to management that the right person is inside the company, not outside.

9. I'LL NEVER GET A PROMOTION—MY BOSS IS A CHAUVINIST AND IT'S A CHAUVINISTIC COMPANY

The tenacity of chauvinism • How to fight chauvinism • Outmaneuvering discrimination • Taking legal action • What to do about the damage caused by growing up in a chauvinistic culture • Power people • The importance of self-publicizing

Male chauvinism—the prejudiced belief in male superiority—is still the norm in business. It can be blatant and brutal: "Women don't belong in business. They're no damn good at it." Or it can be wrapped in rationalizations that attempt to justify the discrimination by blaming it on a quality of the woman: "She's too pretty; she'll get married and be gone." Another defense is someone else's prejudice: "The clients don't have confidence in women." Sometimes the rationale that does you in is well-intentioned and protective: "This is no job for a woman; it's rough and dirty." And sometimes, in a kind of sexist Catch-22, the prejudice is based on fact: "She isn't assertive enough." Society shapes our natures as women and then says we're not promotable because we are misshapen.

The revolution in women's consciousness—our recognition of the pervasiveness of sex discrimination, and of the price we pay for it—has not penetrated very deeply into the corporate brain. While women have everything to gain from eradicating sexism, it's not in business's interest to change the status quo. On the contrary; companies reap enormous benefits from women's inferior position: they get a competent, conscientious, responsible work force at low cost. And while companies do lose out by not moving talented women to higher levels of management, as business sees it, that's not a problem. There are already more candidates for management than business could ever use. And the benefits of a cheap labor force far outweigh the dubious value of having a larger pool of managerial talent. Companies have little reason to put effort into providing equal opportunities for women. Chauvinism has a tenacious hold on business because chauvinism *works* for business—which is why, despite all our efforts and all the talk of recent years, discrimination is still a fact of life for most women at work.

If chauvinistic attitudes in your company are blocking you from advancement, you have three possible courses of action: 1) you can try to force the company to acknowledge your right to the position through a legal battle in the courts or through government affirmative action agencies; 2) you can make a complaint within your own company; or 3) you can take a strategic approach and maneuver your way around the prejudice.

What your best course of action will be depends on your situation at work, the facts of your case, your resources, your obligations, and your goals at this point in your life.

If you go the route of a legal fight, you may win your promotion, as well as advances for all the women who come after you. And, win or lose, you will make great personal gains. A fight against illegal and immoral practices will be strengthening, and once you have gone through the complex stages of such a fight, you may even find yourself equipped for a new, more politically oriented career. You do, however, run the risk of being blackballed within the company and possibly within the industry. Before you decide to engage in legal action, evaluate your emotional and financial resources, as well as your ability to build a network of support among organizations, colleagues, and friends. You need to be able to sustain such an action over a prolonged period.

If you are considering making a complaint within your company, whether to your boss or upper management or even to the personnel department, beware. This is a high-risk option. Management will probably see you as a troublemaker; they may try to block you from advancing or even get rid of you. When you take this route, you are quite unprotected. Before you say anything, seek advice from people who are experienced with this kind of protest.

Even if your company has an affirmative action office, be careful. Before you file a complaint about sex-based discrimination, look at their track record. Affirmative action departments have been notoriously ineffective in getting promotions for women who are being discriminated against. However well-intentioned the individuals within the departments may be, they are part and parcel of the corporate structure. Unlike labor unions that have been organized by workers to fight *against* the company, these departments have been established *by* the company to implement company goals. So unless your company is unusual or has a good history in this area, stay away from this path.

If, at this point in your life, your focus is on your own individual career advancement, your best bet is to try to get around the prejudice with a strategic approach. You need to change the way the chauvinistic boss sees *you*.

That's what Julie did when she managed to become the first woman supervisor in her division.

Julie's Story

Sam, the director of Julie's division, had never promoted a woman to the position of supervisor. His remarks about women indicated that he saw them as entertaining, attractive, and more interested in men than in work. When Jim, a supervisor with whom Julie worked, told her he was leaving the company, she saw this as her chance. She knew Jim respected her work, so she asked him how he would feel about recommending her as his replacement. When he agreed to talk to Sam on her behalf, she gave him some ammunition. She armed him with reminders of her past accomplishments that related to the new job to ensure that he did a good job of pitching for her promotion. Next, she approached several of her good friends in the office who, she knew, would agree that she was the outstanding candidate for Jim's job. Would they mention her to Sam as a good choice for a supervisor's job? They would. Julie discussed with each one why he or she thought Julie would be the right choice and how to present those reasons to Sam, so that different facets of her ability would be emphasized.

At the same time, she met with Dick, a division head who, she knew, was in a very strong position in the company, strong enough to raid Sam's group and get away with it. Julie told Dick that she had found herself stymied where she was; she was interested in joining a group where she had a better chance of getting ahead. Since Julie was very good at her present job, he was quite responsive. He formally requested that she be transferred to his group. Dick's request, combined with the chrous of praise Sam had been hearing, made Sam see Julie in a different light. Just as some men get interested in women when they are "popular," he finally began to take Julie seriously. Her campaign was effective and he offered her the promotion. In fact, her strategy worked so well that a few weeks after her promotion, when it was clear that she was handling the new job well, Sam was overheard taking credit for having discovered this "hidden" gem.

Kim's Story

Sometimes, I find, women blame discrimination for their failure to get a promotion because there doesn't seem to be any other reason. Since chauvinism exists everywhere, it's a natural enough explanation. But, as Kim found out, it may not be the entire answer.

Kim was in charge of order fulfillment for a tool and die manufacturer. She couldn't get promoted because, as she saw it, her company was sexist. As proof she offered the fact that, two years earlier, a man who was less capable then she had beaten her out for a promotion. Now he was her boss, and he was proving to be an inept manager. He had just sent her a three-page criticism of her work, all of it unfounded. Kim fought back by sending him an even longer memo of her own. She disproved every one of his criticisms by simply documenting her work and letting the facts speak for themselves.

Kim was indignant and contemptuous: "He didn't even know what I had been doing for the past four months." But as she told her story, I began to wonder why her boss knew so little about what she had been doing. My mind flashed back to his promotion over Kim two years before. If her boss back then had been as unaware of her good work as her current boss was, he would have had no reason to promote her. Kim apparently did not understand the importance of publicizing her own work to her boss. It never occurred to her that he didn't have a clear idea of what she was doing. She assumed that her boss read all reports, saw the bottom-line figures, and credited her with the improved results.

What held Kim back could well have been management's chauvinism—men *don't* see women's skills very clearly. But it was also true that she played into whatever blind spot they might have had, with her own lack of awareness. As long as she did not highlight those qualities that would make her a good candidate for management, how could anyone see the full extent of her value? Kim had the requisite strengths, but she hadn't made hay with them, as her competitor—now her boss—had. Kim's task was to learn how to operate more effectively in the workplace by publicizing her outstanding achievements.

In a way, Kim's diagnosis of chauvinism was correct, but she had focused on the wrong target. The real cause of her problem was her having been raised female in a society that doesn't give women a chance to develop the key qualities needed to move into managerial positions—independence, assertiveness, a well-developed political and strategic sense, and the ability to toot your own horn. Kim had to learn new tricks and strengthen herself to compensate for the way she'd been brought up.

On the other hand, Julie's boss was clearly prejudiced against women in management. He didn't think women could supervise, so Julie's strategy was to change the way her boss saw *her*. She mobilized her allies to impress him with her ability and thereby outmaneuvered his prejudice.

If you see discrimination as the barrier to your advancement, stop and analyze the situation. Is the boss not seeing you clearly? Is he looking at you through prejudiced eyes? Or are the barriers internal—the effects of discrimination that have been built into you?

10. MY JOB HAS NO FUTURE—I'M STUCK IN A DEAD-END ALLEY

How to turn your job into a job you want • Locating people's needs and meeting them • Using each job function to develop a more important role

Joan's Story

Joan had a typical, off-to-the-side staff job, a situation in which all too many women find themselves. After getting her graduate degree in library science, she had gone to work as a reference librarian in a company that developed and marketed computer programs for business applications. Being out in the business world fired her ambitions, and it wasn't long before she realized that she had made a serious mistake. Her chosen profession had carried her right into a dead-end alley. She was in a job with no future.

But just because you've put yourself into a dead-end job—or, as is more often the case, the company has put you in one—doesn't mean you have to accept it. You can build a bridge that takes you where you want to go.

As a business librarian, one of Joan's main functions was to search out, on request, book and article references that related to various areas of the company's data processing business—anything from news of a rival product to an article analyzing a particular business's special needs in the data processing area. A number of different departments used her services: sales, research and development, engineering, and account representatives. We decided that instead of just handing over files of clippings and articles as she had been doing, she should start analyzing and digesting the material, voluntarily writing it up into easy-to-read reports. People at the receiving end were delighted; it meant less work for them because they didn't have to read through masses of material. But there was another, more direct benefit for Joan. She was becoming a storehouse of business information— and the more knowledgeable she became, the more on-target were her analyses.

We decided that the time was right for her to push on to the next step: to try to work more closely with the people who received her reports. Now, she asked them questions at the start of each assignment to find out what their problems were and what they were hoping to accomplish. She then set to work with such energy, intelligence, and concern that she was soon considered virtually a member of each group with whom she worked. She even got invited to departmental meetings at which the projects she would be working on were discussed.

This brought on the opportunity to take another bold step. Since she now knew what the purposes of the reports were, she began to cast them in terms of their ultimate uses. For example, if the sales department needed the information for drawing up a proposal to a client, she would draft her report in the form of a selling proposal. If it was to be used for a speech to a professional organization, she would draft her notes in the form of an outline for a speech. Her reports became even more valuable: not only did they save even more time for those who used them, but the caliber of her work was so good that the final departmental results were far better than they would have been without her help.

By now, Joan had developed a first-rate reputation as a researcher, writer, and repository of all sorts of valuable business information. When the director of business communications resigned, she was a natural candidate for his job. She proposed that the company combine both the library and the business communications department under her. They agreed, and Joan was out of her dead-end alley. The skills and authority she had acquired by plunging in and taking the next step—and the next step and the logical step after that—built the bridge that carried her up and over the dead-end barrier into the mainstream.

Moral: don't accept the idea that you are stuck in a dead end; dead ends exist on organization charts, but there are countless ways to get out of your impasse.

11. MY JOB HAS NO FUTURE—I'M STUCK IN A LOW-STATUS DEPARTMENT

How to get out of the standard woman's role • How to expand your territory • The job-description box • How to tackle a sticky problem • How to raid more important work from other departments without alienating anyone • When there's too much to do

After a hard climb up, many women find themselves stuck at the top of a very small mountain. They may be managers, but they're managers of relatively unimportant, low-prestige departments. From the start, women get shunted into careers that lead nowhere; they aren't invited into the system that funnels talent into higher levels of management. Consciously or unconsciously, top management chooses candidates for the upper managerial ranks who are like themselves in attitude, education, appearance, and background. In a male-dominated organization, women don't fit the mold.

If you are stranded on top of an insignificant mountain, why not make your mountain bigger by bringing in more important activities? As your department becomes more important, you become more important. A friend of mine from my days as a director of volunteer services did a masterful job of building up her division this way.

Eileen's Story

Eileen was a director of volunteer services, as I was, in a hospital. It was a small department, not generally seen as very important, and she was regarded by her colleagues principally as the efficient shepherdess of nice little unpaid lady volunteers. She had gotten her department running smoothly, she had expanded it by energetically recruiting volunteers, and she'd created imaginative new patient programs. She'd done about as much as could be done with the department as it was then constituted, and she was becoming thoroughly bored. As many people would in this situation, she was thinking of making a career change. She talked to me about it, and I suggested that before she did anything as drastic as abandoning her hard-won position, it would be worthwhile for her to see if there were ways to capitalize on what she had in hand. Rather than change her career, could she change the nature of her department so that it would give her more opportunities? Could she expand the boundaries of her department so it included more important and more interesting work?

She decided to give it a try. First, she looked at every problem in the hospital as if it were hers to solve. Empire-builders aren't stopped by someone else's definition of territorial boundaries or job responsibilities—which are, in actual fact, never as rigid as they appear to be on the organizational charts.

Once Eileen stopped thinking in terms of territory, a logical direction for her expansion suggested itself. As the director of volunteers, she had an entire web of people working under her supervision throughout the hospital: the volunteers. Through them, she heard a steady stream of patient complaints. In the past, she and the volunteers with whom she worked often couldn't do much more than listen sympathetically; the complaints usually involved problems beyond the scope of the volunteer department. We reasoned that since no response was being made to many of the complaints, here was an area she might be able to take over—one that would give her an opportunity to involve herself in all the important areas of the hospital. Why not set herself up as the hospital's "patient advocate"? In this way, the volunteers, operating under her guidance, could be used to forward patient complaints and problems directly to her, and she herself could set about solving them with the appropriate department.

Eileen was in a good position to propose her plan to the executive director. They had worked well together, and he admired the creativity she had displayed in building her department. When she presented her plan, she reminded him how important it was, from a community relations point of view, for a patient to know that someone was going to bat for her or him. She pointed out that as a representative of administration, her view would cut across departmental boundaries and enable her to come up with new solutions to chronic problems. The executive director was enthusiastic, not only because he had confidence in Eileen, but because her proposal addressed two top priorities of his: the improvement of patient care, and the defusing of patient discontent. And he knew that Eileen had the energy, creativity, and political savvy to make the program work. He gave her the go-ahead.

Now, as patient advocate, Eileen had access to every department in the hospital. She would track down the source of a problem, and then work out solutions with the departments involved. If she decided that a situation was especially important or interesting, she would keep it completely under her own wing. She had the knack of taking over a department's functions in the guise of helping. And indeed she was helping, even as she snared work for herself. For example, when the nurses couldn't respond to patient needs because of a growing shortage of staff, Eileen launched a successful recruitment campaign. With her characteristic get-up-and-go, she toured the country, established contact with nursing school administrators and with students, and created a network throughout the country that provided a steady source of new nurses.

Eileen began to concentrate on the arbitration of conflicts between departments. She soon was called upon to handle all sorts of tricky situations around the hospital. On one occasion, she was asked to settle a dispute between two departments that were arguing over the use of certain expensive technical equipment. She was able to fashion a temporary truce between them, and then went to work on the underlying problem—the scarcity of equipment—which was due in turn to the chronic shortage of funds facing her hospital (and most other hospitals). The problem could have seemed too overwhelming to tackle—indeed, it did to almost everyone else—but she wasn't afraid of it. She pared it down to a size that she could manage and went to work on it. (This, by the way, is how all doers operate.) She launched a campaign to raise the funds to buy two extra machines. She used her contacts among wealthy volunteers both to raise money and to meet their friends, whom she interested in the work of the hospital, which in turn led to more donations. She raised the money to purchase the equipment, but, more significantly for Eileen's personal situation, she succeeded in getting new and important people involved in supporting the work of the hospital. When three of these new donors were asked to serve on the board of trustees, she had the start of her own power base.

After a year as patient advocate, Eileen had gotten hold of an impressive array of key activities for her department. She had also broadened her knowledge and experience, sharpened her strategic skills, and built a powerful network of contacts, both in and out of the hospital. She had developed her low-status department into an important, multiservice division, and now was in a position to make a bid to move into top administration—if that was what she wanted.

Following Eileen's example, here are some tips for bringing more important work into your bailiwick, as well as some cautions that will help you minimize your colleagues' resistance to your empire-building.

1. Make sure that any programs you propose fit in with your boss's priorities.

2. Don't worry about "turf" or traditional boundaries. Take the broad view. The person who gets in first with an idea can usually claim the area for her own.

3. If your boss meets your good idea with a routine "We'll pass your suggestion along," counter with the proposal that you get the program started (who, after all, knows the idea better than you do?) and *then* turn it over to the appropriate department. Once you've got it going well, they'll have a hard time taking it away from you. They probably won't even try.

4. Come in with a fully worked-out plan for the activity you propose. It will be that much more difficult for someone to turn you down if you've thought your idea through and are ready to roll with it.

5. Take care that you don't look greedy. Give away ideas and credit. When you do take something for your own, do it in such a way that it will look like you are doing your colleagues a favor. Don't worry about collecting credit from your colleagues, but concentrate instead on getting into a stronger and stronger position. You can claim credit at the right moment—when you are being interviewed for a higher position.

6. Concentrate your forces on getting new projects off the ground. While everyone around you is bogged down and complaining about being overworked and understaffed, you'll be building an image as a go-getter. Everyone will know that if you propose a program, you'll be able to get it done. Let your main work slide temporarily and in ways that won't be noticed. As the achievements pile up, you'll be in a strong position to argue for more staff.

7. Take an aggressive stance, as Eileen did. Plunge into the work. You'll appear powerful, and people will be wary of tangling with you.

12. I DON'T HAVE TIME TO WORK ON GETTING AHEAD

How to turn down work without getting fired • Insights to help you overcome perfectionism • Three straightforward and four underground techniques for shedding work

When I suggest to women who want to move up that they take on new work to prove themselves at higher levels, they often collapse in despair. "That's impossible," they protest indignantly. "I'm exhausted just getting my own work done!"

For most women, the problem of too little time and too much work stems from being overly conscientious or overly responsive to the boss's or the company's requests. We are well-schooled in putting other people's needs ahead of our own. It's difficult to shift gears and put your own career needs at the top of your list of priorities, but once you've made the decision to consider your own needs as primary, you must learn to keep your workload balanced between your boss's needs and your own.

Your goal is to have a reasonable day's work—or less—so that you have enough time and energy to do the extra work that will get you the promotion. Here are some techniques for shedding work that will serve you well at any time in your career. They are as useful and as basic as pencil and paper.

• *Your first line of defense is to say no.* There are many ways to say no. There's a cooperative no that says, "I'm on your side and we'll figure it out together." And there's a hostile no that says, "That's your problem, not mine." Or worse: "I'm not going to do that. Who do you think I am?"

A reasonable no that won't get you any leadership points is: "I'm afraid I can't do it. I'm loaded up with A, B, and C. Could you please give it to someone else?" The boss may retreat, but you haven't done much for your image. You've delivered the problem back to him.

You could easily change your reasonable no into a more effective response that develops your image as a problem-solver and a potential leader. By working on the problem *with* your boss, you convert it to the cooperative no: "I see that it's important. I could do it now, but I think *we'd* be better off if I finished project B first and then went to work on C." Or, "Let me see if Sally can do my statistical tabulations—then I can go to work on it right away." Or, "We have a pile-up. I'll get back to you with some idea of how to work this out" (giving you time to evaluate the priorities and get back to him with the best possible plan under these difficult circumstances).

Your cooperative no can make such good sense that your boss treasures you for it. That doesn't mean he won't be annoyed; he wants the impossible. But if he can count on you to weigh up the elements and give him a clear idea of how to cope with what he wants done, you will become much more valuable to him.

If he continues to pressure you to do the work anyway, and you know he doesn't have the full picture, stand behind your appraisal. Stay with your well-thought-out position and show him in a responsible and informed way that you can only get one job or the other done.

Unless you try holding firm to your position, you will never know that you are able to be persuasive. Many people back away from the unpleasantness of disagreements and then, because they don't argue, are convinced that others can't be influenced. If you give in at the first sign of disapproval, irritation, or annoyance, of course you won't convince your boss of your position—and your belief that he is totally unreasonable and incapable of responding to logic will be confirmed. The strength of your conviction and the way you present your case is what gives you your chance to persuade him.

If the boss still rules against you even after you've set forth your facts and your reasoning, then you have to go his way and follow his priorities. But even then, don't try to do the impossible. Instead, keep him reminded of the slowed-down status of your other projects so that there are no surprises in store for him. He may be under the illusion that when he "won," you would miraculously produce it all, and it's your job to keep him apprised of reality in a constructive, positive way. Give him a steady stream of reports: "The number one project will be completed Wednesday, on deadline. Project number two will take a few days longer."

• *Divert your lower-level work to other people.* Let someone else have a turn at the routine jobs or junk work. Look for people for whom your lower-level work would be their higher-level opportunity. Good relationships with the people you work with are important—if you are overworked you can get help from them just long enough for you to prove to your boss that you have other talents. If you can't get cooperation from your coworkers, then . . .

• *Convince your boss of the advantages of restructuring the work assignments.* Use the cooperative no and suggest reassigning your work to someone else. Show your boss the advantages of shifting your easy work elsewhere. If he has any doubts, sell him on it. Say, "I'm overloaded, but I think I have a good solution." And then proceed to show him how some job descriptions can be reorganized to get the workloads more efficiently distributed. Say, "I'd like to concentrate on A, B, and C. It'll be some time before I get to D. I think I should give it to Dorothy." If he agrees, you're in. If he nods vaguely or doesn't say anything, consider your proposal approved and turn the work over to Dorothy, explaining that "John gave me two new assignments; he would like you to do D."

Don't pick out a hardened old-timer who will storm into the boss's office and refuse to do the work. Select someone who is likely to accept an assignment from you—someone who is new to the company and eager to make her mark, someone who is a compulsive overworker, someone who's overly accommodating or who can't say no.

If these direct approaches to getting the time you need to prove yourself don't succeed, then you have to go underground.

• *Let work go.* Sweep housekeeping chores that won't get you anywhere under the rug. Just do the things that are likely to be noticed. There's an element of risk in pushing work aside, but with a little luck you will prove your high-level value before the rug is picked up.

• *Do less-than-perfect work.* Join the rest of the world. Having everything in meticulous order and working beautifully may not be in your best interests if you need time to work on getting ahead.

This is hard to do if you can't bear the thought of being seen as less than very good at everything you do. It will help you abandon your need to be perfect if you keep in mind that your plan is to dazzle everyone with your surprising new abilities. Although people may notice that you've been remiss, as they discover your new worth, they won't care.

• *Don't make things look too easy.* Resist the temptation to look like Ms. Wonderful by doing a job and a half with your left hand. You may look terrific, but you run the risk of getting even more work piled on you. There's a much smarter way to look like Ms. Wonderful. Do the job and a half but don't make it look too easy. Give your boss interesting information about all the problems you had to surmount: "Would you believe the computer conked out eight times? I talked to several technicians at the manufacturing plant in Boston and at the service department in New York and everyone had a different theory, but they were all wrong. I asked everyone I met about it, even the owner of the local hardware store. Believe it or not, he had the answer. It was a power line problem. The voltage wasn't steady. I had them install a new line just in the nick of time. Another week of problems and the job would have been too late for the client to use."

This won't work if it has the sound of a complaint. You are trying to build an image as a positive, energized, creative, successful problem-solver who is challenged by problems and excited by solutions. Don't slip into the role of an overburdened complainer. And don't miss a deadline to prove how overworked you are. That tactic could easily backfire: if the boss can't count on you, he won't promote you.

• *Give yourself more time than you need to do the work.* The length of time it really takes to do a job is a hard thing for a boss to measure—so take advantage of it. If you exaggerate the time it takes to do something, you have, in effect, bought yourself some free time to do the work that's more important to you. If the boss implies that you could get more done, he's probably guessing. Often as not, he's just applying standard boss pressure.

If he's nervous about how well you use your time, it's important for you to keep him reassured that you are working efficiently, solving problems, and forging ahead. And as you give him your reports, you will also be reminding him that things do indeed take time (how much—or how little—is your secret).

Most women have been overburdened and overworked throughout history. Overwork saps creative energy and will lock you into lower levels of work. However you do it, you have to break out of this cycle and get time to think, to be creative, to concentrate on the more important aspects of your work life and your personal life. That's how you, as an individual, can fight for your equality: you can create for yourself the conditions that will enable you to function more fully.

13. *I'VE BEEN OFFERED A PROMOTION, BUT I'M NOT SURE I CAN HANDLE IT*

Women's inability to evaluate themselves objectively • Thinking that you've fooled people • The fear of failure • Ambivalence about moving up • The danger of the downward spiral • When you have to take the risk • Getting help from outside • Suppose you *are* fired

If your company has offered you a better job and you're worried about your ability to do it, I'd say put your money on the company's judgment and take the promotion. Nine times out of ten when this situation arises, I find that management's favorable assessment of a woman's capability is more accurate than the woman's own estimate. Companies are quite hard-headed about promotions, so it's a good bet that you've given them a clear indication you can handle the job.

In fact, you probably thought you'd be very good at the job yourself—*until* they offered it to you. Your initial feeling is of elation and pride from having your worth confirmed ("I really *am* good!"), but afterward a crisis of confidence sets in ("What if I can't do it?"). In my experience, when women get scared at this point it's usually because they think they've some-how managed to fool the people around them. "They think I'm more capable than I really am. They don't know how much I *don't* know." You waver between wanting to take the new position—and thus becoming what you always dreamed you could be—and wanting to turn it down because you're terrified you will fail. But if you give it up, you are moving away from the achievement and recognition you want. It's painful to resign yourself to being a lesser light. You can't bear either alternative: to go forward is too frightening, and to retreat is too defeating.

Why is it that so many women have difficulty evaluating their abilities in the workplace? Why is our self-confidence so easily shaken?

Images of management are male. The men who run things, seated around a huge conference table of gleaming wood, its very size a symbol of their power . . . working in richly furnished offices overlooking the city . . . they seem almost another breed—so important, so beyond our reach.

Women absorb from these images of male leadership not just proof of male ability, but also evidence of female *inability*. When we compare our inadequate selves with these idealized images, our confidence drains away. With each small step up the ladder we are overwhelmed by the mystique of male executive ability. While men, too, have their moments of doubt when they face new challenges, they are more confident of their chances. Men do, after all, fit the picture.

Even women who take the promotion and succeed still live with the fear that they don't really belong.

Jeremy's Story

Jeremy, a recently promoted department head, reports that she returns over and over again to the thought that she's not good enough for the job—that people will see through her "pose" as a manager. "I catch myself talking in the hall with women at lower levels and I feel just like one of them. I refuse to own up to the fact that I have achieved a high level of responsibility. I don't know how long it takes to get used to a new job, but I feel shy about telling people I'm an executive vice president. I don't think they'll believe it, because *I* don't believe it. I feel the struggle on a daily basis."

She is unable to stay with what she knows: that she actually does the important job her title reflects. She slips back to the childhood view of herself as a follower, not a boss. Her own certain knowledge of her achievement is outweighed by the double burden imposed on her by our culture: our society's contempt for women, and its idealization of male leaders.

Ironically, the men who promoted Jeremy have been able to cast aside the culture's prejudice against women in favor of their own firsthand experience of her talent. They see her through less biased eyes than she sees herself.

Jeremy, like many women, is so battered by messages regarding women's inferiority that she cannot evaluate herself realistically. Even when we understand the source of the bias against women, even as we scorn the chauvinism in the world around us as irrational, we may absorb notions of our own lack of worth. Feelings of worthlessness have a powerful life of their own; once formed, they continue to exist quite apart from their source. We succumb to them, forgetting their origins. The key to breaking the grip of these negative feelings lies in reconnecting them to their origins. When you feel inadequate, remember that what you have learned early on about women and work may have prejudiced you against yourself. Understanding why you have a distorted view of your abilities is the first step toward a more appreciative and more objective sense of yourself.

That's why I urge women to accept the company's evaluation of their abilities when they are in the fortunate situation of having been offered a promotion. If you have internalized the idea of women's inferiority, you may back away from opportunity and, as you do, you set a self-fulfilling prophecy in motion. If you turn down a job because you think you can't handle it, you may *never* be able to handle it. It's a downward spiral: every time you turn down a challenging assignment, you miss out on the chance to learn and develop; and if you're not learning and growing, you will be given fewer and fewer opportunities. You are narrowing your world, instead of broadening it. By depriving yourself of the chance to learn, you will inadvertently bring about what you feared was true all along: through fear of being inadequate, you do indeed become inadequate. You aren't up to handling those more important jobs after all.

By and large, business has a very unsystematic, catch-as-catch-can method of training. Most learning takes place through actually doing the new work. So if you have the usual quotient of ambivalence about your ability to do the job, I'd say take the risk.

Take courage from knowing that no one expects you to perform the job perfectly, right from day one. You'll have a learning period in which to relate to the new cast of characters and to gather information. In fact, the start of a new job is the best time to ask all your questions. While you might be inclined to try to show how smart you are—to prove that you were the right person for the job—people expect you to ask questions in a new situation. If you need more help to master the job, you can get off-the-job aid from friends and colleagues or even from specialists whom you can hire to get you started. While you're learning what they know, you can submit their products as your own. If you have an ethical problem with this option, consider the fact that people at higher levels routinely get outside help for work they submit in their own name—ghost writers, speech writers, and all sorts of consultants.

Suppose the worst happens and you can't keep up with the new job. If you get fired, you'll probably have to deal with low spirits and financial problems.

If you want to avoid devastating mood collapses as you accept the challenge of career growth, it's essential that you put "failure" in perspective. It seems to me that it's impossible to move forward without going down any number of wrong alleys. You need to respect and understand the learning process so that when things do go wrong, you'll be able to think of your error as a natural part of growth—"just a mistake," not "I am a failure." You'll discard the attitude that blames your own ineptness, and will become interested in analyzing what went wrong. No active person can avoid failure, but successful people seem more able to accept their failures and go on to the next task. If you're not psychologically demolished by getting fired, your chances of getting an equivalent or better new job are very good.

If a job doesn't work out, analyze the problem. Do you need abilities you don't have and can't develop in a reasonable length of time? Is there something with which you've had a long-standing problcm? You may want to repair your "deficit," but it's not wise to base your present career plan on new mastery of an old problem—you'd do better at this point to hunt for another route up, one that takes advantage of your strengths.

But maybe you were fired simply because you didn't catch on quickly enough. You were on the right course, but a little slow. If you've learned enough in your brief stay to apply for the job somewhere else—and you probably have—try to get the new level job someplace else. If you need a breather, step back for a few months, and try again. All in all, you will be better off struggling at the new level.

14. SHOULD I ACCEPT WORK WITHOUT THE TITLE?

How to avoid getting boxed into a bad corner by a clever negotiator • How to locate where *your* power lies in the negotiation • Specific arguments you can use to get the title you want • The value of negotiating, win or lose • Collecting the title elsewhere

Not so long ago, women were flattered and pleased to be trusted with important work, with or without the appropriate title. Most of us were relegated to low-level, boring jobs, and if we were singled out as capable and given more interesting work, that in itself was a reward. Indeed, in a world where women couldn't expect much in the way of position or money, you were fortunate to have a job that challenged you. And since most women did not equate personal success with career advancement, titles did not much matter. Women derived status from being seen as special. It was a point of pride to be different from other women who were regarded, generally, as inferior.

Companies are still exploiting women and the limited opportunities they have to do challenging work by offering them the work without the appropriate title and salary. And women, of course, are tempted to take half the pie, rather than none.

I think a wiser approach is this: use the power you have in your situation to negotiate for the title and money. If you put up a fight, you have an excellent chance of getting it all. And even if you don't get it, and decide to do the work without the title, you'll still be better off if you've negotiated. You will have established the fact that you are someone to be reckoned with and that you know what you are entitled to. The matter of your title will already be on the table—and while the boss could brush off people who are less sure of themselves, he now knows that if he wants to keep you, he has to address himself to that issue.

Before you negotiate, you have to understand your respective positions. His negotiating strength is based on giving you the opportunity you want so badly, as if it's a gift. His generosity undercuts your position: your feeling of gratitude saps your negotiating strength. It would seem ungrateful to push for everything. To regain your strength, you must pierce the logic of your adversary, to whit: he's not giving you a gift. There are no gifts in business. People in business give in order to get. And that's where your power lies: he wants something from you. He wants you—in particular—to do the new work. Now the sides are equalized: you want something and he wants something.

Women tend to see themselves as having few choices and many needs—and the boss as having a million choices and no needs. They find it hard to think of themselves as special, as not easily replaced. But if the boss is giving you new, more important work, then clearly he needs you—you are the best solution to his problem. It's *not* easy to replace someone who knows the ropes; it's time-consuming, costly, and risky. Take another look. The chances are excellent that he wants *and* needs your abilities with the new work.

Bolster your case for a new position with arguments like this, tailored to fit your own situation:

"I should have the title to match what I'm doing so that my responsibilities are clear to people both throughout the company and outside the company."

"If I had the title, doors would open more easily and I could handle more work. People at higher levels resist dealing with someone who has a lower title."

"It's to your advantage to have higher-level people working for you. Besides, it's long overdue."

Here's a sample negotiation:

YOU SAY TO YOUR BOSS: "It seems to me the work you'd like me to do fits the job description of a senior account representative. I agree with you that the job is right up my alley, and I'd like the title that fits my new activities."

BOSS REPLIES: "We're not rigid here about things like that." (Meaning, I don't want to give you the title.) "We all pitch in and do what's needed." (Meaning, you shouldn't be so petty and concerned with status.)

YOU: "The job title is important to me. I've worked hard to become a senior account rep, and now that I am, I want it known." (Declaring forthrightly and unashamedly that you don't think you're being petty; that you have a different value system.)

BOSS: "Oh, you're not concerned about things like that!" (Shame on you.)

YOU: "I am. The job title is very important to me." (Escalating your assertion, thus establishing the fact that you have your own appraisal of the situation and that he cannot entrap you in his.) "I would like the people I work with to understand clearly that I've achieved a specific level of skill."

BOSS: "Everyone knows you're good."

YOU: "Yes. And I'd like the title that goes with my new work." (Not letting him deflect you from your main argument.)

BOSS: "Hey, I'm giving you a great opportunity." (Meaning, you're greedy and ungrateful.)

YOU: "Yes, I'm pleased about that. Both the job *and* the title are very important to me."

Win or lose, he sees that he cannot maneuver you out of your position. The final decision of whether or not to give you the title is certainly up to him, but you are showing him that you are not overwhelmed by his arguments. This kind of exchange convinces the boss that you are clear about the validity of your request, and that you are not easily brainwashed out of it. It's important that you stay in the argument and not cave in after one or two objections—that you not give the appearance of being easily manipulated.

More arguments:

BOSS: "There's a temporary job freeze, and the personnel department won't approve a new line and title."

YOU: "Let's talk to them. I think we can convince them that this is an exceptional situation." (Enlisting him in your cause.)

OR YOU SAY: "Well, let's use the title 'acting' or 'consultant' until there's a line for me." (Reserving the next opening.)

Suppose he says no, flat out no. How you respond depends on when he says it. If he specifies no new title early on, you say, "Hold it!" and then give him all your arguments. But if he says no at the end of your discussion, and you are thinking of leaving in utter frustration, you might want to try this first. Take the work anyway and make it part of your campaign to move up. The fact that you are actually doing work that leaps ahead of your title gives you a good basis to claim the new title. That doesn't mean your boss won't argue with you next time, too, but it does mean he won't be on very strong ground.

When you take the work without the title, concede the argument with a statement that indicates it's temporary—that you'll get back to him to collect the title. Say: "Okay, I'm willing to do this for three months without the title in order to overcome any reservations you might have about giving it to me." Not only are you giving yourself the opening for a future claim on the title, but you are showing him that he hasn't intimidated you or convinced you to settle for less than the appropriate job title. Through this kind of exchange he will come to see you as a strong person. And that, in turn, is how he will learn to pay more attention to what you say and to be more responsive to your requests.

Whatever he replies to your concession speech, even if it's a "We'll see" or a grunt, take it as an assent. When the time comes to press for the title, you can say, "I've come to collect the title that we agreed I would get when I proved myself." You've primed him with your past discussions and now your hope is that, whatever he actually felt back then, he'll feel obligated now and will follow your lead.

But, you protest, he doesn't ever have to give you the title; he can do whatever he wants. In a sense, it's true—he does have the final vote, he can say no, he can even fire you. The bare fact of the boss's power often overwhelms women. They feel that he holds all the cards—and they lose sight of their own power. But the source of an employee's power in this situation lies in the fact that the boss has to do things that make good sense. He can't make too many mistakes if he wants to make money or secure his position. You have just taken on new functions, you are doing a good job, you two work well together. You are worth a lot to him. He may be as frightened of losing you as you are of losing the job.

And beyond that, you are in a strong negotiating position. The new work itself is a first-rate passport to the title in another company. If he won't give it to you, you can describe the work on your résumé and collect the title somewhere else.

15. THERE'S NO PLACE FOR ME TO GO—THE NEXT STEP IS MY BOSS'S JOB, AND HE'S NOT GOING ANYWHERE

Strategies to get your boss unstuck • Being strategic for two • Learning what motivates people

When your boss, for whatever reason, is standing still, and the only way up is to follow in his footsteps, why not try to get him moving? Difficult as that may seem, read on. With your help he might be able to do things he couldn't possibly do alone.

First, figure out what's holding him back. Does he need strategies? Does he lack ambition, confidence, or courage? In all these areas, you can help him in order to help yourself.

- *Career counsel your boss.* Give him the moving-up strategies he needs.

Gwen's Story

Gwen, a project leader in a systems development program, had a boss, Bill, who was just as stuck as she was. Their work was highly specialized. Until Bill moved, there was no place for Gwen to go. Bill had been trying for six months to get approval for the equipment needed to begin the work on his big project. There was no apparent reason for the delay: perhaps it was just inertia, perhaps the project had been rejected but no one wanted to say so. It was a mystery. But whatever the reason, nothing was happening; Bill was standing still and so, therefore, was Gwen.

When she heard that a new vice president was coming in to run the division, it occurred to Gwen that Bill might have a second chance to get his project off the ground. The new manager would be looking for a way to make his mark. Gwen had confidence in Bill's project. She urged him to move in fast with a new proposal. While everyone else was scrambling for favor with the new manager, Gwen sat down and went to work on the proposal, writing and rewriting until, after two weeks, she had a presentation that was readable, alive, filled with compelling arguments and documentation—a first-rate selling tool. The new manager read it and immediately gave Bill the needed approvals for equipment, staff, and space. Bill was on his way. His group was growing, the importance of his work was being recognized, and he was now in a position to move up.

Not only had Gwen given her boss the career advice he needed so that he could move upward—leaving a space for her—but also, because he had seen how valuable and helpful she could be, she was his choice to fill the space he left behind.

Gwen's basic strategy had consisted of finding the opportunity for her boss. Its implementation was as simple as coming in with a first-rate, well-thought-out proposal. What was not so simple was her seeing herself as the person who could size up her boss's situation better than he could—and as the person who could influence the top manager's course of action.

Caitlin's Story

Caitlin, like Gwen, was held back by a boss who didn't know how to advance. She gave her boss, Paul, some advice that paid off for both of them. Paul had taken on most of the activities of two higher-level jobs, but still had the same title he had been given when he was first hired. Caitlin could have commiserated with him about how unfair it all was, how the company was exploiting him—an easy way of giving him support. Instead, Caitlin went to work on actually helping Paul by suggesting that he mount a carefully prepared campaign to collect the title that reflected the higher-level work he was doing. Caitlin became Paul's career counselor and helped him to prepare a persuasive case showing why it was in the company's best interest to give him the new title. As Paul got upgraded, so did Caitlin.

Caitlin was able to help herself by helping her boss fulfill his ambitions. But what if your boss has no ambitions? What if he's perfectly happy right where he is? This calls for a different tack.

• *Infuse your boss with ambition.* Trying to fire up your boss with ambition if he's settled back into a comfortable niche is not an easy task, but you may want to give it a try. Win or lose, you will develop your ability to motivate others as you experiment with various approaches and observe your boss's reactions.

If you decide to try to reawaken your boss's long-gone ambitions, think about what might lure him into activity. Perhaps he'd be moved by money, or by new, more interesting work, or by a chance to meet new people, or by an opportunity to garner achievements and/or status. Maybe he'd like the chance to do something worthwhile or important. For Myra's boss, Leo, it was escape from boredom.

Myra's Story

Myra was the assistant to Leo, the administrator in charge of a hospital emergency room. Myra wanted Leo's job, but he wasn't going anywhere. He was perfectly happy to stay where he was. He had talent but no real ambitions; he was more interested in his life outside the hospital than in his job. Myra tried to think of a way to get him more involved. She knew that the head of the hospital's public relations department was doing a rather routine, uninspired job, and she thought that Leo—who had a flair for imaginative ideas as well as the ability to make contacts—had a chance of making his mark in public relations. So whenever she sensed he was dissatisfied and bored with his personal life, she presented him with exciting ideas for publicizing their department. Together they developed publicity events that began to attract citywide attention to the hospital.

Myra anticipated resistance from the public relations department. She and Leo were, after all, crossing departmental lines and doing the work that normally would be done by public relations. Myra raised the issue with Leo, and together they worked out explanations. When the public relations department protested their activities, Leo explained that they had gotten the stories on TV through someone he knew, or someone owed him a favor, or the executive director had suggested he make the call.

Although Leo had settled into the routine life in the hospital, the new work gave him a lift. He took Myra's bait to relieve the monotony, and before he knew it was caught up in his own success.

Myra didn't stop there. She planned ways for Leo to expand his territory into a community relations division with several departments, including under his umbrella not only the emergency room and public relations but, eventually, social services and volunteer services as well. The growth of the department gave Myra endless possibilities for advancing her own career.

Myra's boss had not been interested in moving ahead, yet she had managed to arouse his ambitions. But what if your boss has tried to forge ahead, all his efforts have failed, and now he is thoroughly demoralized?

• *Infuse your boss with courage and confidence.* If your boss has a bad case of demoralization, if his efforts have been consistently rejected, if he feels shelved and is resigned to his fate, you might be able to get him back on track. This, too, is a formidable task, but it can be well worth the effort.

The strategy here is to lend him your energy and ideas. If your boss has a collaborator—a partner who knows how to get ideas accepted and implemented, who understands the politics of the system, who knows how to operate—life might flow back into him, bit by bit. He might do things with your support that he wouldn't tackle alone.

To get past his negativism, swing into action. As he sees things getting done, he'll become more optimistic. As you report your successes, be sure to share information so he feels in charge of the work you are producing. The more he is part of your activities, the more confident he will become.

Hard work? Yes, but many women have been successful with these strategies. Even if you try these approaches and your boss stays hopelessly immobilized, you, at least, will have learned a lot from having tried to get him moving. You will have learned about motivation. You will understand more about what the boss's environment is like, and, through teaming with him, you will have had the chance to practice operating in it. Each thing you do will have been practice for your eventual involvement in the increasingly complex and political arena at higher levels. You will be better equipped to get a job equivalent to your boss's somewhere else—or to stay and compete with him for *his* job. Read on!

16. MY BOSS IS IN TROUBLE—SHOULD I GO FOR HIS JOB?

When sympathy and support are appropriate, and when to take other action • How to position yourself • How to get your boss's job when this looks like a good idea

If your boss is in trouble, you may be torn between trying to rescue him or standing aside, watching him sink, so that you can get his job. It's a pain-

ful conflict. What do you do with your sympathetic impulse to help someone who's in a bad situation when you may have more to gain by letting him
fail?

In general, the best policy in business is to support your colleagues.
You not only earn a good reputation, but you also create an important network of allies. Before you decide to help your failing boss, however, appraise the situation. Is he rescuable? Can he, with a reasonable amount of
help from you, straighten things out and make it? If you think there's a
chance, go to it. Lend a hand. Give him information, advice, ideas,
strategies—whatever you can to help him out of his jam.

Granted, if you are ready for a job at his level, you will be giving up
your immediate best chance to move up. Nevertheless, if you are confident
and if your abilities are developing, there will be many opportunities for
you to move ahead.

But if he's in serious trouble and the problems can't be readily repaired
with your help, then it is time to go after his job. First separate yourself
from your boss so that you are not seen as his sidekick or part of his failing
team. You don't want your ability to be blurred with his inability. Then
take pains to impress management with your competence while you let your
boss fend for himself. If your instinctive reaction is to try to cover up for
him, remind yourself of your appraisal: he's in the wrong job, and your trying to save him won't make a difference. If you were to try, you would only
succeed in jeopardizing your future along with his. Do your best work and
let his work speak for itself. And as the company looks around for a replacement, there you are.

Andrea's Story

Andrea was faced with a dilemma when the head of the division,
Stanley, took her aside and questioned her about her boss's dismal performance. Andrea had already evaluated the situation: her boss, Jim, was
sinking in the quicksand of his own ineptitude. For fourteen months she had
backed him up, given him ideas, repaired damaged relationships, and corrected his errors, all to no avail. She thought it was time to stop trying to
rescue him. Andrea's decision was to use her meeting with Stanley to position herself for Jim's job. Her immediate problem was how to answer
Stanley's probing questions, not knowing exactly how Stanley felt about
Jim. She didn't know how much of what she said would get back to Jim,

and she also wanted to avoid creating a distasteful image of herself by delivering her true—but very critical—appraisal of Jim's performance.

Andrea's solution was to stay with the facts. She reported the bad news: the department's limited progress and the problems with various projects. Without appearing judgmental, she gave Stanley a clear picture of what was going on and let him draw his own conclusions about Jim's competence. Andrea then seized the opportunity to let Stanley draw another conclusion—about her competence and leadership ability. She outlined for him her own ideas for bailing out projects and solving the department's problems. Finally, she let Stanley know that her allegiance lay with him. She proposed that they have the same cover story. She put it diplomatically: "I'm concerned that Jim might resent our evaluating the overall condition of the department. When I report this meeting, perhaps I should focus on the more technical subjects we reviewed—ones that fall in my area." Stanley agreed and their new alliance was cemented.

Andrea's strategy in answering Stanley's questions was to display her own strength while letting her boss's weakness speak for itself. Her estimation of the situation proved true, and her strategy was on target. Jim was fired and Andrea got his job. Andrea was quite sure that Stanley had found it easier to fire Jim knowing that she was there to fill his shoes. Building her leadership image, while letting Jim sink, had paid off.

17. I TRAIN THE INEXPERIENCED YOUNG MEN—AND THEN THEY GET PROMOTED

Women as trainer-mothers • Moving onto the upwardly mobile track • Looking and acting the part • How to enlist your boss's aid • If you're still discriminated against

"Why should they get jumped ahead? It's outrageous. I've been here years getting nowhere. A man walks in and I'm expected to train him so he can be promoted over me!" My client was angry—and why shouldn't she be? She was middle-aged, the head teller in a large commercial bank, and she had seen young man after young man come through her department and then move on to bigger and better things. Now, after years of accepting the "system," she had come to realize that it was really nothing more than a chauvinistic tradition that had robbed her of her chance to move ahead. It had never occurred to her before that she could be a top person. Now, how-

ever, under the influence of the women's movement, women like my client have been discovering their ambitions, *and* the fact that they've been hood-winked. They are furious, and rightly so.

In fact, my client was a "trainer" in a training program, although no one called it that. A management training program is nothing more than a system to acquaint bright young stars with the workings of the company. They are brought in to take a look around, and then, armed with the knowledge which experts such as my client can give them, they move on to another department and another teacher until they know enough to function effectively as managers.

It's an old story for women: at home we raise children, and at work we raise trainees. In both places we nourish the growth of others; in both places they outpace us, leaving us behind. In neither place are we seen as people who will grow in their own right, who can move on, who themselves can reach for higher and higher levels of achievement.

A woman in the workplace can easily become demoralized when she sees a new man apparently outdo her and get promoted. In one of the more insidious ways that chauvinism cripples its victims, she feels she's lost the competition—that somehow *she* didn't measure up. *But she was never in the competition.* The new man was tagged for promotion—consciously or unconsciously, by himself and by management—the day he was hired, while she was tagged from the day she was hired as a helper and tutor.

If you are stuck as a trainer-mother and you want to maneuver past the prejudice that pins you to this role, here's what to do—and what *not* to do.

First and foremost, *don't* protest the injustice of men moving past you, or remonstrate about the discrimination against women. Unfortunately, that kind of complaint almost always falls on deaf ears. For one thing, most people can't own up to being sexist. Discriminating against women is too nasty and embarrassing a flaw for most to admit, even to themselves. If you are too direct with your complaint, you'll put your boss on the spot. He'll just dig in his heels and defend himself. He'll think, "Hey, I'm a good guy. I'm fair. *She's* off the mark. She's just not qualified." Your complaint, founded or unfounded, will seem like an attack. Instead, approach him indirectly. Let him know that he's got you incorrectly pegged by making him see you differently. Find ways to dramatize your potential—the same potential he's been looking for in management trainees. Do new things in new ways. Walk around with a management textbook under your arm. Dress differently. Propose a meeting with him to present some substantial new ideas you have for improving, say, the organization of your department, or increasing the efficiency and productivity of the staff—whatever would fit your situation. Present your ideas in an assertive, organized, and authoritative manner. Let him know that you are ambitious and are working on a career plan. And finally, enlist him in a joint campaign to get you on the upwardly mobile track.

How do you enlist him? You might introduce the subject by saying, "I'm formulating a long-range career plan, and I'd like to ask your help." Tailor what you say to fit your individual situation. If, for example, you have been on your job for eleven years without a murmur, you might begin with: "I've been rethinking my job. When I first came here, I wasn't career-oriented. I thought of work as just a job. Now I'm more ambitious, and I've begun to realize that I'm capable of developing myself and contributing more to the company. I guess I'm what you call a 'late bloomer.' "

Your aim in this meeting is to "guide" him into being your collaborator. Let him know you are serious by showing him you've done your homework. Know what you are talking about. "I've been meeting with people in different jobs in the division and getting a detailed understanding of their work." Make him feel you really want his opinion: "Since my strengths are A and B, it seems to me that I should shoot for X and Y. Do you agree that that's where I would fit best?" Ask specific questions that will elicit specific advice: "What do I need to learn to get there? How can I best prepare myself?"

You want to involve your boss in your future, so play his psychological strings. Let *him* gain something from advising *you*. When people give advice, they feel helpful, useful, and important. Moreover, they have an investment in your success. If you move ahead, they can even take credit for your success—they feel a kind of parental pride. That's not to say that you should play baby to his parent, but whatever his motivation is, take advantage of the help he can give you.

If you run up against resistance, it may be because you've made it too hard for him to help you. Many people wouldn't mind doing worthwhile things such as helping someone get ahead, but they want to do so without a lot of bother. Make it easy for your boss. Don't ask difficult questions or questions that are so general that he may not be able to answer them, such as, "What do you think I could be?" Or, "Where in the company do you think I could use my skills?"

Once you've recruited your boss in your strategy, don't let it rest there. Often women think they've done all they can when they say to their boss, "I'd like a better job; I'd like to get ahead," or, "I want to move up."

Show him that you are really serious by waging a sustained campaign. You have to encourage him to think of you in new ways. Keep coming back to him with statements about your career goals. Let him know how you are using his suggestions. Fill him in on interesting bits of information you've uncovered, or facts you've accomplished in your job research. As you do, you will remind him of who you have become and where you are headed. Most importantly, your calm perseverance over a period of time will speak for itself. Your boss will be impressed with the fact that your ambitions are not to be dismissed. They are not going to disappear.

If you follow this strategy, you may not change management's thinking about all women, but you very likely will change their thinking about you. You stand a good chance of being seen as the exception to their chauvinistic rule.

Of course, it is possible that your company may have a well-entrenched policy against advancing women, in which case your best efforts will fail. Whether you should continue to wage a private battle or mount a public fight against discrimination depends on your resources and the circumstances.

18. I DON'T THINK I SHOULD GO FOR THE PROMOTION BECAUSE I DON'T EXPECT TO STAY WITH THE COMPANY

Conflicting interests: whose needs come first? • Women as over-givers

I overheard one of my clients tipping off a friend to a good job opportunity she had seen posted on the bulletin board in her company. It was a notch higher than either of their present jobs. I interrupted their conversation to ask my client why she wasn't going for it herself. "I know I could get it," she explained, "but I don't see any point in it. I'm going back to school full-time in a few months."

"But," I argued, "why not try to get the new job anyway? With a degree, plus a middle-level management job in your background, you'd be in a much better position when you come back to the job market two years from now. You won't have to prove yourself at this level; you'll already have done that."

"I wouldn't do that to my boss," she protested. "I like him, and I feel I'd be sabotaging him. I don't think it's right. He'd be spending months training me for the new position, paying me a high salary to learn the job—and just as I catch on and start producing, I resign. I feel it would be unfair, even unethical."

"Companies use you, why not use them?" I asked.

But she was unconvinced. "My boss is a person, not a company. I know how I'd feel if someone did that to me."

The issue of conflicting interests between employee and employer was sharply posed by my client's situation. If she did not take the promotion, she would lose out on the chance both to do new work at a higher level and to get the higher title that would serve her well on future job interviews. Her résumé would suffer: it wouldn't reflect the confidence her present employer had in her. On the other hand, if she selfishly took the promotion and left a few months later, her boss would have to start all over training someone new.

Why do so many women find it more acceptable to accommodate the boss's needs than to use a situation on their own behalf? The culture has a fairness code, written by the power structure, that—not surprisingly—puts corporate needs above individual needs. In effect, companies define for us what our priorities should be. If we don't investigate the source of the code, we accept it as gospel.

Women are particularly vulnerable to the definition of fairness that puts the interests of the company and boss ahead of their own needs. It's simply an extension of their role in the family where women subordinate self-interest to the more "important" needs of others—the husband's career, the children's education, the father-in-law's illness. A mother's crucial role in the care of infants and children becomes generalized into a lifelong serving role vis-à-vis the whole world around her. Although this is indeed a convenience to others, the fact is that unlike children, adults (husbands, managers) and institutions (corporations, charities) are able to have their needs met in a variety of ways.

Women, schooled in giving, feel loyalty to their jobs and to the people they work for; men, encouraged in their ambitions, are better able to be loyal to their own best interests.

Women need to break with a tradition of "fairness" that consistently positions them in the giving role. Establish your equality by taking as much as you give. If you have a chance for a promotion, grab the opportunity, even if the company suffers an inconvenience. This time they will have a setback while you leap ahead. Sometimes you give, sometimes you take.

If you are planning to leave the company soon—to relocate, to have a baby, to be with your family, to take a sabbatical, whatever—I say, go for the promotion. Take the new title that will serve you so well in future interviews. It's an ideal time to put your own needs first.

19. I HAVE TO STAY IN THIS JOB TWO YEARS BEFORE THEY'LL PROMOTE ME

Why companies resist using your talent • How to get on the fast track • Teaming with the boss • How to take advantage of someone else's mistakes • Winning out over the competition

"Two years in this boring job? No way! I learned the whole thing in two months." My client, a young, ambitious woman, was outraged at her boss's lack of appreciation for her abilities, as well as his lack of sympathy for her desire to get ahead. She had been working for only a few months when she applied for a more challenging job. Her boss's response seemed more than she could bear: she was told that company policy required her to remain in her present job for two years before they would consider her for a promotion. When she argued that she had outgrown the work and didn't want to stay in a spot where she wasn't learning, he replied coolly, "We're not here to teach you."

Would she have to serve out her sentence? Did she have to live with the company's ridiculous regulations? Or was there some clever way around it?

My client's spirited refusal to put the needs of the company or her boss ahead of her own was encouraging. At long last, more and more women are unwilling to thwart their own development. They are ambitious, competitive, and impatient. Younger women have high expectations; they are fired up by the new climate in business that seems full of promise for women. They want to get ahead, and get there fast. Older women now want to make up for lost time; they want job status appropriate to their experience and abilities. They get angry when they compare their achievements to those of men their own age. As one woman put it: "Here I am, just starting out, and the men I date are talking about their boats, their weekend houses, and their investments."

Nevertheless, my client had to take into consideration the realities of business. By and large, management is not moved by employee needs. Your career advancement is of interest to them only if it serves their purposes. If you press for a promotion too soon, the boss is more likely to fire you than to promote you. He'll think that you are too demanding, that you will always be dissatisfied—and he'll replace you with a more patient, more easily exploited woman. From his point of view, two years in one job doesn't sound very long. And if you have the job down pat and things are running smoothly, then to him two years doesn't sound nearly long enough.

That's not to say you should patiently wait out your sentence. In fact, if you settle in and do a good job, there's little guarantee that you will get promoted even after two years. The put-in-your-time rule is designed to hold you back in your useful spot as long as possible—*not* to give you the date on which you move ahead.

While you can't show your impatience, you should do everything possible to make the boss *want* to promote you. You have to convince him that it's in his best interests to have you move up, that he needs you at the next job up more than he needs you where you are. You have to impress him with your value so that he *wants* to deliver more responsibility to you.

Watch for opportunities. See what your boss's problems are.

Holly's Story

Craig's biggest problem was Anne, his second-in-command. He had gotten the job she had hoped for; she resented working for him, and was more competitive than cooperative. Holly was new on the job and low woman on the totem pole. She worked at strengthening her relationship with Craig by being Anne's opposite. Since Anne withheld information, Holly went out of her way to share it. Anne grabbed public credit; Holly gave ideas to Craig so he could take credit. Anne wasn't very friendly; Holly was always responsive. Holly teamed with Craig, in a cooperative, nonchallenging way. The day after Craig and Anne had an even noisier than usual blowup, Holly asked Craig for more responsibility. She had outgrown her job, she said, and was beginning to understand many facets of the department's (meaning, of course, Anne's) work. Holly had timed her request cleverly. Often a manager will keep an employee he's not happy with simply because the employee knows the work, and it's difficult to find a replacement. But if someone good is available, he won't hesitate to get rid of the problem person. Craig fired Anne and promoted Holly. Holly broke through the two-

year rule by taking advantage of the deteriorating relationship between
Anne and Craig.

Did Holly's impatience to move up lure her into doing something
unethical? No, not at all. She didn't sabotage Anne—Anne had sabotaged
herself. Holly just filled a void. Actually, this is the way competition typically works. People have a misguided notion that competition is like a race,
and that the person who comes in one inch ahead of the others wins. But if
Anne had been working well with Craig, the only way Holly could have
gotten her job would have been to come in ten miles ahead of Anne, out-
performing her dramatically in nearly every way.

If you want to beat the system, remember that your boredom is not the
issue. Your desire for career advancement is not the issue. The issue is
whether your boss sees you as the person he wants and needs—someone
who can do more for him in the higher-level job you are after. *That's* the
way to get around the put-in-your-time rule.

20. I'VE BEEN DOING MY BOSS'S JOB TEMPORARILY— CAN I HANG ON TO THIS INTERESTING WORK?

Going for the job your company doesn't think you're ready for
• How to create your own job description • How to move up before you've paid your dues • Women's tendency to be overcau-
tious about going for a higher-level job • Accepting the work
before the title • Helping the boss move up so you can get his job

Sometimes people have the good luck to be handed their boss's work to
do for a while. Once you've done this interesting work, however, it's painful to have to go back to your old routine. If you have been given your
boss's work temporarily, why not try to hold on to it permanently? While it
might seem impossible, here are the stories of three women with whom I
worked who did just that.

Sara's Story

Sara, a bright, mature secretary, got her opportunity when her boss suddenly resigned. She was asked to pitch in and do what she could to keep
things going until a replacement could be found. Although she couldn't

handle his entire job, she soon realized that she was quite capable of doing a good part of it. She had, through this fortuitous event, discovered her abilities. Now, with more interesting work at hand, she didn't want to be forced back into her purely secretarial job when a new supervisor came in. At the same time, she couldn't apply for the boss's job because she didn't have the necessary technical background. Difficult as it might seem, she *could* hold on to part of the boss's work.

Sara had one advantage she could use: she knew the workings of the department and the new boss would not. When a new man was hired, Sara offered in a helpful way to fill him in on the procedures and routines of the department. "The X is routed through the Y department; Jane handles the pink slips; I distribute the green slip assignments." She drew up her own job description, including the part of the boss's work she wanted to hold on to, and presented it to him while orienting him to the department. He didn't question her rundown but accepted the job assignments as she outlined them.

Could she have handled it more openly? Couldn't she have explained that she had been doing part of his job and would like to continue? Possible, but chancier. If the new boss was worried about doing things the way they'd been done by his predecessors, or if he was a controlling person, or if he felt threatened, he might have decided to take the work back and do it himself.

If you are thinking of trying this strategy, you might be concerned about not telling the whole truth. You might worry about being found out. Consider this: you are presenting yourself as you now really are. The new reality is as truthful as the old one. Yet many women find it difficult to report their new and higher positions in a matter-of-fact way. They feel compelled to give a history of their growth and development, as if they have to justify their new level. Many women feel uncomfortable when they assume a higher position, as if they are not supposed to develop or grow. They feel out of place when they forge ahead. If you can accept your advancement as natural, then you can handle it matter-of-factly. If the boss questions your version of your job description, you can show him how it's to his advantage to leave it alone. Or you can say that you've been doing the job very well, and assumed that he would value your contribution.

Another point to remember: the job descriptions on the records rarely reflect the actual jobs being done. In reality, job descriptions develop and change according to the skills and personalities of the people in the picture.

Job descriptions are created through action, through the process of getting work done. Reality supersedes what's on paper.

Sara's strategy of defining her job for her new boss before he could do it for her might seem simple, but in implementing it she had to define—for herself—both her job and who she was. She had to break free of stereotyped definitions; she had to resist being overpowered by the label "secretary." When Sara was no longer bound by what she thought others expected of her, she could do what had to be done.

Her strategy was effective on several levels. In the very act of formally orienting her new boss, Sara was taking the initiative, thus projecting strength and becoming credible at the higher level. By presenting herself as the competent person she really is, she created an image of an assertive professional. Contrast this to the impression she would have made if she had sat passively at her desk, waiting and worrying about how the new boss might see a secretary's job. If she had waited, she would have exposed a lack of confidence and an inability to take charge that would have prevented management from seeing her as a next-level person.

In Sara's situation it was clear that she would be doing well if she got a secure hold on even a few of the boss's higher-level functions. But if you are filling in for your boss temporarily, maybe you should be thinking about applying for your boss's entire job. I find that most women tend to wait overly long and are overly prepared for the next level before they brave applying for a promotion. Don't underestimate yourself and your ability. If you're doing the boss's job and are able to handle it, sell yourself for it. You know the department, you know the company, and you understand the job. Even if you are rejected, you'll still be ahead of the game if you make a bid for your boss's job. You will have let the company know you are ambitious and confident, and you will have alerted them to the fact that you are definitely someone to be considered for promotion.

Janet's Story

Janet had been with a new company for only two months when her boss resigned to take a job elsewhere. She was temporarily given most of her former boss's responsibilities while management looked for his replacement. She saw that she could handle the work, but being so new she wondered whether it was appropriate for her to approach management for a promotion. She was concerned about management's reaction: they didn't know much about her, and whatever she did now would form their impression of her. She was afraid she might appear presumptuous and, since she was in a conservative corporation, she feared the people above her would be threatened by her ultrasonic pace. Indeed, if she applied for her boss's job, her ambition might earn little more than resentment ("She hasn't paid her dues") and distrust ("She might be after *my* job next").

The odds were so much against her getting the job that it didn't seem worth taking the risk. Janet had to avoid making a direct bid for the job. She decided to test the waters with a nonthreatening request for her division head's advice. "I'd like your opinion. Do you think it would make sense for me to apply for this position?" Then she slipped in her credentials to impress him: "Although I'm new on this job, I have as much experience as many other senior economists. In fact, in my last job as a junior, I was doing a good part of the work that is included in this company's job description for a senior economist."

Not surprisingly, her division head didn't think it was a good idea at all. We shifted strategies. Now Janet's goal was to keep him from hiring someone else for as long as she could while she established herself as the best candidate for the job. She needed time.

Since managers tend to turn their attention to problem areas and ignore things that are running smoothly, I suggested she take over even more of her absent boss's work. In view of the division head's negative reaction, Janet's impulse was to pull back. I suggested that she plunge in wholeheartedly to make certain that things ran well. If the work of the senior economist was being completely covered by Janet, there would be no immediate pressure on the company to hire a replacement.

A month went by without any evident attempt on management's part to fill the vacant job. We then decided it was time for her to try to solidify her position. She presented a proposal in which she offered to take over the whole job *without* the title or salary that would normally go with it. To explain her generous offer, she said that keeping this new work was important to her: she liked it, it was challenging, interesting, and appropriate to her level of training. She laid out a persuasive argument based on cost effectiveness: she showed the division head how this move could save the company $11,000 a year.

Her reasoning was all to the company's advantage: Janet was at the top of the salary range for her grade level, earning $28,000 a year. Her former boss's job paid $6,000 more, but she was willing to do it with no increase—a saving right there of $6,000 a year. Then, to fill her original spot, they could bring in someone at the low end of the salary range for that grade level at $23,000 a year—an additional saving of $5,000. In a tough business climate, it was irresistible. Even though she had only been in the company three months, Janet maneuvered her way into a "promotion." Within six months she had established herself as one of the strongest senior economists in the division, and the arrangement was formalized with the appropriate title and salary increase.

Deirdre's Story

Deirdre was an old-timer who had been stuck in her job for some years. She was handling her boss's job while he was on an overseas assignment. She thought it was quite unlikely that she could find a way to hold on to this interesting work when Dan came back. "Dan's certainly not about to hand his job over to me—what's *he* supposed to do if I do his work? He might even fire me if he thought I was after his job."

Deirdre had shown that she could do Dan's job: while he was gone, she had run the department and solved some knotty problems. She had welded together a team of difficult personalities to develop a rush proposal, which she had then presented and sold to a client. She had hired someone to replace a worker who had resigned. Deirdre could have taken her experience to a new company, but she rejected that option—she had a good collaborative relationship with Dan, the company was solid and had an excellent reputation, and she got along well with her co-workers. She was happy where she was.

Fortunately, Dan, like most people, was interested in getting ahead. Deirdre's strategy would be to play on his ambitions to further hers: we had to find something for Dan to do that would hook into his hopes for himself.

I advised Deirdre to talk to her boss quite straightforwardly about her taking over some of his job functions—in order to free him for bigger and better things. The timing was right: she was in a strong position because she had just shown how well she could do his job. As soon as her boss was back in the office, she made her proposal: "The analysts take up a lot of your time, energy, and creative thought. I could relieve you of this difficult group and free you to develop new business." (This was the great concern of their top management, as she well knew.) After she had broached the idea, she settled down for a leisurely discussion of new business ideas, including a couple of leads for new contacts that she had developed. He took the bait, and she got to keep many of the new functions she found so much more interesting than her old job.

These stories show that there is no ready-made formula for advancement. You have to weave your opportunity out of the threads of your own situation. Each woman had a slightly different variation of the same problem—holding on to some or all of her boss's work—but each had to find a quite different solution to fit her particular situation. The solution for Sara was to define her job on her own terms before her new boss put her in a standard secretarial mold. Janet's opportunity for advancement came too soon, so she stalled for time. Deirdre got *her* chance by giving her boss *his* chance; she got to do what she wanted by giving him the opportunity to do what he wanted.

21. HOW CAN I GET A RAISE?

Publicizing yourself—to yourself and others • How to press for a raise without jeopardizing your job • Why mystique is important • Overcoming the reluctance to talk about money • How to measure your value objectively and feel confident that your request is appropriate • How to keep the discussion going when the boss turns you down—without becoming a pest • His power/your power: equalizing the negotiation • How to argue nondefensively • The arguments management uses, and the answers, word for word, that will earn you respect • Useful strategies for negotiating anything • Threatening to quit

Stepping into the boss's office and asking for a raise can be a scary and painful proposition—and even the boldest and most experienced of us are apt to turn tail and run at the last moment. But maybe that's because we don't actually know how to *ask* for a raise, and maybe we don't understand the dynamics of the entire situation.

One thing you have to realize is that the raise negotiation begins well before you actually walk into the boss's office and make your pitch. I like to think of it as divided into three phases, or stages, extending over a period of several weeks or even months. How you conduct yourself during each of these stages can determine whether you get the raise or not.

I call these stages:

- The Prep-Up.
- Psychological Sparring.
- The Encounter.

Stage # 1: The Prep-Up

You are not ready to negotiate until certain things are in good order. Your raise does not depend on your productivity or the quality of your work alone. First and foremost, you should have a good working relationship with whoever will be deciding on your raise. If that person doesn't like you or respect you, you probably won't be successful. If this is your situation, take hope. I've seen over and over again situations in which a woman, once aware of her problems, has turned a not too good relationship around in a matter of a few short weeks. This must be remedied before you step in and make your pitch. You very definitely want the raise-giver on your side.

Petra's Story

When Petra, a researcher in an economics consulting firm, asked her boss for a raise, she was told coldly that it was just not done that way—"People in this company don't *ask* for raises." When I probed, however, I discovered that a rather difficult situation existed between Petra and her boss. They seemed to be at odds about everything. He told her he expected her to be "pleasant," and Petra, for her part, thought her boss was an absolute bore. He liked nothing more than to chat about personal matters, restaurants, social affairs, his dates, theater, and so on. Petra, who was very efficient and conscientious, thought it was a total waste of time and would invariably change the subject to discussions of office matters. The boss clearly felt rebuffed, criticized, and, in a sense, snubbed by Petra.

She was quite amazed when she came to realize that "getting down to business" was the source of her trouble with her boss. She thereupon set out to see if she could repair the damage: she began to listen to his stories and to respond to them with interest. At the same time, she also made sure to get in her licks on important matters, reporting on the volume of work handled, the reports completed, etc., so that her boss would know that she was still attending to business.

Three months later, she decided to risk making another request for a raise. Despite her boss's earlier admonishment, she felt hopeful that since they were now getting on well, he might be more receptive—and she was right. He replied, "I'll have to think about it." No reprimand this time, and perhaps a raise in the offing.

Being on good terms with the raise-giver not only increases your chances of success, but also minimizes the risk of asking for a raise. If you ask for a raise and your boss is not happy with you or your work, he may seize that moment to fire you.

Before you actually take a deep breath and step into the boss's office, you have to do a publicity campaign on yourself—to yourself. You have to remind yourself that you are worth the raise. At this moment, many women are suddenly thrown into a state of doubt. They begin to wonder: "Am I worth that much money?" "Is my work really good enough?" They think, "After all, I'm not that exceptional." "I did make this mistake and I did forget to do that and I don't know much about the such-and-such." Why does doubt set in? I think it's because historically women have been paid little or nothing for their labor; thus, many women carry with them the feeling that their everyday work is not worth very much. They feel they have to do something exceptional—like being the best in their field—to deserve a raise. They don't comprehend that their value is measured within the context of the office or the department.

You must put yourself in touch with your value as a worker. Think about the things you've accomplished about which you were particularly pleased or proud, or for which you were praised. Concentrate on all the positives you can think of, items or events that make you special.

You also have to conduct a public relations campaign on your behalf to your boss or whoever will be deciding about your hoped-for raise. He has to know that you are worth the raise. Publicizing your activities should, of course, be done on an ongoing basis, but now is the time to concentrate on it—making up for lost time, if necessary. For example, mention that there is an average of four more new customer queries a week, or how you overcame some kind of difficult problem, or casually tell the raise-giver about a compliment you got from the client. In this way, he hears good things about you—and he also knows that you are confidently aware of your value.

You have to set a figure. How much of a raise do you think you should get? Have a range in mind—a maximum and minimum figure. Determine a salary you would hope for and one that you would settle for happily.

How do you know what you are worth? I find that women invariably ask for too little. Try to arrive at a realistic figure by looking at the following factors and evaluating them:

1. What are others in your community in comparable jobs, particularly men, earning? The more people you know, the easier it will be for you to get that information. A tip: keep up your contacts with any employment agency people you meet in the course of your job searches; they can be good sources of information on questions like this.

2. How does your work compare to that of others in a comparable job? Are you producing more of whatever it is you are supposed to produce, whether it's goodwill, ideas, widgets, or profits?

3. How important are you to your boss?

Now, let's answer these questions and work out what your new salary should be. Say people in comparable jobs are getting $18,000 to $21,000, and you're above average in your performance. Set your figure at $20,000. Are you very important to your boss? Increase your figure to the top of the range, $21,000. Now calculate how much more you want to shoot for as a maximum figure.

Your maximum depends on your current salary. If you are already earning $21,000 or close to it, add approximately fifteen percent to the $21,000 figure. Your maximum will be in the area of $24,000.

If your present salary falls far short of $21,000, your realistic maximum might be ten percent above $21,000, or $23,000—but if you are doing a spectacular job and have good ammunition, by all means shoot for the full fifteen percent. Keep in mind that your argument is not based on your present salary, but on what other people at your level of performance are getting. Sometimes, your starting salary was so low or your job functions have changed so dramatically that you can take a giant leap up in the figure you set.

It pays to set your sights high. The numbers may seem outrageous to you at first, but think about them for a while. Say them out loud to yourself. Get used to thinking of yourself as a $20,000-a-year-person or a $50,000-a-year-person or whatever your hopes are—you'll find it easier to ask for the right amount.

Prepare your arguments in advance for the actual encounter. Some sample dialogues showing typical boss reactions to a request for a raise, and some indications of the right ways and wrong ways for you to respond, follow in a moment.

It's very important for you to build the most persuasive case you can. Although you might think a raise is a cut-and-dried matter—that the company is either going to give it to you or not—the fact is, you can influence the outcome dramatically through the strength of your logic. The company's management consists of people, and people are convinceable. Think of how often you have made a concession to someone else's logic.

It's a good idea to anticipate the worst possible things your boss could say. Don't ignore or overlook anything, particularly any skeleton that might be in your closet. Have an answer ready that is assertive and non-defensive.

Suppose the raise-giver says, "What about that big mess you got us into last year that cost us $14,000?" You say, "I made mistakes, of course—everyone does. But fortunately, I learned a good lesson, as proven by my track record in the last few months: no significant errors, and improvements in efficiency have already saved us over $8,000."

Or, suppose he says, "You lied about your salary on your employment application." Your response: "Yes, I did. My skills when I came on board were considerably in advance of the salary I was getting then. I gave you the figure that in truth represented what I could do for you."

Suppose he asks, "Did you resign from your last job—or were you fired?" You say, "Fired. The conservative management there did not agree with my proposed innovations. You do, which is why we get on so well and why we are producing so well together."

Although it's unlikely that any such skeletons will be dragged out, if you are ready with an appropriate response, you will enter the negotiation confident that you can handle any attempts to invalidate your position.

Stage # 2: Psychological Sparring

Psychological sparring takes place before the actual encounter or moment of truth in the boss's office. Sometimes a woman may not even be aware that it is going on or how important it is. By "psychological sparring" I mean the passing back and forth of signals and propaganda—whether artic-

ulated verbally, or in the form of memos, or even unspoken attitudes—
between the company's management and yourself.

One thing you have to realize: any raise is on the minds of all concerned
long before it's talked about. You're thinking about how to ask for it and
the boss is thinking about how to avoid being asked for it. If you handle
yourself well at this stage, you'll come into the nitty-gritty of requesting a
raise with a decided advantage.

The boss has to be made to realize that you are an independent person.
He has to know that you will not cling endlessly to your job—that you are
not the kind of person who will stay there no matter what happens.

He has to know that while you're not dependent on him, he *is* dependent
on you. He never has to worry about your area. With you around, the job
gets done. He's also dependent on you because he doesn't know quite how
you do it. You've created a mystique about your job.

Drop subtle clues that other offers are coming your way. "A friend of
mine who works for such-and-such company called the other day and asked
if I knew someone who is interested in a job as (the job you're holding
down now). Do you know anyone who's looking?" Or, "I just had a
strange call from a headhunter. How would she have gotten my name?"
But at the same time let the boss know you're not interested in leaving the
company. Subtlety is definitely the order of the day here. At this point, you
don't want to say anything that could be interpreted as a threat to leave, or
that would give the impression that you were actually out there job-hunting.
If he has an idea that you are thinking about leaving, he won't be interested
in making a further investment in you.

Make him aware that you live well, that you have a good standard of
living. Let him know, for example, that you are looking at condos on Park
Place—the good side of town. You don't want him to think that the raise is
a big deal. "Oh, she never expected to see that kind of money." You want
him to think that your personal style fits a certain income level, and that the
raise won't be out of line with your standard of living.

He should know that you anticipate things going well and that you expect to stick around. Talk as if you have long-range plans to be with the
company. "This may take several years, but I think we ought to get started
on it now." Or tell him that those condos you are looking at, for example,
are convenient to the company. The message is that you expect to be with
the company for a long time, and that you are therefore a good investment.

The wrong way for you to set the stage for a salary negotiation is
through heavy-handed jokes or snide remarks. For example, the boss says

do this-or-that—and you come back at him with: "I don't get paid enough for that kind of work." Or he asks you if you've ever been to Greece, and you say, "On my salary? You're kidding!"

While you're prepping management, they in turn might let you know that profits are down, that there's a moratorium on raises, that there are no automatic raises anymore, that there is a ceiling on grade levels—all trying to convince you that you shouldn't even ask for a raise (it's hopeless), or to frighten you into silence (if you press for a raise, you might lose your job).

During this period of psychological sparring, the aim is to get in your propaganda while not being knocked out by theirs. To learn how to defend yourself against their arguments, read on.

Stage # 3: The Encounter

This is the actual moment when—all prepped-up and (you hope) having gained the upper hand during the preceding psychological sparring period— you step into the boss's office for the decisive meeting.

Some people, men as well as women, go into the encounter fearful that they will be turned down cold. Perhaps you're afraid that the raise-giver will say you're not worth more money and you will feel humiliated—you're afraid to learn that he thinks so little of you. But if you enter into this discussion knowing that what you are asking for is reasonable, and if you can hold on to the sense of your own worth—regardless of the raise-giver's opinion— you will be able to maintain your own negotiating position and your dignity. If worse comes to worst, you simply have a difference of opinion. You're not a child asking for a favor; you're not at his mercy. In fact, you are anything but helpless; you can argue intelligently and persuasively for your position.

It's also helpful to understand that likely as not, whatever he says is part of his negotiating strategy—nothing personal. You have to counter with your own negotiating strategy: your strongest arguments.

Pick the right time in the company's calendar to bring up the raise issue. Ideally, this might be three or four months before raises are officially going to be announced—that is, before budget decisions are made. If you don't know when this time is, take a guess—better early than late. If you speak up after the raise decisions have been made, it will be more difficult to influence the outcome of your encounter. If you're told it's too soon to think about raises, ask for budget decision dates and get your negotiating meeting scheduled.

However, don't be overly intimidated by the company's calendar. You can go for a raise any time you think you are entitled to one and have a good reason to request it.

Even where the size and frequency of the raise is automatic, you ought to discuss the issue. If you conduct your three-stage campaign well, you stand a good chance of increasing the size of your predetermined raise.

Also, try to choose the most opportune moment to go into the raise-giver's office and make your pitch. Speak with him when things are going particularly well—you've just chalked up some noteworthy achievement, and, more specifically, he's in a good mood and you feel self-confident.

Many women ask me: "How do I start the negotiation?" They seem to feel awkward when asking for something for themselves. Start as you would in any meeting—with the usual greetings and comments and perhaps a couple of reports of good news. Then, open the discussion by saying forthrightly: "I set up this meeting to talk to you about my raise." (Your directness shows him that you are not afraid to talk about it, and it's not an uncomfortable topic for you, and that there's no way he's going to be able to put this on the back burner.)

Then, review your achievements and your effectiveness. Tell him the things that you are proud of and pleased about. Don't take it for granted that he appreciates your worth. You've been giving him regular reports; now, summarize them. This may sound like strange advice if he knows you and your work well, but you have to put him in touch *at this moment* with your importance to him. Your "achievement statement" might go something like this: "Since I've been handling the mailing lists, things have gotten much better. I've increased efficiency and have reduced the number of angry callers. In the near future I think I can do some list breakdowns, which will save the company money."

Or, "The year before I came, the hospital was placed on probation as an institution accredited for continuing medical education. Ten months after I started as director of training, that restriction was lifted. Now we have the opportunity to develop the areawide reputation that will ultimately upgrade the quality of care and the image of the hospital."

Rehearse scripts in your mind and even out loud with friends until you find it easy to argue. The chances are your boss or whoever you are negotiating with is quite experienced at turning people down, and rehearsing is your way to get practice and equalize your positions.

Now for the dialogue. Here are examples of some typical management arguments, plus wrong and ineffectual employee responses, and for each situation, a good assertive response.

Your boss (or whoever is representing the company in the negotiation) gives you one variation of the times-are-tough speech: "Things are pretty bleak this year. The economic picture really doesn't look good."

COMPLIANT RESPONSE: "I guess there's nothing you can do." (You're making your boss feel more comfortable by taking him off the hook. You've solved his problem, not yours.)

MARTYR RESPONSE: "I understand. I don't really mind. It's not so important anyhow. I can manage."

AGGRESSIVE RESPONSE: "Well, that's not my problem. I'm worth more. You know it and I know it." (This might be effective but there's a risk: you've put yourself in the opposite corner of the ring by declaring your lack of sympathy with his problem.)

SARCASTIC RESPONSE: "Times aren't so bad that the president couldn't buy a new Mercedes." (Sarcasm is a form of aggressiveness.)

GOOD, ASSERTIVE RESPONSE: "Yes, I know *we're* in trouble. I understand that in a bad economic climate you can't give raises to everyone, and you can't throw money around like in the old days, but I think the company would want to use its resources in the areas that count and motivate the people who can really produce." (Acknowledges the validity of what the raise-giver is saying, but then moves on to your persuasive case.)

Or the company negotiator might hit you with a second variation of the times-are-tough speech—the out-and-out threat: "There are plenty of people out of work who would be very happy to have your job."

COMPLIANT RESPONSE: Silence. (Thinking: "Oh, God, I better shut up. He's going to fire me.")

AGGRESSIVE RESPONSE: "Don't threaten me." (A counterattack—which he deserves, but which will get his back up.)

SARCASTIC RESPONSE: "They can have it—and the pleasure of working every night until nine o'clock."

GOOD, ASSERTIVE RESPONSE: "Yes, I think what you say is true. But I don't think many people could do as good a job as I do. I would like to tell you why I think a raise is appropriate."

Or he might give you a third variation of times-are-tough: "We don't have any money to give you, so maybe you just better cut down on your life-style."

COMPLIANT RESPONSE: "Okay, but can we talk about it next year?"

AGGRESSIVE RESPONSE: "That's an excuse. There's money wasted around here all the time."

SARCASTIC RESPONSE: "What's left to cut? You mean I've got to stop eating?"

GOOD, ASSERTIVE RESPONSE: "I do enjoy a nice life-style, and I also think my level of skill is worth more to the company. Here's my reasoning . . . (your pitch)."

The negotiator may give you some version of the you-don't-need-the-money speech: "You're single. You can get along pretty well on your salary."

COMPLIANT RESPONSE: "I can't dispute that." (To yourself: "Well, it's true. I don't need it *that* badly. There are a lot of people who need it more than I do.")

AGGRESSIVE RESPONSE: "That's discrimination." (A statement that accuses the other person of doing something wrong generally makes the accused feel under attack. It puts him in an unsympathetic mood.)

SARCASTIC RESPONSE: "What am I supposed to do—get married in order to get a raise?"

GOOD, ASSERTIVE RESPONSE: "I'm single, but I don't see that as the central issue. Salaries are based on the individual's expertise, creativity, ability to do a good job, and more. In the past year, I've . . ." (Choose qualities and accomplishments that suit your situation. By expressing your view without attaching a derogatory label to the other person's view, you are being assertive, rather than aggressive. And it's safer—you're not unpleasant or insulting.)

Or he may come up with this variation: "You're married. You've got a husband to provide for you."

COMPLIANT RESPONSE: "That's true." (Well-to-do woman thinking: "I probably shouldn't be working and taking this job away from someone who needs it." Not-so-well-to-do woman: "Well, we are luckier than most; we *do* have two incomes.")

AGGRESSIVE RESPONSE: "That's chauvinistic. I'm an independent woman."

SARCASTIC RESPONSE: "I've got to get a divorce to get a raise?"

GOOD, ASSERTIVE RESPONSE: "I don't think marital status is the issue." (Pick up the rest from the previous assertive response.)

The raise-giver tries the my-God-you're-never-satisfied gambit: "You've already gotten two raises in the last eighteen months."

COMPLIANT RESPONSE: (with her voice fading out at the end) "But I am doing a lot and I think I deserve it." (Most compliant people would not have been able to make this request in the first place; they would have already talked themselves out of asking by anticipating what the boss would say.)

AGGRESSIVE RESPONSE: "Yeah, and I still don't earn as much as some of the incompetent people in this department."

SARCASTIC RESPONSE: "Big deal. You started me at nothing."

GOOD, ASSERTIVE RESPONSE: "I started with a low salary and I've moved ahead fast in my development. I'd like to see my salary catch up to the level of the work I'm doing. Last month I . . . ."

Suppose the company negotiator pulls the you-don't-deserve-a-raise routine: "Well, you've made some mistakes. You still have some things to learn."

COMPLIANT RESPONSE: "I'm sorry about that. I'm trying harder and I think I've done a lot of good work since then." (Thinking: "I'm probably not that good." Note how the raise-giver has hooked into the employee's ambivalence about her worth.)

DEFENSIVE RESPONSE: "They weren't entirely my fault. I didn't have support and I don't think they should be held against me." (Defensiveness is one form of compliance. You're responding to his accusation as if you have to convince him that he's wrong, instead of presenting your own very different and distinct point of view.)

AGGRESSIVE RESPONSE: "What mistakes? You're just playing games with me."

SARCASTIC RESPONSE: "So does Reggie Jackson."

GOOD, ASSERTIVE RESPONSE: "To me the question of the raise has to do with my ability to supervise the group, run a tight ship, and produce increasingly creative work—as I have been doing during the past year." (You're not defending yourself against his accusation; you're focusing on the totality of your work and putting forth the criteria *you* believe are valid.)

Or he might try this variation: "Your department spent a lot of overtime money. You should have gotten things done without those overtime expenses."

COMPLIANT RESPONSE: "Yes, I know. But we're doing the best we can—and I think we'll do better next year."

AGGRESSIVE RESPONSE: "Yeah, and I should walk on water too."

DEFENSIVE RESPONSE: "We tried, but we had a lot of problems we couldn't do anything about."

GOOD, ASSERTIVE RESPONSE: "I did spend $4,000 on overtime—and at the same time I saved $14,000 on staff salaries, plus the expense and headaches of hiring another staff member. I think I made a wise choice."

Or he might try to put you off with a friendly wisecrack: "Oh, you want to buy your boyfriend a Porsche."

COMPLIANT RESPONSE: Laughter. (You appreciate his joke; you want to be a good sport—and that's the end of your case. Your request doesn't have to be taken seriously.)

AGGRESSIVE RESPONSE: "It's a joke when I ask for money. Everyone else gets taken seriously."

SARCASTIC RESPONSE: "You don't seem too unhappy in your Caddy."

GOOD, ASSERTIVE RESPONSE: (An amused smile.) "Not a bad idea." (And then forge ahead.) "I'd like to take some time now and tell you how I see the job situation. I've been working at this company for three years, I've taken on a lot of extra higher-level work, and I know that people at my new level of skill earn a great deal more than I do." (The wisecrack does not stop you from pursuing your goal. You're a good sport, you appreciate his joke, and then you go on to discuss the serious side of the matter.)

Or he might try to disarm you by using the old we're-in-the-same-boat maneuver: "A raise in this place? You must be kidding. I can't even get one for myself." (You're in this together.)

COMPLIANT RESPONSE: "It looks pretty hopeless, doesn't it." (Thinking: "This company is impossible." You're defeated.)

MARTYR RESPONSE: A resigned sigh. "I guess I'll never be able to get out of debt."

AGGRESSIVE RESPONSE: "You're the one that's supposed to fight for us!"

UNCONVINCING ASSERTIVE RESPONSE: "I'm not kidding. I need the money."

GOOD, ASSERTIVE RESPONSE: "I'm not kidding. I'd like to take some time now . . ." (Continue with the assertive response to the first wisecrack above.)

He tries to brush you off by going into a passing-the-buck routine: "Well, I don't know about this. I'll have to talk to Mary about it, but I don't think she'll go for it."

COMPLIANT RESPONSE: "I think she should understand that I deserve a raise." (Leaving it up to your boss and Mary. You feel your fate is out of your hands, that you can't influence the outcome, that management has all the power.)

AGGRESSIVE RESPONSE: "Well, if you people don't see it my way, I'll have to start thinking about my options." (The threat is a form of aggression.

In this case, you are saying to the other person, "You have no alternative. If you don't do what I want, I'm leaving." You may want to say this, but since it might quickly end the negotiation—either by your winning or your being terminated—it would seem wiser and more interesting to go through the entire negotiating process. Use the threat only after you've decided it's the raise or nothing—without it, you're leaving.)

GOOD, ASSERTIVE RESPONSE: "I'll prepare some notes to back up your case to remind Mary of the reasons I should get this raise. I think when she hears *our* case, she'll see the point." (You've made your boss into an ally and now your quest for a raise has become a collaboration between the two of you on your behalf. You're also giving yourself a chance to reinforce your best arguments.) Or you might say: "Let's set up an appointment with Mary. If I go with you, I can deliver my arguments first-hand." (He might welcome the suggestion because it gets him off the hook; you'll do your own fighting. But even if he doesn't, you are creating the image of someone who's not afraid to present her case higher-up.)

The raise-giver might try to brush you off by postponing the issue: "Oh, we're going to do a general review of salaries. I'll get back to you." Or, "I'll see if I can get it for you. I'll take it up at the next executive board meeting."

YOU: "Okay. I'll get some notes together for your meeting so that everyone can see what I've accomplished—and can you tell me when the meeting is taking place so I can get back to you?" (You are politely and assertively forcing the issue by trying to pin him down to a date. You will begin to see whether he has any intention of giving you what you want.)
BOSS: "Well, I can't tell you exactly."
YOU: "Okay, I'll check back with you next week and see what has happened." (In effect, you're saying, "If you're planning to brush me off, I'm not going to accept it.")

In this situation, check back a little sooner than you said you would. If you say a week, get back to him one day sooner; if it's two weeks, get back two days sooner. You can be sure he won't have the answer for you, but by getting back to him you're reminding him of his commitment. *Don't* fall into the temptation of putting it off. Don't wait longer, as so many people do—for example, two weeks plus two days—because you want to avoid something you see as unpleasant.

If the raise-giver misses the date that he has set with you, or says he hasn't had a chance to discuss it, or says he hasn't gotten around to it yet, or—if he's even nastier—says, "That's not exactly my first priority," don't let him off the hook. Your response might be: "I know you are very busy, but I really would appreciate it if you would put the request through this week and I'll talk to you about in on Monday. This is important to me."

Some people manage the first assertion but then they weaken. You need the ability to hang in there, regardless of what response you get. Have your sense of yourself and your work well-defined, and no matter what comes at you, stick with your point of view. Don't be persuaded by the company negotiator's reasoning. Here's an example of how to hang in there: You've given your boss your pitch, reminding him of your achievements, and he says: "Sure, that's your job. That's what you're supposed to do. That's what you're getting paid for."

YOU: "I'm basing my request on a track record that I think clearly demonstrates not only that I'm doing good work, but also work at new levels. I've been gradually moving into activities that normally fall into the job description of a such-and-such (use the next level title). The company is benefiting from my innovations. I'm worth a lot more to you than I was last year."

BOSS: "You're just doing the same work so-and-so's secretary is doing."

YOU: "I don't think I'm doing the job of a secretary (or someone at the next level down). I am carrying on many of the functions of an associate administrator (someone one level up from your actual title), and I think my salary should reflect that." (He's put you a level lower than your present job; you've asserted your belief that you are a level higher.) "I'm taking a lot of initiative. In fact, just the other day I had a thought about how we could reorganize things so we could make both Jane and Carole happier. I think there's a way that would solve Jane's complaints about being interrupted and Carole's complaints about being over-worked." (You start dangling some carrots. He's already paying you to do what you've been doing well. He'll be more enthusiastic about giving a raise if you are going to function with increasing creativity, and right now he'll want to keep you motivated.)

BOSS: "Tell me about it." (Naturally, he wants to know your good idea.)

YOU: "When I get it totally thought out, I'll write it up." (Look cooperative, but don't tell him your plan.)

BOSS: "I agree with you. You should be earning more. Let's get the blah-blah squared away and then I think we'll be getting the X project, which you can take over. I know that's the kind of project that would give you the experience you've been wanting." (He's dangling his own carrots—promises of future goodies that will make you willing to stay, even without a raise.) The good company negotiator tries to keep you filled with excitement and hope about the coming months on the job. The more glowing the future picture he paints, the more awkward you feel about bringing the subject back to anything so crude and mundane as your salary, and the more you worry about losing your standing in his eyes—you want to seem like the kind of person who's involved with the work, and you don't want to jeopardize your chances by asking for too much. However, you, the counter-strategist, understand what he is doing.

YOU: "Yes, I've been counting on getting involved in developing some of these challenging projects. It looks like things are really perking now, and I'm very pleased to be in on them. It's a wonderful opportunity for me. Now, I'd like to get down to brass tacks and see what figure you have in mind for my raise, and what the timing will be. My last raise was ten months ago and I want to shoot for an increase on my anniversary." (In your book, there's nothing crude about talking money.)

If you were to take his bait and refrain from pursuing the question of your raise, perhaps feeling it would be unladylike, you would be playing right into his strategy—but by staying with your request and your belief that you are worth more money, you increase your value in his eyes. Because you project your belief that you are worth more, he's much more likely to come through with the money *and* the carrots.

As the dialogue unfolds, let him know that you expect a sizeable raise. Once you feel you have got him on your side—when you have reminded him of all that you have done and can do, when he's feeling more dependent on you, and is even, possibly, concerned that you might leave—then indicate the level of your expectation, and overstate it slightly. "This year, I think the company owes me a substantial increase." Or, "I think a merit increase in addition to the cost-of-living increase would be appropriate."

Try to get him to respond with a figure. Then, compare his figure with those you have in mind. If he comes in low, you can argue. "I'm really unhappy about that. It's much less than I expected and much less than I think I'm worth." Then tell him your thinking—what the standard in the field is, and why you are worth it.

The danger for you at every point in the negotiation is in feeling overpowered, helpless, overwhelmed, or angry. If he's firm and you begin to feel helpless and powerless, then you are in trouble.

Remember, you still have the power you had all through this discussion. Keep in mind your own view of yourself and your worth, and that you are going to stay with that view—regardless of his opinion. In a negotiation, displaying the strength of your conviction is often what wins the day.

Reinforce the dialogue with your body language and your voice pattern. If your voice is hesitant, or too soft, too questioning, too high-pitched or girlish, your assertion will be undermined. Even if your *words* are assertive, your message won't be credible. For example, if you put a question mark at the end of each phrase, it sounds as if you are questioning the validity of your request: "I'm here about the raise? That you promised me? When I joined the company last year?" You sound childlike, as if you believe that it's all up to him—as if you don't have any conviction about your raise. You've weakened your case because the "melody pattern" of your voice is weak and tentative. Your message is that you are not a person to be reckoned with.

Instead, convey the force of your decision and your resolve about the raise in both your voice tone and your physical demeanor. Don't appear to be shrinking into the seat. Sit back comfortably in your chair, as if you belong there.

If you've done your homework and have handled yourself well during the prep-up, the psychological sparring, and the encounter, the odds are in your favor that you will get your raise.

But what if you don't? You might be turned down—even if you've done everything right—for good and bad reasons. At this point you might want to start looking for another job. Or, if you are willing to risk your present job, use the ultimate weapon: the threat. "I've decided to leave. Everything about this job is right except the money, and I just can't afford to stay." Make your threat a positive, nonbitter statement, and you will leave room for the boss to rush in and save the day with a raise.

The threat is risky and may result in your getting fired. But what if you don't get fired—*and* you don't get the raise? Many people feel they have to leave because they've said they would, but you can always double back on a threat. Just say, "I changed my mind. As you know, I like working here and I like working for you. I don't want to leave. I decided it's not worth the money to me."

Don't quit, or threaten to quit, prematurely. Go through all the negotiating stages first. It's to your advantage to use every opportunity to develop your negotiating skill. If you want to remain on your job, raise or not, you can see the negotiation through one more phase: The Post-Encounter.

The Post-Encounter

First, evaluate the company's reason for not giving you the raise. Then, if you plan to stay, set the stage for putting the topic of your raise back on the agenda.

The company negotiator may give you this typical turn-down: "Listen, I agree with you. You are entitled to a raise. I have presented all our arguments higher up, and I simply can't get it for you. There's no way—they're just not giving raises."

YOU: "We have tried everything we can. I will think more about it, and when I think the timing is right, I'll get back together with you and maybe we can think of a new approach that will work." (He's closing the door, but you're keeping it open.)

The raise-refuser might try a variation on the turn-down: "You can't get a raise until you can do the blah-blah (get published, learn to keep the accounts, whatever)."

YOU: "All right. I didn't realize it was such a central issue—but I'll get published, and I'll get back to you."

I've spelled out many sample dialogues to try to make the negotiation easier for you, but at bottom, what really will make it easier for you is your attitude: your belief that you are entitled to more money and that it's up to you to go after it. If you still find it difficult and painful to ask for a raise—if you are still inwardly protesting, "Why should I have to do all this? Why don't they just give it to me? They know I'm worth it!"—then perhaps your feeling flows from a resistance to taking responsibility for yourself. As mentioned before, the wish for a different world, one in which you would be taken care of, is a dead-end course.

Speaking up for yourself, asking for what you want, negotiating for what you believe is reasonable, clarifying the conditions you want to work under, and attempting to persuade people to your point of view is the only way to move closer to the satisfying state of being an independent person.

Chapter Four

BUILDING THE RIGHT IMAGE

CONTENTS

Introduction

Part 1: Counteracting Stereotypes
 1. You Are Seen as More Interested in Your Personal Life Than in Your Work
 2. You Are Seen as Too Emotional
 3. You Are Seen as a "Girl"
 4. You Are Seen as Past Your Prime
 5. You Are Seen as Weak
 6. You Are Seen as Naive, Not Political
 7. You Are Seen as Too Dependent
 8. You Are Seen as Hard and Cold
 9. You Are Seen as Having Nothing Important to Say
10. You Are Seen as Good for Only One Thing

Part 2: Match Your Image to Your Job
 1. How to Publicize Yourself
 2. What's the Right Image for You?

Part 3: Your Professional Self-Image
 1. I'm Afraid of Losing my Femininity
 2. I'm Afraid of Becoming a Cardboard Corporate Character

INTRODUCTION

How do people see you at work? How would they describe you? Do they see you as you really are? Do they appreciate your true value and competence? Or do they view you through prejudice-tinted lenses that exaggerate your weaknesses and diminish your strengths? Do they fail to recognize your potential for more responsibility?

Having the right image—the way people see you—is crucial to getting what you want from work: respect, raises, promotions, good working relationships, and an easier time of it all around. This holds for everyone in the workplace, but the "right" image is particularly essential for women because they have to overcome the handicap of being the "wrong" sex.

In our culture women are generally regarded as unsuited for important jobs in business. "Women are too emotional," "They're not tough enough," "They're too tough," "They're not ambitious," "They're not team players," "They're too soft-hearted." The list, however contradictory, goes on and on. Such stereotypes are projected onto all women long before an individual woman ever walks through the office doorway. For all the recent changes in the status of women, chauvinism—refined and passed along from generation to generation—dies hard. Women as well as men can be susceptible to it.

Driving along a small country road near my house, I mentioned to my friend how pleased I was that Phil, my neighbor, had cleared acres of trees and brush surrounding his lake so that it could be seen by all who passed. No sooner had I said it than I wondered why I credited Phil instead of Kathy, his wife. Well, why had I? I, who had thought and thought about these issues, who had worked so hard at casting prejudice out of my head? I did it because the belief that men make the big decisions has been part of our culture from time immemorial, and it was handed down to me years ago just as it was handed down to everyone else in our world. And I know I do the same when I witness a decorating change in someone's living room—if I don't stop myself, I'll automatically give credit to the wife.

To get the picture straight and see women as we truly are, we have to fight these old assumptions, both in ourselves and in others—particularly those who have the power to give us better assignments.

True, some women escape the consequences of prejudice, at least in their immediate environment. But given the pervasive bias in our culture against women in business, the odds are high that you are seen stereotypically in some way, and are paying a price for it, whether you're aware of it or not.

I find that women often seriously underestimate the discrepancy between the chauvinist's image of them and their own image of themselves. They don't comprehend that, when viewed through prejudiced eyes, they and their accomplishments are reduced to suit the chauvinist's distorted notion of the way women are. The woman accountant is mistaken for a bookkeeper; the woman with an important title is said to have slept her way to the top; the executive is said to be just a figurehead who doesn't really do the job—the important work is handled by someone above her. This process of diminishing a woman is so automatic that it is almost as if over the generations it has become built into the circuitry of their brains.

It is with people we've worked with a long time—the boss, for example ("He knows me—he *knows* how good I am!"), that this discrepancy can be most seriously underestimated—and hurt us most.

Not only does a woman have to be twice as good on her job as a man in order to succeed, she also has to work twice as hard at building her image. In essence, that is what this chapter is about. It is divided into three parts.

Part 1: Counteracting Stereotypes tells you about the most pervasive stereotypes that face women, and what you can do to counteract them.

Part 2: Match Your Image to Your Job tells you how you can find your "right" image for the job you presently have, or hope to have in the future, and how to show this image off to your own best advantage.

Part 3: Your Professional Self-Image addresses the fear working women often have of becoming "unfeminine" or "cardboard," and tells you how to cope with these added pressures.

PART 1
COUNTERACTING STEREOTYPES

1. YOU ARE SEEN AS MORE INTERESTED IN YOUR PERSONAL LIFE THAN IN YOUR WORK

How to dramatize your ambition and interest in your career
• When to reaffirm your commitment to your work • How to play
down your home life • Tips for working mothers • Professional
behavior

> THE STEREOTYPE: *If you're single, you're just marking time until you find a husband; once you do, you'll quit. If you're married, you're unreliable; your family comes first.*

What image would work well for you?

To be taken seriously in the workplace you have to project the image of
a highly motivated woman who is in for the long pull, who works because she *wants* to work, whether she has to or not, and who sees work
as central to her life in the same way that men do. If you think you are
seen as more interested in your personal life than your work, take the
following actions:

*Find ways to dramatize your commitment to your present and future ca-
reer.* While no one doubts that a man's involvement in his career will last a
lifetime, women are regarded as temporary members of the work force until
they prove otherwise. Talk to the managers above you, formally and informally, about your career path, your five-year plan, your ten-year plan.

Let them know that you are continually learning and preparing yourself for more responsibilities.

• Make it a practice, on strategic occasions, to arrive early and stay late—not to look like a hardworking slave, but to enhance your image as someone who takes her work and her career seriously.

• When you are *asked* to work late or to take on extra assignments, don't just say, "Sure," like a good scout, or agree because you feel you have no other choice. Instead, make it clear that although you have an outside life, you want to do what's needed because you are thoroughly involved in your job and your career. Perhaps your boss comes in and says, "We've got to get this report finished and on the last plane tonight or we'll lose this account." You say, "You're right. Mr. Jones told me yesterday he was fed up with Paul's procrastination. I think it's best for me to stay. I'll call off my plans for the evening." By offering your independent assessment, you show that you grasp the importance of the task—and you also demonstrate that you are not simply a willing order-taker, but someone who thinks about her work in all its ramifications, as people do who take their jobs seriously. Even better, you yourself might propose that you stay late and get the work done, before anyone asks.

• Come alive talking shop. You can go a long way toward making yourself credible as a woman committed to her career if you respond with keen interest to discussions of work-related subjects.

• If someone tries to lure you into discussing personal topics, resist the temptation. *You* determine the subject matter for discussion. When a colleague says, "Oh, you had a date last night," a polite smile and a yes are enough, or you might answer with news about a good restaurant or movie. But whatever you do, don't entertain them with tales of the ups and downs of your social life.

• If you want to avoid being seen as "just another disinterested female," let your boss know that you carry important business problems home with you. "I was reading an article last night on such-and-such that suggested a solution to . . ." Or, on Monday morning: "Mountain climbing is a good way to clear the head. I've solved some business problems. I think I've got the answer to such-and-such."

Demonstrate that you are ambitious. Because management sees ambition as a key measure of a worker's potential to produce for them, it's vital that you show you are determined to get what you want, whether it's more money, more responsibility, or more challenging situations.

- Project the image of a woman who takes total financial responsibility for herself. Don't let people think you are working just until you get married or to supplement your husband's income or to send your kids through college. Instead, find ways to indicate that you are committed—as a matter of principle—to supporting yourself, now and in the future.
- Let it be known that you expect to be paid more as you become more valuable. When people talk about things that are beyond your present income, don't put down your earning power with a wisecrack: ("That's for the rich; I'm lucky if I can get away for a weekend!"; and don't say, "That's what I'm going to do when I marry a rich man," as if you feel you can't make it on your own. Instead, say confidently, "When I earn enough money, that's one of the things I want to do."

It may be hard for some women to demonstrate that they are ambitious because the word has unfeminine connotations. Women were supposed to have more "noble" things to do than strive for money, power, and success. But today, ambitious women are seen in much more positive and realistic terms. Almost everyone today would agree that women have a need and certainly a right to look out for themselves, to develop their potential, and to earn as much money as possible in the same way as men do.

If you are going to get married or have a baby, reaffirm your commitment to work. When there are big changes in your personal life, you can be quite sure your boss is going to be wondering whether you will remain at work. Because his uncertainty, warranted or not, may restrict your career opportunities, it's important that you discuss with him (and any other managers whose input might affect your assignments) the fact that you see your career as a permanent part of your life. Explain that you are not about to give up any gains you've already made. Drop hints that indicate you plan to be around after the big event: "Next fall I'd like to expand the X department," or, "I want to learn more about the public relations side of the business. I'm thinking about taking these two courses (showing him the catalogue) at the Publicity Club. Do you know these instructors? What do you think of them?"

Megan's Story

One young woman, Megan, thought that by returning to the office only four weeks after she had her baby, she would put an end to any doubts about her future plans. Even though she came back in near record time, she noticed a dramatic change in her boss's attitude: he no longer gave her important assignments. We tried to analyze why he was cutting down her role. Perhaps he interpreted this first baby as only the beginning? He may have thought that she would go on, as many women do, to have more children, and sooner or later give up work.

Taking aim at what *we* thought *he* thought, we designed a campaign to impress upon him the fact that Megan had no intention of leaving work. At appropriate moments, she would say things like, ''My baby is a delight but, believe it or not, I missed my job. I'm very glad to be back.'' She had to choose her words carefully to avoid stepping into another image problem. Since most people disapprove of mothers who aren't caring, she had to emphasize her commitment to work without rejecting her mother role. She couldn't say things like, ''I could hardly wait to get back to the peace and quiet of work,'' or, ''Home life is not for me—I'll take work any time.'' Her campaign was effective: in a few weeks she had apparently reassured her boss that her work remained a top priority, because he started giving her good assignments again.

Leave your home life at home. In general, it's not a good idea to remind people at work that you have another major commitment. If you have children, do what's necessary to meet your responsibilities, but play it down at the office. Make your calls with the baby-sitter short. If something has gone wrong, don't stay on the phone and try to set it right. Take a coffee or lunch break and try to work it out privately. And don't discuss the situation with your colleagues. If you need help, call outside friends and talk it over with them. Then, when you've got the solution, telephone the baby-sitter privately.

Kids are a worry, and when something goes wrong at home (and it will), it's hard to look like you are thoroughly involved in your work. And then there's guilt. You think you really ought to be home taking care of your kids. Our culture is full of guilt-giving messages for mothers (''No one can provide the love and care that a mother can give,'' ''Children of working mothers get into trouble,'' ''What if something happens to them?''). These are manifestations of exaggerated ideas of a mother's importance. I personally think they persist because they serve society's need to keep a woman's nose to the baby-care grindstone. After all, a mother at home, working long hours at little cost, is still the cheapest way to raise kids. The wealthy have never had any qualms about leaving their children's care to others. Men, too, seem to find it easier to turn over much of the rearing to others.

Perhaps women are more susceptible to the premise that they ought to be with their children twenty-four hours a day because mothering is one of the few areas where we are in charge. Society wants us to play a role—the role of mother—and it tells us how wonderful we are at it and how only we can do it. We buy this because it makes us feel important, valued, needed, even gives us a sense of power.

But in terms of the world as it is today, the indispensable, twenty-four-hour-a-day mother is not a believable or persuasive concept. While a mother's role is certainly crucial, most of us now believe that children do benefit from the rich variety of experiences that they can gain from having contact with a whole range of people, personalities, ideas, and interests.

If you are working, try to use your imagination in finding people or situations that can give your child or children some special advantages. As a single parent, I found a wonderful teenage boy who enjoyed teaching my child how to fly kites, climb mountains, study bugs through a microscope, and all kinds of things that at the time I wasn't interested in. Another time, I discovered an ex-actress, eighty-two years old and full of fun, who had retained the capacity to play delightful children's games hours on end. While she wasn't much on neatness—I had a lot of toys to pick up when I came home—that was not so important to me. What was important was that she enchanted my son with her games and stories. With both these sitters I was confident that my child was doing things he liked doing, was learning a lot, and was being well taken care of. I never felt guilty.

Another tip: if there are big doings at home—if your baby has taken her first steps or the kids are graduating—don't dwell on it as if that is where your real interest lies. Just share the news with your co-workers, show your pictures, enjoy the oohs and ahs, and get on with the business of the day. That's not to say you shouldn't bring in a tale of family fun or a child's achievements once in a while. You should, because reports of a smooth and happy family life can underscore your competence. It's proof that you are a woman who manages two major assignments—job and family—with ease.

When personal problems get in the way of your work, don't ask for sympathy—give reassurance. If you have a pileup of problems and need time at home, don't try to arouse your boss's sympathies by explaining your difficulties. Although he'll probably be understanding and give you a break the first time, his tolerance will soon run out and he'll see you as having too many problems to be reliable. If you have to take a lot of time off, let him know you are not overwhelmed with your problems; you've got them under control. Most important, assure him that the end is in sight—even if it isn't—and forestall any thoughts he might have of replacing you. If your situation appears to be complicated and unresolved, your boss almost certainly will get worried and begin to think about bringing in someone else, so take a guess and set a date on which he can count on you to return—"It's rough going, but I have reliable help coming in six days"—and then work like mad to make it happen.

You might find it difficult, as many women do, to speak with such certainty when there is doubt in your mind ("How can I say that? Suppose I can't make my deadline?"). We are so afraid of being wrong, and at the same time we lack confidence in our resourcefulness in making things work out. Promising something uncertain seems too risky. But if you can look at the situation objectively, and weigh the advantages and disadvantages, you can see quite clearly that there is more to gain by taking a confident position and striving to make it work than by letting your boss wait around nervously—in this case, without any idea of when you'll be back.

Don't flirt. If you want to emphasize your orientation toward work and your value as a member of the group, refrain from behavior that conjures up images of boy-girl fun. When men flirt with you, keep an air of easy friendliness with no coy or sexy overtones.

Don't come in yawning. And if you do, expiain that you were up until 2 A.M. reading technical manuals.

2. YOU ARE SEEN AS TOO EMOTIONAL

The things you can't talk about • Keys to presenting an image of calmness and strength • Female chauvinism • When your emotions *are* too near the surface

> THE STEREOTYPE: *Women get upset over little things, panic under pressure, and fall apart in crises. They can't take criticism, and are easily hurt. They are not objective.*

What image would work well for you?

You need to be seen as a person who stays calm when the going gets rough, who doesn't need reassurance but is a source of strength for others, who can cope with crises, who can take criticism in stride. In short, you want to be seen as someone who is governed by reason rather than emotion.

If you think you are seen as overemotional:

Slow down. Cultivate a calm manner. Adopt a take-it-easy posture: sit back and relax. The aim is to look like you go with the flow. When you have a lot of responsibility and the pressure is on, an excitable demeanor is not reassuring to those around you—you won't convey the impression that you can handle still more pressure and more responsibility, and you won't look like a good candidate for moving up.

Don't talk about your nerves, your anxiety, your depression, your moods. Talk is good therapy, but if you are seen as too emotional, you don't have that luxury at work.

• Don't discuss your emotional difficulties, if you have any. So don't say things like, "I was very upset when I heard that siren," "I can't stand arguments," "I hate yelling," "I didn't do a thing all weekend; I was too depressed," "This place drives me crazy," or, "I need a vacation." You would do better to display your emotional strengths rather than possible weaknesses.

- Don't discuss psychosomatic ailments—ulcers, headaches, insomnia —and if you happen to be on any kind of medication, don't take it in public.
- If you are in psychotherapy, keep it to yourself. Unfortunately, in our culture, there is still a great deal of unresolved prejudice against anybody with "psychological problems."
- Don't let co-workers "take care" of you. Don't bring them in on your personal problems, and if anyone tries to give you advice and support regarding your personal problems, politely reject it. Say, "I appreciate your thoughtfulness, but I really don't need help," or, "Thanks, but I'm working it out. Things are under control."
- If would-be chivalrous men treat you stereotypically as a frail and volatile female, disabuse them of their theories about you.

Martina's Story

When Martina's marriage broke up, she noticed that the men she worked with were tiptoeing around her. They would ask her with great concern how she was doing. As she put it, "I tell them I'm fine, but they still handle me with kid gloves; it's as if they're afraid I'm going to fall apart." She knew they were trying to be considerate, but she didn't want to be seen as someone who was so fragile that she needed special treatment.

Apparently, they were projecting onto her their ideas of what women were like, or how they would prefer women to be—or, most likely, a little of both. Martina had a reserved, soft-spoken manner on the surface, which they misread. Instead of seeing her as the strong, psychologically sturdy person she was, they saw her as a romanticized movie character whose life revolved around her man and who wept, got hysterical, broke down, and wasted away when things went wrong. Martina had to correct their misperception. She had to dramatize the fact that she was a woman who had considerable inner resources and who was quite capable of taking care of herself during this admittedly difficult period of her life.

Now when they asked with great concern, "How are you doing?" she would report some piece of good news: "I just found an apartment and I'm really quite pleased. It's only four blocks from the beach." She also took every opportunity she could to plant the idea that she wasn't collapsing. One evening when they were all caught up working late on a fascinating and important project, she remarked, "Marriage has its advantages, but it's nice to be free to work late without any pressure to get home." The special treatment abated: she had made the point that she was resilient and wouldn't sink under the weight of her divorce.

Avoid the language of impatience and intolerance. If you are seen as one of "those emotional females," even such everyday expressions as, "I can't stand it when she does that," or, "He gets on my nerves," can be damaging to your image. Don't join in emotional gabfests with your colleagues in tearing others apart. You need to be seen as more evenhanded. Any critiques or evaluations you make should be balanced, thoughtful, and fair.

Emphasize your cool, reasonable side. No stereotype for you: when others panic, you take hold and show your confidence by moving toward solutions. "Let's see what can be done about this." Let them lean on your strong, capable shoulders.

Some women find it difficult to present a composed, "unemotional" image. Men, as everyone now knows, are conditioned to suppress emotions while women are encouraged to display theirs openly; somehow, this is "feminine." While this seems to operate in the woman's favor ("We're letting it all hang out, we're 'healthy' ") and is seen as detrimental to men ("Holding back makes your feelings fester within you"), in actuality the entire thesis is vastly detrimental to women. We are too prone to glorify our "feminine" capacity to feel and express emotions. While we should indeed take pride in this ability, it's important to realize that not all emotions so glorified are admirable. Some, like crying or panicking or getting angry, can spring from weakness; they are often the response of someone who lacks the tools to cope actively and successfully with challenges and who therefore feels powerless. There's a big difference between crying out of sadness and crying out of a feeling of helplessness and sheer frustration. It's important that women, when they pity a man who is unable to weep, distinguish between the inability to feel and express sadness, and the ability *not* to cry from a feeling of helplessness and frustration. This latter comes from strength and from possessing the power to do something about a situation. It is our own brand of female chauvinism to praise those characteristics of women that flow out of weakness and not, as some would have us believe, out of sensitivity.

If you think your emotions are too near the surface, try to track down the igniting sparks. One way to focus your attention on what causes your emotions to flare up is to keep a journal. When you do react emotionally, pinpoint what happened just before the emotion welled up. What was said that made you cry? What were you thinking about when you suddenly got anxious? Did someone do something that triggered your anger? Did you become anxious when you walked into the office and looked at the large pile of work on your desk? You hung up the phone and immediately sank into a depressed feeling—was it because the person to whom you were speaking mentioned a meeting to which you were not "important" enough to be invited? Were you just criticized? Do you get furious when people don't do what they are supposed to? Are you upset because you expect more support from someone than you are getting? Be aware that much emotionality flows from feelings of helplessness and dependency and from not feeling approved of.

But many women tell me that awareness alone doesn't help; that their intellects and emotions are not synchronized. When I start to talk about women's need to surmount the feelings of powerlessness which come out of our historical conditioning, they say, "But I know all that, and it doesn't help me."

It's true: it is not enough to be aware of the general premise—one must apply knowledge and insight to the actual situation. This must be done at the moment of impact; that is, the moment you feel beset by the emotion.

Now, let's see how this should work. Let's say you feel unfairly criticized. Your boss comes in and finds fault with your work. You start to try to justify yourself and explain what happened. He interrupts and escalates his criticism, and then you get all choked up, tears come into your eyes. You can't talk. You feel helpless. He doesn't understand why you committed what appears to him to be an error; he isn't giving you a chance to explain what happened. He's judging you harshly. Now, insight to the rescue: you're not a child, a helpless female. You don't need to be thought of as perfect. You are now an adult, who is perfectly able to deal with criticism. You can agree or disagree with your boss's judgment—you don't have to feel wiped out by his criticism. In sum, you are an independent, thinking woman.

Stay on the objective side. Demonstrate that you don't take things personally. Even when you are attacked, keep your eye on the issues and not on who's right and who's wrong. For example, the boss says, "That was a useless idea you had this morning." Instead of coming back with a hurt, "If you don't like my ideas, why do you ask for them?" you might say calmly, "I think it would work. It solves the problem of the plates. Although the steel is thicker, the extra cost is made up by eliminating the spring.'' You have defused his attack by responding with your own solid reasoning; you set yourself in a dignified position, and you certainly haven't taken his remark personally.

As a woman who is seen as overly emotional, you can't afford the luxury of coming back at him with a personal attack of your own; you would be feeding into his stereotyped view of you—and even if you did come back at him with a personal retort, he would answer you in the same vein and you would both become trapped in a fruitless series of personal jabs and counterjabs, all to the detriment of reaching a solution to the problem at hand.

Disguised personal remarks present even more difficulties. ''Where did you learn to write reports like that?'' If you take this personally and come back with a jab of your own, the offender will surely plead innocence. ''What's wrong with my asking where you learned this? You take everything so personally.''

If you persist and back him into a corner, he will just deny it all the more, sometimes to the point of believing in his own defense. He's convinced there's something wrong with *you*. And even if he was taking a personal swipe at you, what's the point in challenging him? You only succeed in this instance also in proving to him that you are another one of those ''hyper-emotional women'' because he's convinced he's a good guy and definitely not being hostile.

3. YOU ARE SEEN AS A "GIRL"

Highlighting your problem-solving abilities • How to avoid putting others into the parent-teacher role • Romanticizing girlishness • Keys to projecting a worldly image

THE STEREOTYPE: *Women are childlike and need protection and help. They are not quite smart enough or strong enough for the big jobs.*

The stereotype of woman as child is everywhere. It's even built into our language—''I'll have my girl take care of that,'' or, ''Ask the new girl in accounting.'' The ''girl'' may be five-foot-ten and over forty; it doesn't matter. Any woman of any age or size is in danger of being treated like a child.

What image would work well for you?

On the job—as well as off—you need to be seen as a self-sufficient adult who can handle responsibility and act independently on her own initiative.

If you think you are seen as a girl:

Take hold of problems. Children report difficulties (''I cut my finger!''). Adults do something about them (''Put this antiseptic on.''). If you want to grow up in the eyes of the people around you, make a dramatic move that will highlight your problem-solving abilities.

Betty's Story

Betty, a secretary and the only woman in a department of middle-aged men, was known as ''the kid.'' Although the nickname was well-meant and affectionate, it not only revealed how she was seen but served to exaggerate the difference in status between Betty and the men with whom she worked. She had the ambition to move up into the professional ranks of the company—but to do so, it was clear that she had to find a device that would appreciably change her image. She needed to shock her boss out of seeing her as a ''kid'' and into seeing her as a grown-up problem-solver. Finally she came up with a real attention-getter. While her boss was away on a business trip, Betty went into his office and wrote her name down in his appointment book. When he returned, he was astonished to find he had a formal appointment with his own secretary. ''You want a meeting with me?'' he asked. ''Why?'' She looked him straight in the eye. ''Yes. I want to discuss my cost-cutting program.'' In disbelief, he said, ''Are you putting me on?'' But Betty was prepared for his reaction. She had drawn up a long list of possible economies for the department, giving concise, logical reasons for each suggestion. She immediately brought in the list to her boss and watched as he read it. When he finished, he looked up. ''You did this,'' he asked, as one would a child, ''all by yourself?'' ''Yes,'' she said. ''What do you think?'' ''Hmm,'' he answered, ''very interesting.'' And he proceeded then and there to discuss and approve every item on her list.

They never did have the meeting she had written into his book; she had achieved what she wanted.

After her first bold move, Betty continued to work in this new, independent way. She began to look around to see what other problems she could handle on her own, without involving him. Now, when he asked her about something, more often than not she could say, "Don't worry, it's been taken care of." He would give her strange looks and walk away. But it wasn't long before he accepted her newly projected image. He stopped referring to her as "the kid"—proving that the name had indeed been more than just a term of endearment—and in three months asked her if she would be interested in the job of junior analyst.

Don't put others in the parent or teacher role. Avoid an asking-for-permission manner. When you think your point of view has merit, take a position. Put yourself on the line and stand behind your idea. *Don't* say: "Do you think we should follow up the direct mail campaign with telephone calls?" *Do* say: "I'm planning to follow up on the direct mail campaign. Here's my thinking . . ." Instead of "May I?" and "Can I?" use "I've decided to," "I'd like to," "I'm considering a new approach to . . ."

• Don't avoid adult responsibility by deferring to a "parent"—"I have to ask my husband," or, "I don't know if my boss will let me." Instead, be your own decision-maker. "I'll think about it. I want to do more research and I'd like to get other people's input." When you formulate things this way, it's clear that while you are getting other people's opinions, you are going to make the decision.

• If you think you are seen as a "girl," don't ask a lot of questions. You remind people of a pesty child. But unlike good parents who will respond patiently to a child's quest for knowledge, your colleagues are likely to take your questions as an imposition on their time and knowledge. They will feel resentful: "What the hell does she think I am? Does she think I'm here just to answer her questions?" They don't see your education as their responsibility.

No matter how desperate you are to get answers, avoid being the constant questioner. Limit yourself to queries that flow out of a need for specific information that you can't get anywhere else. Put yourself in an adult role by getting your own information. Ransack libraries, study technical manuals, and, if you need to, take courses.

Sometimes a "questioner" remains stuck in the child role when she doesn't feel she can rely on herself. She may continue to be childlike in the hope that people will watch out for her, protect her, and not make too many demands on her. It's hard for many women to let go of the child position, but it's helpful to understand that being an adult does not exclude getting assistance when you need it. Adults support each other in many ways, all the time.

Relating as one adult to another implies sharing and flexibility—sometimes giving, sometimes taking. The roles are fluid, shifting according to the needs of the situation. Relating as a child to an adult implies a one-way dependency in which the roles are fixed.

When I say don't ask questions, I'm not saying you should be totally self-sufficient, but I am saying you should reject the idea of manipulating people into taking care of your needs by acting like a little girl. Being child-like is only *one* way to get help, and in fact it is the most painful because you thwart your own development and thus become increasingly dependent.

Cut out "girlish" femininity. Although our culture romanticizes youth, helplessness, innocence, and naivete as being ideal feminine qualities, these are not traits that inspire confidence in a woman's ability to handle responsibility. Nor are they any longer so universally appealing—they are leftovers from times past, and you will do yourself a favor by trying to erase any traces of childlike femininity.

• Don't use a little-girl voice—one that's too soft or too high-pitched. Speak out loudly and clearly. Avoid a questioning melody pattern: don't speak in a tentative voice that swings up at the end of a declarative sentence as if you are asking for permission ("I'm going to Mary's office?"). Instead, drop the last word a note or two.

• Don't use a little-kid name. You may have been Debbie all your life, but it's time to call yourself Deborah. If your boss is Mr. Smith, then be Ms. Jones; it demeans you to be a childish Anne to an adult Mr. Smith.

Sometimes women find it unimaginable, even in fantasy, to address Mr. Smith as Bob. Inequality is so drilled into us that we really don't perceive ourselves as equals—and that is why we can't imagine addressing higher-ups without their titles. It's true that these people are more important to the company than you are, but don't confuse their job status with their being more important as human beings. Human equality is continually being fought for in the workplace today, and one of its demands is equal respect for people in lower positions. Courtesy titles that signify and per-petuate the inequality between student and teacher, patient and doctor, worker and boss, are gradually fading out of style. If you can find a way to address other people as they address you, you strengthen your image as an equal adult.

When you are new on the job, position yourself immediately by sug-gesting your preference: "I prefer being called Ms. Jones." If you know your boss well, involve him in your concern: "I've been thinking about a long-standing custom in our department, and I'd like your thoughts. I'm uncomfortable being called Anne when so many people in the department are Mr. or Ms. How would you feel about calling me Ms. Jones? I'd appre-ciate it."

Sometimes, depending on your relationship, you can be more direct and raise the issue by saying, "I'd like to be addressed in the same way as other people in the department—by my last name, rather than as Anne." Or, "I've noticed that all the managers are referred to as Mr. or Ms. or Mrs. or Miss, and all the secretaries are called by their first names. I don't know how the others feel, but I'd be more comfortable either being called Ms. X., or referring to my managers by their first names, as they refer to me. Do you have a preference?"

You do, of course, have the option of fighting this feminist issue in a political, confrontational way. In one recent case in the Midwest, one young woman dropped an idea for equality for women in the company sug-gestion box. She proposed that since all male executives were addressed as Mr. by the women in her office, the women, all of whom worked as stenog-raphers and secretaries, should likewise be addressed by their courtesy titles: Miss, Mrs., or Ms. Two weeks later she was dismissed. Fortunately, having gotten into trouble, she put up a good fight. She sued, and was awarded back pay and damages. One could choose this route for many of the issues raised in this book and be the gainer by it. (See Chapter 3, #9, "I'll Never Get a Promotion—My Boss is a Chauvinist and It's a Chauvin-istic Company," for a discussion of the risks and rewards of such a fight.)

• If you're seen as girlish, it behooves you to avoid remarks and ac-tions that suggest a lack of worldliness: "I never heard of such a thing!" "Really?" "You did *that?*" Wide-eyed expressions of amazement are ap-propriate reactions for children as they experience new and strange events; children haven't been around for very long—but you have. And if you *are* inexperienced and unworldly, play it down. The company doesn't want a babe in the woods; it wants and needs someone who can be relied on, some-one who knows her way around.

• Avoid fads, teenage and collegiate styles, the Alice-in-Wonderland look. Don't dress in anything sweet or ruffly. Instead, wear clothing and hairstyles that are sophisticated and businesslike. Changing your appearance is an easy way to grow up fast in the eyes of the people around you—at least on the surface. Not long ago, while I was conducting a group workshop with women who have been meeting weekly for some two years, a total stranger entered the room. As I wondered who she was and why she was there, the intruder—a tall, handsome, rather athletic-looking woman—sat down. She looked at my face: "Is something the matter?" When I heard her voice I realized it was one of the members of the group—but what a dramatic change in her appearance! She had always seemed so fragile and vulnerable, with an unformed and timid sweet-sixteen air about her. Now she seemed robust, taller, more imposing. She looked confident and forthright—she had presence. Actually, she had made only a few surface changes. Instead of her usual demure pastel outfit, she was wearing a bold striped dress and large sunglasses. She had pinned back her fine, straight, shoulder-length hair into a French twist, thus opening up her face, her neck, her shoulders—and herself—to the world.

For more pointers about adjusting your image to reflect independence, responsibility and maturity, it might help you to search out role models whom you particularly admire. Figure out what there is about their behavior and appearance that could help you with your image.

If you find it difficult to leave girlish femininity behind, think about the fact that women are discouraged from growing up, in part because of society's prejudice against older women. Many women cling desperately to youth when they see older women being devalued and discarded right and left. The very words "mature woman" conjure up the distasteful image of a matron—gray-haired, thick in the middle, old-fashioned, and completely undesirable. In contrast, the mature man with graying temples and a prosperous pot is sought after. He's come into his own; he's powerful, thoughtful, worldly, filled with wisdom.

To compound the problem, too many women have had the unpleasant experience of witnessing their own mothers' dreary or deteriorating lives. These earlier generations of women were often soured and embittered or apathetic, their dreams destroyed by baby bottles and diapers, by lost struggles. The more we understand and sympathize with these women, the less we will worry about becoming like them.

But to be middle-aged and "unattractive" or girlish and "attractive" isn't your only choice. These are the images of women that are presented to many of us by the culture we live in. Take a fresh look. If you can see beyond the stereotypes and reject the notion that women whose development is thwarted are attractive, you will find more and more women—middle-aged and old—who are sought after because they are delightful, growing human beings, enjoying their own lives. If you have resisted maturing and are seen as a girl, women like this—who have chosen the only satisfying alternative—should motivate you to grow up. There's something much better ahead for you.

4. YOU ARE SEEN AS PAST YOUR PRIME

How to show off the advantages of experience • How to react to new ideas • Checking out your own prejudice • Keys to a dynamic image

THE STEREOTYPE: *Middle-aged women aren't good for much.*

While there is plenty of prejudice against older men, the prejudice against older women starts earlier and is more intense. In too many instances, women are chosen for jobs on the basis of their youth and their attractiveness, and likewise, in too many instances, they are rejected for their lack of youth and "attractiveness." Since many women don't get their careers going early on, this prejudice is a virtual killer.

What image would work well for you?

You need to be seen as a woman who is a repository of a wealth of information and judgment that can only be gained through experience. You are a woman full of energy and enthusiasm. Whether new in the workplace or a veteran, you are a dynamic, growing human being; you are going places, you are not a has-been.

If you are seen as too old:

Go out of your way to display the best qualities of youthfulness. Show that you are interested in everything you do and in making contributions— new products, new ideas, new systems. You're not just sitting there, waiting to collect a paycheck, waiting for retirement. Work is a challenge for you, not a routine. You are always looking at problems with a fresh eye. Never say, ''That's the way we've always done it.'' Bring new solutions to old problems—and avoid ruts.

Show that you expect success in everything you tackle. You don't fit the stereotype of the defeated, disillusioned old person. The knowledge and understanding you have gained have energized you because you've learned through experience to make things work for you.

Don't react negatively to new ideas or new situations. Interest and enthusiasm are among your greatest image-building assets. Be receptive to other people's ideas. If you've heard an idea a hundred times, you need to hear it this time in the context of who is delivering it, how he or she sees it. Your response should have a definite end in view—teach the idea-giver, or challenge his reasoning without humiliating or discouraging him, or use the idea to spark your own solutions.

Don't make a point of age, yours or anyone else's. Construct a world, including your social life, inhabited by people of varying ages. Don't run away from younger people because you think they are rejecting you. It's hard for women to hold on to a sense of their own worth in a culture that is so categorically rejecting of older women. We suffer enormous discomfort and self-consciousness when we are in a junior position at a relatively senior age. But wherever you see prejudice, it's important that you find a way to break through if you want to survive. Don't encourage the supposed prejudices of the younger people around you by withdrawing. If you do so, you are viewing *them* stereotypically. Display your valuable qualities and give people a chance to react to you in their own individual ways; some may see you as a has-been, and some will not.

Walk fast. Move your body. Dress in a contemporary way. Many women as they get older lose interest in fashion and dig up old things out of the closet to save time and money. There's nothing wrong with this, but the prejudiced observer may be apt to write you off because of your "old hat" look. You can very easily handle this prejudice by keeping your wardrobe relatively up-to-date.

Watch your language. Don't say, "I'm too old for that." If someone carries a heavy package for you, say, "Thanks"—not, "I can't carry those heavy things anymore." Don't talk about your arthritis, or how you never had to wear glasses until recently. Don't say, "Oh, to be young again." Talk about current events, not memories. You can tell wonderful stories about the past, but don't sound as if you live in the past—as if then was better than now. "How wonderful it was then, when I was pretty and I could do more." It's better to focus on these facts: first, that older faces are attractive to many people; and second, that now—because of your greater knowledge and broader interests—you can do more things than you ever could before.

5. YOU ARE SEEN AS WEAK

Claiming your territory • Why women have trouble being assertive • Being strong without being aggressive • The importance of sticking to your guns

> THE STEREOTYPE: *You are compliant and easy to manipulate. You can't stand up to people. You're not tough enough—you can't withstand pressure, and you can't put pressure on others when it's needed. Therefore, you are unable to protect the interests of your boss and the company.*

What image would work well for you?

You need to be seen as someone who is forceful enough to make good deals; who is out to win, not to please or appease. You are not afraid of other people's power, but feel, in fact, quite powerful yourself.

If you are seen as weak and manipulatable:

Counteract the stereotype with a consistent show of assertiveness. Once-in-a-while assertiveness won't do it. The conviction that many men share about women is that they can be pressured into doing things they don't want to do—so declare your position boldly on even the most minor matters and stick with it, particularly in the face of disagreement and pressure. Don't back off in an attempt to create the image of a more reasonable person. Of course, you may decide to change your position if the evidence warrants it, but no one is going to push you into it.

Don't worry about going overboard and being too forceful. The big danger for you—and for most women—lies not in looking aggressive, but in seeming too malleable.

Shira's Story

Shira, a new supervisor, was invited to a planning meeting with Vincent, her boss, and Howard, the head of the department. During the meeting, Howard turned to Vincent and said, "I want you to take care of . . . (and named one of Shira's important functions)." Shira jumped right in. "Hey, that's *my* job." Howard responded, "You're too busy. I want Vincent to handle it." At this, Shira could easily have caved in, thinking, "He doesn't have confidence in me; he doesn't think I can do the job." Or she could have thought, "Maybe he's being considerate— he's trying to help me get established by not burdening me down right away. I shouldn't reject his thoughtfulness." But Shira didn't give up. She knew that, whatever Howard's reasons might have been, it was crucial for her to establish herself in the new job in more than title only. She stuck to her guns and addressed his stated concern about her being "overworked." "It's no problem for me, Howard. In fact, I *want* to follow through on that." At that point, Howard gave way. Shira had made it clear that she knew what she wanted and she knew how to go after it. No one was going to take away important parts of her new job without a fight, boss or no boss.

If you demonstrate such assertiveness on your own behalf with the people who are in a position to judge you, they in turn will have confidence in your ability to fight for them when *their* interests are at stake.

If you should fail to make an assertion because you are inexperienced and things happened too fast, or the issues seemed too difficult to deal with, you cannot afford to let your mistake go by. If you do, you train people to ignore you. You must reopen the discussion and regain your position on the company chessboard.

If Shira had permitted her valuable assignment to slip through her fingers during the meeting with Howard, I would have suggested that she correct her error as soon as she realized what had happened: "Howard, I've rethought the decision we made at yesterday's meeting. I don't like the idea of giving the blah-blah to Vincent. I want to follow through on that myself." She would then argue her point and offer succinct and tangible reasons to support it. Win or lose, she would thus have solidified her image as someone to be reckoned with.

It is indeed difficult for a woman to be assertive. Why? Because we feel we are being aggressive and arrogant when we stand up and declare our differences with others. We are expected to be pussycats, and we are taught and conditioned to be agreeable in order to be successful with people. But in my experience, exactly the opposite is true: being assertive and standing up for your rights result in your becoming noticed and respected and valued.

There is, however, such a thing as what some women call being "too assertive," that is, aggressive. Fortunately, Shira did not say, "You guys gave me the title, but you don't want me to do the work. Why? Is it because you feel threatened by me?" Or, "You don't take important assignments away from the men!"

Never confuse the discussion with the deed. No one else will. Don't think you are making an assertion just by making a protest. Take, for example, this dialogue:

FAINTHEARTED ASSERTOR: "You charged more than we agreed on."

OVERCHARGER: "The job took longer than we thought it would—two extra days. Actually, I didn't even bill the whole amount. It should come to $60 more. I gave you a break."

FAINTHEARTED ASSERTOR: "Well, I'll let it go this time. But in the future, I think we should stick with the agreed-upon price."

The fainthearted assertor thought she was making an assertion by raising the issue, but actually it was an ineffectual protest. In reality, she didn't make an assertion at all. She merely postponed the issue—and in doing so, she displayed her weakness and compliance, and overpaid to boot.

Of course, sometimes there are circumstances that call for compromise, but not in this case. The "assertor" did not believe the bill was valid, yet she paid it anyway. She "compromised" because she couldn't tolerate head-on conflict. Perhaps her rationalization—in which many women take refuge—was that if she were "reasonable," her adversary would respond by also being reasonable, and thus a confrontation would be avoided. But it usually works the other way around: a "reasonable" statement will be interpreted as weakness and the other person will push even harder to get the best deal he can. This is especially true in the case of women who are seen as compliant to begin with.

Here's how our fainthearted assertor should have proceeded:

ASSERTOR: "Listen, we agreed on X dollars. I won't pay more."
OVERCHARGER: "You didn't tell us about all the difficulties. We lost hundreds of dollars."
ASSERTOR: "Sorry you lost money, but the agreed-upon price is X."
OVERCHARGER: "You're unreasonable. Everyone knows things have to be adjusted when there are problems."
ASSERTOR: "A deal's a deal."

There can be other problems, however, that do not quickly meet the eye. For example, sometimes a woman will make a properly assertive statement, but when the other person seems to give way or act abjectly, she immediately begins to feel sorry for him—to empathize with his supposed plight in the time-worn, archaic "woman's way." She will give in before he does, thus handing him the victory—because she felt terrible about besting someone.

Speak for yourself. Use "I" language to show that you don't need consensus or approval, that you have a strong belief in your own judgment, your own convictions, your own decisions. Instead of: "Well, try it my way. I think *you* will find it looks better in red," say, "I don't agree. I've considered all the arguments and I prefer red." The first way may suggest that you cannot tolerate difference, that you want the other person to change. This puts you into a weak position and paradoxically can lead to further argument. The second statement declares that you have a point of view regardless of disagreement—which puts you in a psychologically strong position.

If you are seen as sure of yourself, these subtleties of language are not important. But if you are in danger of being seen as ineffectual, then your choice of words and the tone with which they are delivered are crucial.

Eliminate apologetic, defensive, I'm-in-the-way expressions from your vocabulary. Don't overuse "I'm sorry," "please," "excuse me." You're not being polite, you are indicating that you feel like you are imposing. You have to learn to be considerate without subordinating yourself. The overapologetic person will say, "Excuse me. I'm so sorry I interrupted you." (Like a servant—you are supposed to know what the other person needs and wants.) Compare this with the considerate response: "I see you're busy. Would tomorrow be a good time?"

Use assertive body language. Your body posture—the way you carry yourself—reveals your feelings. Your poise can either back up and strengthen your assertions, or can undermine them. Imagine someone mumbling, "I won't pay more," with her body folded, eyes averted, head down. Now picture yourself leaning forward, looking someone in the eye, and saying loudly and clearly, "I won't pay more."

• Avoid a timid, tentative walk. Enter a room as if you belong there, as if you are entitled to take up space. Be there with all of you, your whole presence. You are not hiding or wishing you were not there.

• Don't smile too much; it might seem as if you are begging for approval or a pat on the head. Don't smile at all if a smile is not congruent with the seriousness of what you are saying. "I don't agree with your solution (smile)."

• Don't sit on the edge of the chair as if you want to run out of the room.

When you use assertive body language, you may feel at first that you are coming on too strong—especially if you are accustomed to comporting yourself as an unobtrusive, modest assistant. But the message you are giving out is not overdone; it is that of a person who feels like an equal.

6. YOU ARE SEEN AS NAIVE, NOT POLITICAL

How to break a commitment gracefully • Humanistic values in the workplace • When to keep your empathy to yourself • Why being judgmental can keep you from getting information

---

THE STEREOTYPE: *You don't understand how to play the game. You're too straightforward. You believe everything people tell you. You're simplistic and are inclined to see things in black-and-white terms.*

What image would work well for you?

You need to be seen as business-tough. The people above you should know you are shrewd—that you can maneuver your way around as well as anyone. Yet they also must know you are on their side—that you are loyal to them.

If you decide you are seen as the stereotypical naive woman:

Keep your "people" concerns to yourself. No matter how tenderhearted the individual managers, including your boss, may seem to be, in the final analysis they are primarily motivated by the philosophy that "what's good for the company is good for everybody."

Some women recoil in horror when advised to be discreet about their humanistic "people" concerns because this seems to conflict with the qualities we admire most about ourselves. Indeed, they believe that this deeply ingrained humanism of women one day will change and upgrade the morality of the workplace as more and more women join the work force. But I'm afraid that this attitude can be the most naive of all. Certainly, women's humanism should be treasured, but such a formidable change cannot be accomplished by women as individuals, only collectively, and then only through enormous effort and struggle. Meanwhile, you would be well-advised to manifest your humanistic "people" concerns selectively.

Valerie's Story

Valerie, a purchasing agent for a chemical firm, had been told by her boss, Dan, to select a supplier for a new product line. She went through the arduous process of interviewing and evaluating wholesalers and finally found one, John, who could deliver exactly what she wanted. She then spent on and off some ten hours with him sorting out problems and using his expertise. Suddenly, when she was about to place her order, the president of her company told her to scrap John, that he had already lined up a supplier—and he wasn't interested in the people she had found, or how good they were, or what they had to offer. Valerie understood the politics of the game, figuring that probably her boss had a buddy in the other company, or had other deals in the works. Whatever the reasons, it was clear to her that there could be no arguing. She knew enough not to appeal to his sense of fairness (''How can we do this to John? He put in so much time!''). In sum, she realized that the president had made a political decision and that she had no recourse but to cooperate with it.

Going along with the president's choice was easy. The tough part was facing John. She felt that he had gotten a dirty deal but she realized she was trapped: she just could not give him the job. Some people faced with Valerie's dilemma would try to sneak out of it by not telephoning John and by not returning his own anxious phone calls. Others might play nasty: ''Your work isn't up to par and we decided against you.'' Others might pass the blame onto the president himself. But what Valerie did was to confront the situation in a straightforward manner. She telephoned him: ''Unfortunately, there was some confusion here. I just found that the president himself had made a prior commitment to someone else, and that wholesaler got the order. However, we've cleared things up and when I approach you for future orders you can be sure there won't be any last-minute shifts.'' She also told John that she had recommended him to a colleague and suggested he follow up on this. In addition, some weeks later she telephoned him to ask if he would like to serve as a member on a panel of experts at next month's meeting of her professional trade association. In this way Valerie was able to preserve her image with her president as a company-oriented person, while at the same time keeping her own self-image intact as a people-oriented person.

There are much larger ''people'' problems that arise in the workplace—for example, layoffs or plant close-downs in which you have to fire, say, two hundred people at a time; or having to order speedups on the assembly line that may seem inhuman; or issues of safety in the plant; or vast environmental concerns such as pollution, waste disposal, and so on. Some of these you can handle in a humanistic way by proving that your solution is in the company's own best interests—for example, by arguing for better health conditions that will benefit the company itself as well as the worker. But other solutions of yours may be not at all in the company's interests, particularly where bottom-line, dollars-and-cents issues are concerned. Discussing those solutions won't be tolerated, and raising them will change nothing, only making you appear naive and disloyal. Since companies won't deal with such problems, they become societal concerns; thus, if you want to help correct them, you have to do so in a larger context, such as in the political or organizational arenas. If you do opt for social action or, more directly, to blow the whistle on immoral business practices, keep in mind the risks and rewards of such a fight. These are discussed in the section advising women who want to conduct a political struggle against chauvinist practices in their companies (Chapter 3, #9, "I'll Never Get a Promotion—My Boss Is a Chauvinist and It's a Chauvinist Company).

Don't be openly critical of what you see as unsavory business practices. If you are, you may find yourself cut off from possible channels of information.

Women often say they are excluded from discussions, conversations, etc., at work, and this is too often true. But sometimes they react with naive shock when they have been brought in on the real and nasty truths of business—leading their male co-workers to the conclusion that "a woman just can't take business morality in stride." Consequently, the men tend to keep their business secrets to themselves.

Amy's Story

Amy was a newly hired secretary in a large department store, eager to get ahead. Her boss, a young, on-the-move executive, basked in her admiration of him and loved to boast and confide to her about what went on in the executive suites. One day he gave her a long discourse about the internal strategies, schemes, and political maneuverings that he was in the process of learning. At the end, she turned to him and asked, "How could *you* do things like that?" Seeing her unexpected dismay, he reacted in the most obvious way: in order to maintain his image as a hero in her eyes, he clammed up—and that was the last that she heard about the tricks of the trade. It was also the end of her own personal pipeline to information that would help her to understand what really goes on in business.

Show that you know when and how to cut corners without getting into trouble. Indicate that you know how to make friends in the right places—and get things done. Let people know that you are something of a wheeler-dealer. You will learn more about how to do that in Chapter 8, *Survival Tactics.*

7. YOU ARE SEEN AS TOO DEPENDENT

Why women find it hard to be the ultimate decision-makers • How to depend on people without being dependent • The hallmark of independence • If your wings are truly clipped

THE STEREOTYPE: *You're unable to make things happen on your own; you need too much help and support. You're okay as a helper or backup person, but not as a leader.*

What image would work well for you?

You need to be regarded as a take-charge person definitely able to do what has to be done without waiting for direction. A leader makes her own decisions, and if she happens to be wrong, she simply deals with the consequences.

If you think you are seen as too dependent:

Emphasize your decision-making role. Whatever the level of your job, *you* make the decisions it requires. You are the leader of *your* work. Taking full responsibility for something is an unaccustomed role for many women; we are used to doing things under the supervision of parents, husbands, bosses, teachers—and are inclined to hold fast to this dependency. Until you experience actual independence, there is something quite comforting about the belief that you have someone you can count on for all the answers, who knows better than you what should be done.

You can be a decision-maker and still get help from others when you need it. Just don't ask people to *tell* you what you should do. Don't say, "Do you think I should order in bulk, or in smaller but more expensive quantities?'' Don't formulate the question as if the other person is the actual decision-maker. Instead, ask for opinions, information, and input: "I'd like to order in bulk and save the $3,000, but I'm concerned about storage space. Do you have any thoughts?'' You ask a colleague's thinking, but retain the decision-making power for yourself.

Demonstrate that you are an independent person. Show that you understand the crucial difference between knowing how to depend on other people and being personally dependent on them. Turn to people for aid and assistance in areas of assigned expertise and specialization—but if they don't perform to your satisfaction or fail to come up with the answers you require, turn to others. Leave losers behind. A dependent person will wait endlessly on people who aren't producing because she feels desperate and imagines she has no other recourse.

The hallmark of independence is finding ways to get things done. The independent worker knows how to use the resources that are available in the larger world. You must not be like an overly dependent homemaker who waits endlessly for her husband to remodel the kitchen or rewire the broken doorbell. If he procrastinates, you find other solutions. *You* check out costs. *You* interview labor. Or you learn how to do it yourself.

Many women feel stuck in their dependency on a boss who doesn't give them information or on a peer in another department who holds things up. The independent person will find other ways of working. And if there are none, she leaves. She's not dependent on one job.

8. YOU ARE SEEN AS HARD AND COLD

How to tell if your tough image is working for you • How to tone down your sharp demeanor • How to criticize

THE STEREOTYPE: *You are rigid and uncompromising, you're tough, even cruel. You're an emasculating bitch.*

Chauvinists view women either as too softhearted or too tough. There's no in-between. Whichever way your personality tilts, prejudice pushes you the rest of the way. Your tendency will be exaggerated and you'll be pigeon-holed at the extreme. If you're not seen as too caring, you are probably seen as an emasculating bitch.

What image would work well for you?

You need to be seen as assertive but not hostile, businesslike but not ruthless—a judicious balance.

If you think you may be seen as a "ball-breaker," first decide whether your image is working for you. Many "tough" women do very well, getting what they want when they want it. People admire them for being strong-willed and aggressive, "like a man." If that's your situation, don't worry about the negative labels—they go with the territory. But if you feel your style is hurting your career—if, for example, the people you work with resent you for it and won't cooperate—or if you are concerned about your seeming lack of humanity and "femininity," then you can soften your image using these tips:

Concentrate on responding in a positive way to the people with whom you deal. Be sensitive to their feelings.

Situation. Someone comes to you for help and you are under heavy pressure. Instead of a brusque "I'm busy," be more responsive to his or her needs: "I do want to talk to you, but I don't have time today; I'm jammed up. How about Thursday at ten o'clock?"

Situation. Someone who works for you comes for help that would be inappropriate for you, in your position, to give; you have more important work to do. Thoughtless response: "Why are you asking *me?* I can't get involved in that sort of thing." Positive, image-softening response: "I'd like to help you out, but unfortunately I don't have time to teach. Maybe Jim can do it." Or, "I'm afraid you'll just have to do the best you can. If I think of a way to get you some help, I'll let you know." Each response gives the same message—that your work is too important and the helpless employee will have to get assistance elsewhere—but when your answer is given in a considerate way, it's not a put-down of the other person.

Situation. You're annoyed. Someone has barged into your office and interrupted your work. Instead of "Don't interrupt me! Can't you see I'm busy?" try a gentler response: "I'm in the middle of something; I'll get back to you as soon as I get in the clear."

It may be hard for you to respond in this gentler way if you fear you will lose authority and/or be taken advantage of. It is true that until fairly recently the only way many woman could get authority and respect in the business world was to be super-tough and pushy—and it is also true that it is difficult for women to gain authority, even today. But I believe it is possible to be strong without being harsh, and likewise one can be considerate and respectful of others without appearing weak. Keep in mind that your authority and force don't come from looking tough and sounding tough, but from being assertive, and from sticking with a decision once you've decided it's right.

Treat people like people, not objects. Let them know that *you* know they are human beings and not machines.

Situation. One of your staff leaves an hour early to prepare for a dinner party. The next day you ask, "How was your party last night?" This shows that you acknowledge her as a person who has a life apart from serving you. The boss who is seen as using people should avoid appearing to see everybody else's abilities and time solely in the framework of the boss's own needs.

Show those around you that you are aware of their opinions and personal likes and dislikes.

Situation. There's a discussion of where to go for lunch. Someone says, "How about that new Mexican restaurant?" The interested-in-people you replies, "No. Toni (a third person) doesn't like Mexican food." Toni notice your considerateness: "Oh, you remember that."

Also show that you are sensitive to people's special qualities—their uniqueness.

Situation. You can't remember something. Acknowledging Jean's special quality, you say, "Jean, you have a good memory. What did Bill say at that meeting?"

Be careful how you criticize people. Criticism can be constructive, but a great deal depends on how it is expressed. Often as not, when you criticize or evaluate someone, he or she tends to see you as a judge or an authority, and as a result, to feel childish, resentful, humiliated. Thus, it is important for you to try to avoid presenting your criticism in a parental, judgmental way.

Situation. Someone asks you the same question three times. Instead of a parental reprimand ("I told you that! You just don't pay attention"), say, "We discussed that the other day when we were in Barry's office. You recall I suggested the such-and-such approach and gave my reasons for it?"

Criticism in public can be particularly devastating to the recipient. You may be able to take good care of yourself when you are criticized publicly, but many people cannot.

Situation. Someone says something irrelevant during a large meeting. Inconsiderate response: Rolling your eyes at the ceiling as if to say, "How dumb can you be!" Image-softening response: A respectful "Unfortunately we don't have time to get into that side of it right now." Then you move on to the next point.

Situation. Someone keeps interrupting your speech. Instead of "Stop interrupting me!" or, "I'm talking!" say, "Hold on to your point for a minute. I want to round this out—and then I'd like to hear what you have to say." Or, "I'd like to hear your point, but unfortunately we don't have time for a discussion."

Don't bad-mouth people. If you say nasty, mean, or cruel things about anyone—your colleagues, your kids, your husband—it will just fuel the image of you as a tough, heartless bitch. I know that it's often tempting to make a negative remark about some other person. Among other things, it's one way of forming alliances—you isolate him and thus make common cause with others who may feel the same way about him. But it's a good idea to resist any temptation to do this. Your alliances should be built of sturdier, more positive stuff.

Don't look like you are out to get someone. Don't go after people publicly, even when you know you can win the fight—it will simply help build up sympathy for the person you are attacking. Others in the room are apt to identify with his or her humiliation. If you are at a meeting where you feel compelled to tackle someone's ineptness, you can best do so in a way that I recently witnessed.

Walter, the town's zoning enforcement officer, was manifestly incompetent at his job. Many of us at that evening's town meeting were aware of this fact. But when one of the disgruntled citizens jumped up with a dossier of criticism and demanded an immediate public debate on Walter's shortcomings, Kenny, one of our town's leading activists, suggested that because of the magnitude of zoning problems, a committee be appointed to investigate the general zoning situation. Within a few weeks, Walter was quietly dismissed from his job and a new, more competent zoning officer appointed. The message was made clear, but without subjecting poor Walter to further humiliation.

Soften both your verbal and nonverbal communications. If you are already seen as tough, go easy on four-letter words and tough talk. Watch your body language: don't walk like a football player. Avoid a mannish look. If you do wear man-tailored clothes, soften them with accessories or makeup.

Don't get gooey, but do some favors.

9. YOU ARE SEEN AS HAVING NOTHING IMPORTANT TO SAY

Training people to listen to you • When to talk and when to stay quiet • How to get—and hold—people's attention • What to do with interrupters

THE STEREOTYPE: *You're a dumb broad. When it comes to important discussions and decisions, you are not consulted. You're told, "Don't bother your pretty little head." When you do speak up, nobody notices—your contributions are ignored. People talk to one another and you are totally overlooked. It's as if you aren't there.*

What image would work well for you?

You want to be seen as a solid thinker, business-smart. In the chauvinist's eyes, you are the exception—you "think like a man." You are a woman who has significant things to say about your particular area of work. When you start to speak, everyone listens.

If you are seen as a "dumb broad" who is not worth noticing:

Don't talk until you have something important to say. Also, don't say the obvious. Remember, the first idea that pops into *your* mind may well be the first thought on everyone else's mind, so don't try to beat them to it. Sit back, listen, and hear out the others. Save your thoughts and information until you have something you are sure is original and valuable and can advance the discussion. In this way, you train people to listen to you. They'll begin to expect something interesting when you start speaking.

Stage your contributions. When women are ambivalent about speaking up, they tend to speak so softly that they will inevitably be ignored or interrupted. When you do talk, make sure you are heard.

Once you have decided to speak, don't hesitate. Pick the moment, enter the discussion firmly so that you get the floor, and keep it until your point is made. Keep your voice in a low-pitched, confident tone, and don't rush. Your ideas are important; treat them that way.

You will rush if you are worried that people aren't interested and don't want to hear what you have to say, or if you're concerned that what you have to say is inappropriate, or if you feel that you are wasting everyone's time. Then you are apt to cut corners, your story gets garbled, and you come across as a "dumb broad."

My thought is that you should present your story as a jeweler presents a prize diamond: on a velvet cushion. He doesn't just display it in his hand or on the table. He makes an event out of it.

Don't let people interrupt you and take over. Keep talking, or pick up again and get back to your point.

Situation. You are speaking. "The X of the Y is about . . ." Someone interrupts: "What about the A, B, and C?" You respond, "Yes, and as I was saying, the X and the Y is about . . ." or, after a lengthy interruption, say, "That's an interesting point and I want to give my reaction to it. First, however, I'd like to say . . ." and restate your point, this time completing it. It may seem difficult or even strange to restate your point this way, but you dignify your idea by not letting anyone dismiss it or drown it out.

If someone turns away from you while you are speaking, or picks up some papers and starts looking at them, don't continue making your points. You should pause. You should try to make an attention-getting or dramatic statement that will cause him or her to put down his paper. Call him by name. "Angus, this is the core of the issue." Or, "Angus, I think I've got the answer." Or, "Angus, you'll be interested in this."

If he continues glancing at the paper, say, "Would you rather discuss this later? This is valuable stuff and I think the issue rates your attention. How about this afternoon at three?" Pin him down to another time and then leave.

Don't take too many words to tell your story. If you bring in too much detail, it undermines, rather than strengthens, your point. Sometimes I think many women bring in a great deal of extra material because they truly want to avoid taking an assertive stand. They want someone else to verify their conclusion and put a stamp of approval on it. They want to present all the evidence, just in case their thinking might be wrong. They lack confidence in their own judgment regarding what are the relevant facts, the important facts, the key facts—so they pour it all out, hoping the other party will separate the wheat from the chaff and draw the suitable conclusion.

Women tend to overtalk for another reason: in the past they generally haven't had to count their words; their time wasn't assessed in dollars and cents. In the workplace, use the time-is-money principle.

Women also are more apt to feel responsible for "filling" silences than men. We want to make everyone comfortable; to entertain them. ("The thing that really throws me off is other people's *silence.* I come out with my idea, and nobody says anything. So immediately I think my idea needs more explaining and I start babbling away, trying to get them to understand. And that makes me feel even more stupid. And I get more and more embarrassed.") Because of our own discomfort, we don't seem to allow time for the natural pauses that occur in thoughtful discussions. If you're puzzled by a silence, you have the option of asking those around you—in a meeting or whatever—*why* they're not saying anything. "I am wondering what your silence means." Or, "I just proposed an idea and I would like some feedback." Or, "How do you feel about my idea? Are you disagreeing with it? Do you have anything to add to it?"

Work on your small talk. Make it big. Read the best newspaper in the city; at the very least, the front and editorial pages, and all the lead stories in the business and financial sections. "Dumb broads" don't usually comment on the situation in the Middle East or third-quarter profits.

10. *YOU ARE SEEN AS GOOD FOR ONLY ONE THING*

How to minimize come-ons • Ways to say no • Why women rely
on their sexual attractiveness • Why you can't have it both ways

THE STEREOTYPE: *Women are sex objects. The aim of this particular
game can be anything from a flirtatious diversion to serious sex.*

Men who view women as sex objects evaluate them according to just two
criteria: "Am *I* interested?" and "Is *she* interested?" Nothing counts but
your looks and whether you'll "come through" or not. Otherwise, you are
of no importance at all.

What image would work well for you?

You need to be seen as a multifaceted person who has any number of interests—people, books, politics, sex, sports. You're certainly not a prude,
but in the office you are concerned, first and foremost, with work. Further,
you are a woman who knows who she is and who is comfortable with herself.
     If you think you are seen as a sex object:

*Don't get entrapped when a man comes on to you in a sexual or flirta-
tious way.* If you respond coyly, flirtatiously, or angrily to a man's advances, or if you become embarrassed or start arguing, you are joining the
discussion on *his* terms. You are allowing him to set the agenda: you as sex
object. Instead, you need to act out of your own personal definition of yourself.

Situation. He says "My, my, don't you look sexy today!" You smile or
nod and promptly disengage with something like an easy "Come on, Joe,"
then move on to what you want to talk about. If he persists ("What's the
matter—frigid today?"), stay with your casual dismissal, like a relaxed
hands-in-the-air, eyes-to-the-sky show of confidence that says "What am I

going to do with this guy!'' Then, keep on with your subject. ''Did you hear about the recall of so-and-so's silicon chips?''

In a sense, his attempt to keep the conversation on a sexual level is a power play. He is trying to draw you away from any territory where you might be his equal or superior and put you, figuratively, in bed—where he sees himself as your conquerer. But you can keep this from happening by adhering to your own style, your own personality, your own professionalism. You will thereby express your view of who you are *and* you will rule him out of order, all without any put-downs, long discussions, or verbal battles that might incite his revenge and, in any case, would be inappropriate to a work relationship.

To help you stay with your agenda, you should be prepared with a good-sized arsenal of mutually interesting subjects ready to discuss—news of a good restaurant, stories about the latest antics on the pro tennis circuit, or last night's political debate. Then it won't be so easy for him to catch you off guard with a sexual put-down.

Some women have difficulty following this advice. They are worried about rejecting a man's interest and hurting his feelings. That's understandable—women are taught to flatter, not to criticize. Moreover, since many women themselves feel so hurt when they are rejected, they assume that everyone else reacts to rejection in the same way. Certainly, there are men who take rejection badly and are hurt by it, but even with this type you are pretty safe if you reject the *behavior,* not the person, just as you would with a child who acts out of turn.

You might also find this advice difficult to follow if you become angry and would much rather say, ''Get out of here, slob!'' I admit it's tempting to do so, but unfortunately, it's usually ineffective. A Don Juan thinks he's flattering you with his attentions, and he'll never understand why you are insulting him when he's ''complimenting'' you. He'll just hate you for it. So remember your goal: to be able to function effectively at work.

Watch your body language and dress. Take note of any possible cute, coy, or sexy signals that you might be giving out. Although it's not fair to ask you to change your behavior when it's the other person's obsession with sex that is causing the problem, I don't think there is any other immediate solution. It is in your best interest to minimize the nuisance by shifting to a direct, assertive style and manner. Dress for work, not play. Go overboard on "safe" clothing. Play down the curves.

There are some women who have trouble projecting an image based on professionalism because they depend—as women have for centuries—on their sexual or "feminine" attractiveness for attention. They lack confidence in everything *but* their sexuality, and at work they feel completely lost without their flirtatious behavior.

To learn better ways of relating to men in the office, you might do well to observe the women around you who seem to get along easily and effectively with their male co-workers. How do these women handle themselves? What specific things do they say and do that elicits respect? Your role model can be anyone—a receptionist, an office manager, or a top-level executive; it's not her office rank that counts, but her office style.

Since you have an image gap to overcome, it will take you time and experimenting to work out a relaxed, businesslike manner for yourself and feel comfortable with it. The only way to get past this awkward stage is to practice until you have developed a solid repertoire of new responses, phrases, gestures, looks, and topics.

It may be difficult to do all this if you also have some interest in playing the sex game. The office can in fact be a good locale—perhaps one of the few places in your life—where you can meet men. But, unfortunately, there is a choice to be made. If you opt for too much fun you are feeding right into the stereotype of woman as sex object and you won't be taken seriously at work. Consequently, you will be undermining your career, and in turn your ability to support yourself and to be independent in the future, come what may. So if you are seen as a sex object and your career is important, you'll just have to turn off the fun-and-games behavior—at least while in the office.

PART 2
MATCH YOUR IMAGE TO YOUR JOB

Many women report that they have difficulty making their outer image—that is, their demeanor and presence, their way of working, and even the way they talk about themselves—reflect the importance of the job they are doing. They don't look or act the part. Their style lags behind their titles. As a result, they run into all kinds of problems in carrying out their jobs.

The reason for this is that although they are moving into more important jobs at higher levels, with more status than women in general have ever before achieved, they are stuck with behavior patterns that were molded to suit lower-level roles. While women often recognize the need to act in new ways in order to command the respect required for them to do their jobs successfully, they are at a loss as to exactly how to do that.

Claire's Story

Claire was an office systems consultant, and although she was tops in her field, she had a run of disasters when she set out on her own. During a period of several months, a rival in Philadelphia encroached on her territory; a client left her over an apparently minor squabble; and a potential customer had a series of meetings with her, picked her brain for her expertise—what equipment he should get, what systems he needed, and how they should be set up—and then walked out and gave the contract to someone else. It began to look as if these were not isolated incidents.

As I discussed them with Claire, I began to notice more and more that she did not have a very impressive demeanor. She was quite tentative in her manner. It took me several meetings to discover how high her standing was in the office systems field. I began to wonder if that was the way she presented herself to her clients. Could it be that people found it easy to leave her because they didn't see her as valuable and important—as a top-level expert who could provide the answers to their problems?

I began to question Claire about this. She told me that she did, of course, let new clients know of her excellent track record. But I suspected that she did this diffidently—and I saw that she didn't realize the necessity of letting people know how important she was on an ongoing basis. Claire needed to hear the old you-are-only-as-good-as-your-last-press-notice truism, and be reminded that she had to be her own press agent. People tend to forget your accomplishments if you don't keep them informed, and their confidence in you begins to erode.

Claire agreed that it was natural for her to play down herself and her achievements. "Once I had gotten a certain standing in my field, I assumed that was that." She felt it was immodest to call attention to her exceptional track record. Like so many women, she had a lifetime habit of diminishing herself in the service of making other people important. She simply didn't appreciate how crucial it was to impress people, both with her style and with news of her accomplishments.

If you find yourself in a situation like Claire's, you should, first and foremost, try to analyze what it is you've been doing that undermines your image as a person of importance. Once you know what is happening, you can start to work on substituting behavior that will help you build the image you need.

In essence, there are two aspects to building up an impressive image: first, a personal public relations campaign is called for (as mentioned in Chapter 3); and second, you have to find the right image and work hard to change over into it. These two tasks must be done concurrently. Here are some tips on how this can be accomplished, gracefully and effectively.

1. HOW TO PUBLICIZE YOURSELF

The danger of assuming people know who you are and what you have achieved • Overcoming modesty • How to toot your own horn without bragging • How to impress the people above you when your boss won't let you near them • Measuring the risk of bypassing your boss

Recognize your achievements and be sure to take credit for them. It's a mistake to look upon your accomplishments as routine. I often hear women say: "Why should I tell my boss I did such-and-such? That's just part of my job." But doing good work *is* an achievement, and if you do it better than someone else in your position might, that's important. Just because something comes easily to you, don't underrate its value.

Some women are so modest that they give their laurels away without even realizing it. Take this classic scene: the boss says, "That's a great layout." Modest woman: "Thanks, the printer suggested it." The printer may have done the final layout, but she directed the project, brought her original designs to him, established a good relationship in order to draw out his suggestions, and gave him the go-ahead when he had a good idea. Now she is downgrading all this in her mind, while exaggerating the role of the printer. In fact, it was a collaboration for which she could rightfully take credit.

Many women feel this need to move into the shadow and push someone else into the limelight. It seems to be a deeply ingrained female response to praise: our skill as women, gained through years of practice, lies in diminishing our role and enhancing that of someone else—child, husband, boss, colleague. If your modesty overwhelms reality and causes you to play down your achievements, you will lose many made-to-order opportunities for image-building.

Toot your own horn—without bragging. It's a subtle art, and one worth learning: getting your message across in such a way that people hardly know you are sending it.

• One of the best ways to disguise your self-publicizing is to weave in as a secondary point that which you in fact want to highlight. For instance, tell a story about the obstacles you've overcome, and incidentally mention your triumph: "Sorry I'm late, but I was conducting a workshop at Union Carbide to teach them how to use the new X-400 I designed for them—and in the middle of everything the power went out! It took forty-five minutes and ten phone calls to get it back on." (You've casually let people know that Union Carbide is your client, and you did it without bragging.)

• Tuck your accomplishment into an interesting tale. "Wait until you hear this horror story! A friend of mine at such-and-such corporation told me that all their paychecks went out last week with two extra zeros before the decimal point. But don't worry, it can't happen here. When I set up our system, I put in a glitch control that will prevent that."

• Sandwich your "commercial" within a compliment to a co-worker. Instead of saying, "I designed a new program that became famous in the field," say, "Joe (the public realtions director) is a really ethical guy. There was a lot of pressure on him to write up the news release about the

XYZ program without mentioning anyone but the executive director, but Joe gave me full credit for the idea.''

• Another way to present your standing is in the form of other people's evaluation of you. For example: ''I was asked to make the keynote speech for the second day of the trade association convention this year.'' Or, ''I was chosen to do the research project.''

• Use facts—statistics, dollars, whatever—to give people the evidence that leads them to draw the right conclusion: that you did a great job. For example: ''I solved the layout problem that was holding us up. I widened the margins and used large print. Now Saul (the client) is very happy with the result, and we've already begun discussing a new project. I think if we move in with a proposal, he's ready to buy another design.'' Conclusion: you know what you are doing, and you're good with the client.

• Learn how to angle your stories to highlight the qualities with which you want to impress people. For example, if you want to show that you are aggressive, you would say something like: ''I fought Saul (the client) to get it through the way we thought it should be, and now he loves it.''

When I advise my clients to talk about their achievements, many women report that it feels as if they are bragging. There is that danger when tooting your own horn, but the tips I've outlined here should help you avoid this. Also, you should understand the different motivations behind bragging and strategic self-publicizing. The braggart boasts to shore up his ego; he's looking for an audience to join him in a chorus of praise. What I'm suggesting you do is quite different: a carefully calculated reporting system designed to let people know what you are doing—so they will give you the opportunity to do more.

Make your personal publicity campaign a permanent part of your repertoire. Memories are short, so keep reminding people of your achievements—of what you did in the past and of what you are doing now. If you don't, people will take you for granted.

Focus your campaign on the right people—those who have something to give you (raises, promotions, cooperation, support) and who will give it to you if they see you as an achiever. (Don't aim at those who are resentful and envious and would rather see you done in.) Sometimes they will be those in your own department—your boss or the people who work for you. Or you might want to aim at the people you work with outside your department, or those at the higher levels of management throughout the company, or people in the industry itself.

By and large, the most difficult people to reach with news of your achievements are those at the higher levels of management. This is usually because of the structure of the company itself. Most bosses don't like their staffs to have contact with people above them, and usually the upper levels of management prefer that you work through channels. If these are the people you want to impress, I feel you have three options. The first is to work through your boss. If he sees you as a team member and understands that your work enhances his own position, he will most likely come to trust you and include you in meetings, informal gatherings, and other contacts with the higher-ups. Then, at the right moment, you can get your message across.

Your second option is to bypass your boss and go directly to the top people. You do this only if you feel it's worth the risk or you are in a strong position—for example, if you are an obvious company star or someone higher levels of management is interested in keeping around. If you win out, you get your message across. If you don't, you might find yourself looking around for another job.

Here are the stories of two women who took the risk and won.

Alana's Story

Alana wanted to make sure that Robert, her boss's boss, knew about her good work. Not only was Robert in charge of raises and promotions, and therefore a key target for any personal public relations campaign, but also Alana had discovered that her boss, Allen, had been downgrading her role to Robert. We decided that in this situation it was worth the risk for her to approach Robert directly. She began to send Robert a carbon copy of the weekly report she prepared for Allen. She knew this might threaten Allen, so to minimize the risk, she included in her report compliments to him. "As you suggested, I did such-and-such and it turned out very well." Or, "Thanks to your good idea . . ."

Her strategy worked: she got her message through to Robert, and she didn't alienate Allen. On the contrary, in a surprising turn of events, Allen began to bring her along to his meetings with Robert—meetings she had been trying to get invited to for months. Thanks to her compliments, Allen now saw her as being on his side, as part of his team, and Robert saw her valuable contributions firsthand.

Angela's Story

Another of my clients, Angela, tried an even bolder, if somewhat riskier, maneuver. She wrote a letter to the president of her company, explaining her idea for improving the efficiency of the sales force. He was impressed, asked someone in her region who she was, and then asked her to develop the idea. It was eventually put into practice, but even if it hadn't been, Angela had accomplished her objective. She had set herself off from the pack; in the president's eyes, she was a comer.

The third option is to take indirect routes to getting your name and your message across to upper levels of management. You might take an active role in professional associations—joining committees, making speeches, preparing reports, running for office. Or you might endeavor to get your name in print by writing for trade journals or contributing to your company newsletter. It's a long-range plan: it takes time, and it requires the development of a variety of attributes and skills—writing, speaking, the ability to take a public role, to compete for office, to lead a group. But the rewards are great in terms of both your public relations goal and your own self-development.

2. WHAT'S THE RIGHT IMAGE FOR YOU?

What image will get you what you want? • How to sound, look, and act the part • The pitfalls of looking too rich—or too poor • How to look well-connected when you need to

While you are getting your name and your achievements known, you also have to attend to your style and demeanor.

Sound, look, and act the part. One very important aspect of building your image is dressing in tune with the intangible requirements of the job—that is, the inner qualities of forcefulness, confidence, creativity, authoritativeness, or whatever your particular position requires. Dress rings psychological bells, and you want to be sure that what you wear strikes the right ones. You should look as if you can do the job you are supposed to do.

Sometimes it takes a lot of thought to figure out just what look will help you put your strengths across.

Laura's Story

Laura was recently turned down for a job because, as she heard later from a friend, she didn't have the "corporate look." She was outraged: "I *was* presentable, I've got superior qualifications, and I really did well at the interview. If this was what turned them off—that I didn't wear a suit—I don't think I'd want to work for them."

What had Laura worn? A simple straight skirt, a white blouse with a Peter Pan collar, a belt, and a short bolero jacket. The overall effect, she admitted, was more casual than tailored, perhaps even a bit girlish. What was the job she was applying for? That of Washington representative of a large food products organization. It would involve negotiating, persuading, and arguing with the Food and Drug Administration about the correctness of product labeling, advertising, etc. Such a job obviously required an authoritative and commanding presence, someone who is to be taken quite seriously. Clearly, that's what "corporate look" meant in this context. Laura had not understood the kind of subtle signals she was giving off with her choice of clothing—and therefore, she simply looked all wrong for the job.

If you want to develop an image to match your job, it is a good idea to observe the way people dress and act at different levels within your own company. You'll see pretty quickly that, as in most organizations, style and manner change according to the status in the hierarchy. At the extremes, blue-collar workers dress and speak and have a different style than board-room management. I'm not saying which is superior; I'm only trying to help you figure out how to fit in at the level you occupy or are hoping for. It's important that you train your eye to see the subtle differences.

At a company training seminar I attended recently, all the managers wore tailored clothes in muted colors. When the lecturer recommended these somewhat somber shades as appropriate for the authoritative, managerial look in that industry, a new supervisor-trainee next to me leaned over and whispered: "I wouldn't wear those drab colors. I like cheerful ones." I turned to look at her, and sure enough she was wearing a dress as brilliantly colored as the most vivid sunset I'd ever seen. While she certainly looked cheerful, she would never have been mistaken for management in that particular company.

What if adapting to the style of upper-level managers is a step down for you? What if you are *more* cultured, *more* educated, *more* wealthy than the people you work for? I'm not suggesting you downgrade your standards of behavior. The way to fit in is to be careful not to set yourself above people. If you have genuine respect for them and if you are not snobbish, you have an excellent foundation on which to build a good relationship with them. For example, if you have a wider range of knowledge and interests, you can use that to find points of mutual interest. You can take responsibility for establishing rapport with them.

It pays to let people know that you are financially successful. Looking prosperous is more important in some businesses than in others, and you will have to decide for yourself how this advice applies to your situation. Earlier I explained how the appearance of having a good standard of living can affect such things as the amount of your raise and even whether you get promoted or not. I'm not suggesting that you engage in competing with your co-worker to have the biggest car or the fanciest designer-label suits, but I am suggesting that you try not to look as if you worry about money. For example, don't take small advances from your company for business expenses. If you need an advance, ask for a good-sized one. And don't borrow money from the company or people with whom you work.

Don't undermine your image in small ways. Don't look petty as you would, for instance, if you gathered up the leftover cookies from the business lunch, or took the pad and pencil from your place at the conference table. You want to give the impression that you have more important things to think about.

Don't let yourself be labeled as a penny pincher. If you go out to dinner with someone, and you are each paying your share, don't get out the old calculator when the check comes around. Either pick up the check yourself or split the bill down the middle. Of course, if your bill is a lot bigger than anyone else's, quietly put down enough money to pay your share. Be big about small amounts of money. Many women find this hard to do because traditionally the woman's role has been to stretch money, watching their nickels and dimes. Living more expansively is the habit of people who feel their power to generate income.

One warning: don't look *too* affluent. Your boss may be intimidated and resentful. He may feel you are more on a social par with his superiors than he is, and worry that you will get on better with them than he does. Also, be careful on a job interview. If you look like a woman with a lot of money, you're in danger of not being taken seriously. The interviewer may decide that since you don't need the money, you won't be properly motivated, and therefore won't stay in for the long pull.

Let people think you are well-connected. Better to go around looking like you have friends "upstairs" than to say things like "You think *they* care what I think?" One client of mine was new on the job and needed to impress her subordinates with her clout with the higher-ups. The only problem was that she actually had no clout. Since she didn't know anyone at all in the upper levels of management, I taught her to refer to "them" and "they" (*"They* wouldn't go for it") and to look upward, as if she did have contacts "upstairs." Everybody concluded that she did indeed have clout, and that was enough to tip the balance in her favor.

PART 3
YOUR PROFESSIONAL SELF-IMAGE

1. I'M AFRAID OF LOSING MY FEMININITY

What kind of a woman does a man really want? • The new femininity • Why being strategic feels unfeminine

Many women may fear that if they act as I suggest they do in the workplace, they will somehow be losing their "femininity" and attractiveness, and be regarded as having become "masculine."

I think that women who feel this way are still hung up on long-since mothballed ideas of what "femininity" and "masculinity" actually are. In the old textbooks, "masculine" was defined as strong, tough, aggressive, and dominating, and included thinking for oneself, ruling the roost, running things, etc. "Feminine" was construed to mean receptive, docile, acquiescent, and unselfish, and involved caring, nurturing, supporting the roost, being empathetic, being compassionate and sensitive to the feelings of others. You can fill in a lot of the adjectives on both sides of the ledger yourself—you know them well.

Women today, by becoming more independent, assertive, and ambitious—by learning to take charge and move strategically—are losing a deformed type of "femininity" made up of qualities that flow from weakness, and instead, are taking on a more realistic type of new femininity, with qualities that are bound to bring them a more interesting and productive life and better relationships. Also, these women are enhancing the qualities that have traditionally been considered most admirable in women—using them more effectively, and in a broader arena.

Women who worry about losing their femininity do so, I believe, because they have had little or no experience with the qualities of this new femininity. They are frightened at the very idea of becoming more powerful. They become anxious when confronted with situations that cry out for these qualities. They are also afraid that if they act in this new way, they will no longer be considered attractive.

But let's look at how these fearsome qualities really add up:

• *Being independent means being self-reliant.* The independent woman is able to search out ways to get her needs met, and if her support system or any part of her support system collapses, she has the capacity to find new solutions.

The dependent woman hasn't yet had the experience of relying on herself. She fixes on particular people whom she thinks are her only means of getting what she wants and needs. In desperation she pulls on them with no realistic appraisal of what they can do or want to do for her. She cannot afford to see her "rescuer" as incapable of meeting her needs. Although her rescuer may disappoint her over and over again, she doesn't let go.

The dependent woman is attractive to those with misplaced Galahad complexes, who have a need to rescue people—but she ultimately becomes tiresome to most people, would-be Galahads or not. In addition, the supporter who doesn't attend properly to her needs begins to feel guilty—and the guilt casts a pall over the relationship. The supporter looks for ways to avoid the contact that makes him or her feel inadequate.

But as you develop more independence, more resourcefulness, and more options, you are increasingly able to be selective and ask only for those things that others are realistically able to give. When you draw on their abilities, those around you can perform well. Now, you've enhanced the relationship. Now people can be genuinely helpful—and you can be genuinely appreciative of what they have to give.

• *Being assertive means standing up for yourself without knocking down the other person.* The assertive person is able to express her wants, opinions, ideas. She's not manipulative, or hostile; she's not shy, she's not afraid to speak up for herself. Is the expression of difference in the assertion of your own point of view "unfeminine"? On the contrary, an expression of difference—without aggression—is what makes you interesting. In the olden days, women equated "femininity" with accommodation and agree-ableness. These days, men and women alike enjoy and respect women who are distinctly themselves.

• *Being strategic—a necessity for moving up in the workplace—means maneuvering and outmaneuvering others.* It means playing it cool and clever, being political, and playing to win. Somehow being strategic seems "unfeminine" to many women. The reason is that it acknowledges the need to be self-reliant. The strategist is separate from the adversary. Being simply direct, forthright, and open—as opposed to strategic—is based on the hope that the world is your ally. This (unrealistic) hope flows from the fear of being separate, of standing on your own. The refusal to strategize is not a quality of feminine attractiveness, but is instead a product of fear— fear of autonomy, fear of having to outsmart others, fear of successfully outsmarting others.

• *Being a leader means taking charge, guiding.* It's a necessary role in every business endeavor. There's a great deal of admiration in business for people who take over, shove obstacles aside, and get things done. But it's not a good idea for a woman to carry this take-charge style back home and into her personal life. Neither is it a good idea for a man. The boss role at home is not appropriate for either sex. In the best of all relations, there are no bosses. Mutuality is the truly attractive order of the day.

• *Being competitive on the job is relatively new to women.* Many of us are afraid of giving up the noncompetitive aspects of our natures. Tradition-ally, we've been noncompetitive at work because we didn't want to get anywhere. Now that we've established goals, we have to compete—which implies racing ahead, giving our all, beating other people out, upstaging them, wanting to be bigger and better. In its worst sense, competition means winning at any cost. In its best sense, competitive behavior means not withdrawing for fear of being done in, not being intimidated by a com-petitor's strengths. It means playing the game—win or lose—and not aban-doning the field to your rivals. It means being your most productive self, forging ahead, and not holding back for fear of losing—or winning. It can mean simply going after what you want, and not withdrawing.

In the workplace, you can in fact use the idealized qualities that so many people admire in women—and that women admire in themselves—such as compassion, empathy, sensitivity, concern for others. In truth, you can put them to even better use when you combine them with assertiveness, strength, leadership, strategy.

With all this, you become a whole new animal. Will people like this new animal? You bet! And, more important, you will too.

2. I'M AFRAID OF BECOMING A CARDBOARD CORPORATE CHARACTER

How the pressure is exerted • How to resist it • How to make concessions without paying a price

As soon as you step into the workplace, you are under pressure to blend in, to tone down your own special brand of individuality and become the "corporate man." The company has well-defined goals; they don't want any interference, and anyone who doesn't think or act in the prescribed manner is a hazard—a possible red mark on the year-end profit-and-loss report.

These pressures are exerted on your life in the office as well as your life outside the office. They can encompass the clothes you wear, your manner of speech, the way you act in business meetings; your public attitudes, the people you spend time with or do not spend time with, both in the office and out; your life-style; the organizations to which you do or do not belong; the car you drive; what you drink or do not drink; even whom you marry or do not marry.

How does management exert the pressure? The message is given subtly. The company hires and promotes people who are most like those already in the company—"their own kind"—in terms of behavior, dress, life-style, talk, personality. The message, though unspoken, is clear: if you want to advance, you have to be the way they want you to be.

But that's only half the story. The outcome—whether or not you *become* a cardboard person—has to do with you. Management's relentless pressure must find a receptivity within you. It is your eagerness to be what they want you to be, to have what they have, that traps you into conformity.

If you want to resist, then start right now by not succumbing to every pressure. You may have to make some concessions to play the game, but you don't have to make them all—and you *never* have to make them in your head. Give way on small things and hold firm on those issues which are crucial to you.

Chapter Five

MOVING IN

CONTENTS

Introduction

INTRODUCTION

Women often come for career counseling when they are moving into a new job, or when they've just been promoted to a higher-level job, because they are anxious. They know it's important to start off on the right foot—but they don't really know how to do it, or what, exactly, "starting off right" means.

Other women come because they've gotten into trouble on their last jobs and are worried about making the same mistakes again.

Then there are others who have just started in their new jobs and have already run head-on into problems and are in dire need of solutions or ways to counteract problems fast.

The start of a new job, particularly one of higher status and with more authority than you've had in the past, can be a crucial time because the conditions under which you come in, as well as what you do during the first few weeks on the job, shape the way your co-workers will respond to you in the future.

If you seem weak, you are inviting rebelliousness.

If you seem too well-connected, your co-workers might move to get rid of you before your influence carries you above them.

If you line up with the wrong people, you're an outsider before you've even had a chance to be an insider.

If you move in too fast, you'll be in trouble. But not taking hold fast enough can also be a danger.

If you have taken someone else's hoped-for job, you can stir up a nest of resentment.

You can do a lot to short-circuit these problems before they arise—but if they do arise, then you have to deal with them properly and quickly.

Let's look at some common "moving in" problems together and see what we can do about them. (For more on moving in as a boss, see Chapter 6: *I'm Having Trouble Being the Boss.*)

1. THE JOB ISN'T WHAT I THOUGHT IT WOULD BE

How to claim the job you were promised • When cooperation does
not earn respect • How to create your own job description

Often the realities of your new job turn out to be dramatically different
from the position described to you during the interview courtship. At that
time, the talk can be relatively lofty and may not descend to grubby details,
which leaves a lot of room for misunderstanding—and if the company
wants or needs you badly enough, the interviewer is apt to tell you anything
at all. Then, over the first weeks, as the on-the-scene realities unfold before
you, you discover that the job is not as important or as interesting as the one
you'd been sold.

Here's how a client of mine stepped into this problem but was then able
to claim the job that had been promised to her in the interview.

Santha's Story

Santha's boss, Ralph, persuaded her to join his company with promises of
activities that were right in line with her ambitions. He described the job as
a conference communicator in glowing terms: her days would be spent attending meetings and seminars, speaking with the top people in the field,
and then discussing and evaluating her findings with the management group
above her. Thus, on her second day there, she could not believe it when
Ralph walked into her office with a carton of papers, dumped it out on her
desk, and said, ''The first thing I want you to do is to redesign these statistical charts and analyze the data in these reports.'' This was work that he
himself was supposed to handle, but which he never seemed to have time to
do.

Santha was annoyed and surprised that he would bring her his work—
and, moreover, it was work that had nothing to do with her job and that
didn't interest her in the least. She had a fleeting concern that maybe she
should reject the work or at least talk to him about it, but she said nothing.
She did not feel on sure enough ground to challenge him. ''I owe him a
lot,'' she thought. ''After all, he really has been very nice to me, he just
gave me this great opportunity; and twice in the past he's given me free-

lance assignments when I needed them. Don't make an issue of it," she cautioned herself. "You can't start a new job with a fight. Better to be co-operative, get off on the right foot." So she plunged in and tackled the distasteful job with determination: she'd do him a favor, get the chore out of the way—and then, on to the conferences.

Predictably, two weeks later, when the pile was down to two inches, in came Ralph with another carton. "Here's some interesting stuff we should tackle." Despite her protests, he responded with another promise: "Take it easy. Don't worry. In a few weeks we'll be structuring up the conference teams, and you're going to be a part of them." Clearly his needs were very different from those he had presented on the job interview.

At this point, Santha knew she was in trouble, but she didn't know how to stop the downhill course her job was taking. We analyzed what was going wrong. Santha had an all too common misperception about how to create a good impression on her new boss. She tried to show how exceptional and cooperative she was by going along with his requests. But look at the impression you actually make by being "cooperative" and taking on work that is uninteresting, or below your level, or not in accord with your ambitions. Your boss is likely to see you as malleable, as being available to the service of his every need, and, therefore, as lacking a clear sense of your own importance. Your willingness to accommodate his desires does not always earn you respect. On the other hand, if you refuse the work, you are clearly a determined, goal-oriented person, someone who understands the value of her expertise, as agreed upon in the interview.

The job description is determined not in discussion during the interview, but in practice during the early days on the job—as the boss takes your measure. He's observing how you operate, and getting ideas about the level at which you are *willing* to function and at which you will say, "Enough!"

Don't, therefore, sign a blank check of endless cooperation. Only those who are doing routine work—assembly-line work or "women's work"—are valued for uncomplaining obedience to the "superior" person's decisions. You need to be seen as a *selectively* cooperative person, one who, together with others, decides which projects will—and which will not—serve a good purpose for everyone involved, including you, the boss, and the company.

Women in Santha's position often see the logic of taking a stand early on. They understand the need to hold firm to their job description at the outset. And yet, over and over again, they sink back into an accommodating silence. Why? The silence allows them to keep the illusion that others will take care of their interests. In order to be able to say, "Hold on—that's not the job I was hired for!" you have to give up that fantasy. When you are able to speak up for yourself, you've relinquished the hope—and the wish—that someone else will do it for you. And, win or lose, you've declared to the world that you intend to take responsibility for yourself.

As you become clear about the fact that it's up to you to establish your job description—as indeed, you must try to establish the conditions of your existence in virtually all situations in this world—speaking up for yourself will become easier.

Santha now did what she hadn't been able to do in the first place. She confronted the issue with Ralph.

SANTHA: "There seems to be a problem here. The work you are giving me is not really up my alley, and I would like to get started on the conference reporting."

RALPH: "First things first. The basic work of the department has to be done."

SANTHA: "I can appreciate that, but at the same time I do have very specific job goals in mind. And as I understand it, the conference reports and evaluations are essential to the work of the department and needed by top management." (She is not diverted.)

RALPH: "Yes, of course. But we have to get this urgent stuff out of the way before we can go on to conference work. Please be patient."

SANTHA: "In the interests of doing a good job for you, as well as working at the level of my ability, we have to agree on my job description. I really am not willing to fill in wherever there is a need. From time to time, sure. But not as a way of life. Maybe you can tell me more about what you see as my role here." (She clarifies her position; she takes a very definite stand.)

RALPH (irritated): "We don't have to get into that. I keep telling you—you'll be doing your conference work in a few weeks. You know I'm in a pinch with all this other work."

SANTHA: "I'm willing to help in a pinch, but I'm very concerned about the direction my job might take. Maybe we can work this out with some specific limits and a date on which I can turn my attention to the work I was hired to do.''

RALPH: "I can't do that. I can't tell how long this stuff is going to take."

SANTHA: "Well, if the job requirements are not quite clear, if you need someone who can do the charts and graphs and then, at some point, the conference work, then maybe I'm not the right person for the job." (By forthrightly bringing up the unspoken issue, she puts herself in a powerful position. He is forced to confront the question of whether or not he wants to lose this valuable person.) "As you know I am very anxious to work with you, and I'm not precluding the possibility that you will have other assignments that will be up my alley." (Reminding him that he does want her.) "But it seems important to me that we agree on what I'm to do here." (Her openness makes it clear that he can't dismiss her concerns.)

Ralph backed down. Even though he would have liked Santha to clean up his desk, he did not want to lose her expertise.

Over and over, I've seen women take a stand in this diplomatic way with good results. Conversely, I've seen many Santhas who were unable to reject the undesirable tasks and got more and more buried in distasteful work.

This is not to say you can't compromise, but whatever you decide—whether you do the work or not—your boss has to know that *you* are making the decision, that you are not being manipulated by him or by your own weakness or inability to negotiate the situation.

What if the boss did mislead you, and has no intention of giving you the desirable job he had described during the interview—the old bait-and-switch game? What if his plans were vague and the job you wanted is far off in the future? By taking a stand you will bring the facts out in the open. You will then know the score, and can make your decision about whether to leave or stay.

2. THEY DON'T WANT TO ANNOUNCE
MY NEW TITLE—YET

The hidden danger in accepting the delay • When a woman is promoted over men • Arguments that make a good case for your title • When to announce it yourself

Simone's Story

"We don't want to hurt John's feelings by giving you his title while he's still around," the foundation's director explained to Simone. "So, until he actually retires at the end of the year, we feel we should keep him listed on the organization chart as chief librarian—but the job and all authority with it are yours as of today. Congratulations!"

There are a number of reasons bosses withhold titles, or give titles and then don't announce them. In Simone's case, the rationale was not wanting to hurt someone else's feelings.

Simone was quite pleased to have taken this big leap forward in her career. She was now in charge of the library of a small foundation, specializing in funding inner-city projects. The title would come in due course. Meanwhile, no point in offending anyone.

Then, a few months later, the director, Eric, hired a new staff member as a media specialist to develop—under Simone's direction—the library's audiovisual section. The media specialist, Marthetta, soon began acting as if she were a peer on an equal level with Simone.

Marthetta insisted on representing the library department at meetings of the grants committee—"to get them to understand the audiovisual angles involved"—and she also began giving assignments to Simone's assistant. When Simone explained tactfully that attendance at these meetings and supervision of the assistant librarian were the responsibilities of the chief librarian, Marthetta's answer was: "We're *both* 'chief librarians.' We each head up our own divisions."

This led to a series of clashes between them, and Simone realized that the only way to get her authority established was to get her rightful title. On November 30—the day that the old chief librarian, John, retired—Simone marched into the director's office to get him to announce her title officially.

Eric hemmed and hawed. Simone then explained some of the difficulties she was having with lines of authority and clarifying job responsibilities—but it was too late. Eric met Simone's arguments with a series of excuses: "We have a budget problem and it's not a good time to approach the board with a title change." "We can't be so concerned with things like that." "It's not important; the work is what's important." "In time, in time. Don't worry." She couldn't budge him; she had to share her authority with Marthetta.

Why would the director not back up Simone in her attempt to resolve the inner-departmental disputes? Because now Eric had to consider Marthetta's feelings. He was looking for a safe position where he would not injure or offend either of his two skilled and capable workers. Hands-off was his easiest route at this point.

Although the issue of your title may seem of minor importance, it can, as in Simone's case, invite a good number of problems. The correct title doesn't settle the issue of authority—but using the wrong title can be an invitation to other people to move in on you.

By not nailing down her title at the outset, Simone had left the path open for Marthetta's attempt to move in—and had also allowed the boss to blur the reporting lines between the two women. He had probably never even told Marthetta that she was actually *under* Simone on the organization chart. "I guess he just wanted to be Mr. Nice Guy," Simone decided, ruefully.

Charlene's Story

Another reason why a boss may not give a title to a woman straight out is because he wants to allay the possible resentment of the men she's going to supervise. A friend of mine, Joe, a manager in a small engineering firm, told me this story.

Joe promoted Charlene, an engineer, to a supervisory position on a bridge-building project that was already under way, but he deliberately did not announce the promotion. "I thought it would be unwise," he told me. "I wanted to ease her into the job without stirring up the men who would be reporting to her."

But Joe's strategy—to help Charlene gain acceptance in a male-dominated field—turned out to be a disaster. Charlene faced rebellion on every front. When she wanted technical information from the draftsmen she supervised, they often refused to cooperate, challenging her authority: "Why should we teach you how to do a job when we're getting paid less than you are?"

Finally, in desperation, Charlene complained to Joe. He tried to help her out, giving her suggestions on how to deal with these difficult men. He also spoke to some of the men under her, giving them the old we're-a-team-and-we-all-have-to-pull-together line. But from there on, it was all down-hill. Joe's intervention did not improve matters with the men, who saw that Charlene couldn't handle the job on her own. And Joe, when he saw that Charlene needed his help, began thinking that maybe he needed a man in the supervisor's job after all.

Joe unwittingly had contributed to Charlene's failure by treating her differently *because* she was a woman—and when she did fail, he found himself saying, reluctantly, "Well, I guess a woman just can't handle a supervisory job."

These two stories teach us that even when the boss's reasons for withholding your title seem pretty good, it's essential to look at the implications of that decision. In most situations, you need everything you can get to establish yourself in the best possible way, including the right title. If you don't get it, you have to argue for it. Read on.

Diane's Story

"I fought so hard for this promotion and this title, and now it's as if I hadn't been promoted at all. No one knows I'm a supervisor because Tom refuses to announce it."

Diane had been given a promotion to senior economist in a large agri-business corporation, but three months later it was still a deep secret. "When he promoted Sally to senior economist two months before I got my promotion, he sent a memo to the whole staff announcing it. But when I asked him to do the same for me, he said, 'Don't you worry about it, I'll make the announcement when the time is ripe.' And that was that. Nothing happened."

Why was Tom being secretive? Because he hadn't really wanted to promote Diane in the first place. His staff was already top-heavy and management wouldn't take kindly to more promotions in his department. But Tom's resistance had been low, and Diane had been able to pressure him into it, using the fact that he had just promoted Sally, a relatively new em-

ployee, as leverage. Poor Tom had just learned that when you move someone up, you are going to get rumbles from the ranks. So he resolved his dilemma by ducking the issue: he gave Diane the title, but he didn't advertise
it. In fact, he may not even have told anyone else about it. But he couldn't
very well reveal his fears of both management and staff to Diane, and when
she queried him, he made light of the whole matter with another "Don't
worry about it."

If your boss doesn't want to announce your new title, you might be
tempted to ease his discomfort by letting the matter go—but that's too high
a price to pay. Don't collude with him, as Diane did, to keep the secret.
Although your overall strategy is to team with your boss and help him solve
his problems, in this situation you are adversaries.

Women find it particularly hard to place someone else in an uncomfortable position. Remember, though, that you did not cause his problem. He
opted for his position as manager, and his dilemma goes with the territory.

Let him struggle with this one himself. He has to learn how to give promotions, when, and to whom. Your task is to use the leverage that you do
have to get the promotions, money, perks, and projects you deserve.

When you are confronted with a title problem, muster your arguments:

"I think it's important that everyone in the company, especially those
who work for me or with me, understands exactly what my functions and
responsibilities are. The incorrect title is confusing."

"If the men are going to resist a woman supervisor, I want the relationship clarified right away. I want to start off with the authority of the title,
using my own strength to back it up. I think pussyfooting around the issue
can only serve to feed the stereotype that a lot of men have of women as
weak supervisors."

Buttress your arguments with reasons that show the advantages that will
accrue to the boss:

"Clients feel more important when they're dealing with higher-level
people."

"It's easier to get things done around here with a better title. It gives
you clout."

If you are in the peculiar position of having been granted the title and,
despite all your arguments, the announcement memo is not forthcoming,
draft it yourself and submit it to your boss. By writing it for him, you show
him you are not going to drop the issue, and you are making it easy for him

to resolve his dilemma in your favor—all he has to do is sign it. With a little luck, he'll just scribble his name and hand it back for you to distribute.

Your best bet is to get the word out as soon as you are promoted. *Use your new title right away.* If your boss fails to let people know about your promotion, do it yourself. Don't let any self-doubt interfere with your use of the title. Tell your colleagues, and begin to use your new title in memos, letters, and on the telephone. Send a copy of your first communication or report with your title on it to the boss. Having subtly announced it to him, you'll feel more comfortable announcing it to the world.

3. I TOOK A NEW JOB AND I'M AFRAID I'M OVER MY HEAD

The fear of failing • Getting past the panic • Putting your performance in perspective • Getting outside help

Emily's Story

"Maybe I made a mistake; maybe I shouldn't have taken this job. I don't know if I can handle it." Emily was in a state of panic. She had taken a new job as a producer in network television, a big advance from her former job as assistant producer. One of the requirements of the new job was that she write her own scripts. Previously she had had to do some writing, getting together research and blocking out first drafts of scripts, but it had been the producer who had written the finished scripts. Now, suddenly, *she* was the producer and the responsibility for the finished scripts was hers. She was worried that her writing just wasn't good enough for that.

I had suggested that she hire a professional scriptwriter sub-rosa to help get her through the first weeks. I thought that this would give her an opportunity to see if she could do the job, and also provide her with her own private on-the-job training program in this new area. Hiring help is expensive, but women must invest in the security offered by their own successful careers. Those who in the past have been willing to spend money on appearance and social activities as investments in their future security (marriage) must shift their sights. Women need to mobilize their resources as men do, for whatever is needed to further their careers.

This turned out to be a good solution. Together, she and her secret consultant had turned out a series of perfectly acceptable scripts.

But a few weeks after she had started on the job, her worst nightmare had come true. She was suddenly told to have a new script finished in the next twenty-four hours—and her consultant wasn't available on such short notice. Now, she was terrified that she was going to fail and lose her job.

"But," I reminded her, "you've learned a lot in the last few weeks. Why don't you just try it and see what happens?"

"It's the failure," she said. "They'll think I'm stupid." She was apparently panicked not so much at the prospect of losing her job, but at the thought of how she would look to her boss and co-workers. "They won't respect me. And I'd feel humiliated, incompetent—diminished, somehow."

I thought that if I could help her step away from her feeling of possible humiliation, her panic would not incapacitate her and she could give the scriptwriting job her best shot. I had known too many women who had badly underrated their own abilities. I tried to help her gain some perspective on the situation. "Why," I asked, "would they see a not-so-great-writer as 'stupid'? And why should you feel humiliated at failing at this one skill?"

Emily answered, "In my particular job, it's a weakness that's critical—and it would be a bad mark against me."

"I can't honestly see that," I told her. "So you're not so good at this one thing—but you're very good at others. What's so terrible about that? Don't forget, they've known you there for a long time and have already formed their judgment about you, personally. Everything isn't riding on whether you do a thousand-percent, bang-up job on this script or not. Maybe they won't see you as right for this particular job—and maybe they'll be correct. That does not make you a 'failure.' "

I continued, "Let's say there's a job that calls for running up and down an extension ladder and lugging a hundred pounds on your back, and you can't do that—you're not muscular enough. Does that make you a failure? It just means you're not qualified for that one job."

After we looked at her situation in all these different ways, she began to realize she did not have to try to be what she was not. She felt relieved; now she could get down to the business of writing the script without feeling her whole life was at stake. She could step away from her anxiety and present the skills she had, thinking, "What you see is what you get." Instead of trying to give them perfection, she would give them her best shot.

This is what Emily did, and her best shot turned out to be good enough. Twenty-four hours later, she appeared at the studio with a script that proved to be usable. As a matter of fact, she is still holding down the job of producer on the TV show—minus the assistance of her secret consultant.

Emily's situation was typical of all too many women in the workplace. So many of us underestimate our skills and qualifications and have this universal fear of moving to unaccustomed heights—imagining that we can't measure up to a job; that we are the world's eternal children, unable to assume adult roles and challenges. We must discard society's disproven stereotypical notions of women's supposedly lesser abilities. We, like Emily, have little to lose by getting past the fear and giving the job our best shot.

4. I JUST GOT A PROMOTION AND I DON'T KNOW HOW TO HEAD OFF THE RESENTMENT

The roots of fear • The temptation to play yourself down • How to keep the resentment from harming you • If you're the fair-haired girl • Evaluating your competition • The importance of power alliances

Ellen's Story

"How can I move into my new spot," asked Ellen, a newly promoted director of marketing, "without treading on toes? I don't want to threaten anyone."

She was particularly concerned about the sales manager and the public relations director, whose areas of responsibility bordered on hers. Ellen was in a young, fast-growing electronics game company, where, as assistant to the executive vice president, she had initiated a wide range of activities dealing primarily with marketing. After some eighteen months of increasing responsibility, she proposed the creation of a new marketing department with herself as director. She was moving fast, taking over more and more turf that could just as easily have gone into the sales or public relations departments. Her department was collecting data from the sales force from coast to coast, designing in-store promotion campaigns, and planning the development of international markets.

Now, she was worried that the sales manager and the public relations director would see her as a threat to their jobs and to their importance in the hierarchy. She feared that her new title and expanding activities would engender resentment, envy—and retaliation. She was afraid that the sales manager would somehow stop her from functioning, or try to make her look bad, or form alliances with other managers against her, or not cooperate, or sabotage her work. He had already shown himself—even without provocation—to be unethical, stealing Ellen's good ideas and cleverly presenting them as his own. The public relations director, on the other hand, was not a fighter. Ellen figured he might resign when he realized she was building important public relations functions into her own marketing plans.

This sounded like one of those typically dangerous situations that arise in business. If you are a fair-haired boy or girl and a fast mover to boot, you *can* get hurt when the competition gangs up. But sometimes your fear may be so much a built-in part of your psyche that you are unable to estimate realistically what, exactly, is going against you—that is, how much power the supposed competition has against your own.

Ellen and I sat down together to figure that out. The situation as she had originally presented it to me turned out to be remarkably inaccurate. Most of the power cards were in her hands—though she had failed to realize this. For one thing, in her capacity as assistant to the executive vice president, she had had a lot of contact with the company's president. Her abilities were so highly regarded by him that he had specifically carved out for her this new marketing department. Moreover, all along she had been doing much of the work of this new department—title or not.

However, what was most contraindicated by realities was the picture she had drawn for me of the sales manager who terrified her. He turned out to be vastly unpopular with his peers. His devious maneuvers were crude, and management was generally aware that his ideas were rip-offs of Ellen's. All along, Ellen herself had known that management had many reservations about his work.

Her fears regarding the public relations director were equally far off. Since she was so close to top management, Ellen had, all along, been passing on their directives to him and informally supervising much of his work. It seemed unlikely that he would expect their new relationship to be any different.

Why had the picture that Ellen had drawn for me been so wide off the mark? Because she was playing a paramount role—and when a woman does that, she is committing the crime of outshining others. Women are supposed to stay in the background, offstage, except in certain specific situations such as in the home or in social life.

If you're not supposed to be on stage at all, the moment you walk on, you feel like you are upstaging everyone else. And a good woman doesn't diminish others, a good woman supports and helps other people to shine. The taboo against breaking this code is so strong that, the unconscious reasoning goes, you will be punished severely for it. Ellen was so worried about being attacked that she could not objectively take the true measure of the situation.

Ellen was reacting to the message she got as a woman; she was not responding to the reality of this situation. So preoccupied was she with this unconscious message that she couldn't look at the situation objectively to see if there was any real resentment, or, if there was, how much power the supposed competition had to act on it—and how much power she had to protect herself. Her mind never turned to an evaluation of exactly what they could do to her, or she to them, in return. As we uncovered the real problem, it became clear to her that she had nothing much to worry about.

What if the people who resent you do indeed have power? When your promotion is officially announced, you should take steps to offer reassurances to those who will be affected by it. In Ellen's case, that would mean drawing them into her plans, showing how they would be working together from now on, explaining what her new department would be doing for their departments and for the company at large. Long before you get the promotion, you can forestall resentment and keep people from acting on it by seeking out well-placed allies and building power alliances of your own.

The temptation may exist to play yourself down—to pretend that you are not so smart, and not in such a good position—in an attempt to gain acceptance. Although women are taught not to look smarter than men—to hide their intelligence and build up the man's ego—the opposite tack is necessary here. Be nice enough to people, but be sure they know that you are smart, well-connected, and part of a powerful network. They'll be very careful about doing anything harsher or more concrete than merely grumbling.

5. I'M AFRAID I DON'T LOOK AS IF
I'M ON TOP OF THE JOB

Taking a strong independent stand versus being a team player • Four ways to get control of a new situation • Why you can't count on your title for power

When you move into a new job, and people are taking your measure, it's important for you to be seen as strong and confident. In the case of a managerial position, many expect a woman to be weaker. Some are very hostile to women in a superior position of any sort, and are just waiting for a chance to move against her. If you don't look like you are on top of the job—if you have the appearance of weakness—you will encourage them to move in for the kill. If your new job is nonmanagerial, there is probably someone around who is ready to engage in a contest to establish a pecking order.

Looking like you're on top of the job—which means taking hold firmly—is not easy for many women to do. It goes against their experience as well as their deepest, most ingrained beliefs. Even those women who have caught on to the fact that the way to look on top of the job is to be assertive, even "tough," at the very outset are not able to put the idea into practice. It is one thing to recognize a general principle, such as "Be strong," and quite another thing actually to *be* strong.

Mavis's Story

Mavis had just been hired as director of the new elite products line of a large beauty-products manufacturing company. She was not altogether un-worldly; she understood that she had to show her strength on this new job. But as her story unfolded, it became clear she did not understand what that really meant.

Mavis had gotten this job because of her technical brilliance as a product developer with a much smaller company, where her relations were mostly with other technicians and professionals on her level. She had not previously worked on a managerial level, and she did not realize that "being strong" meant exerting her authority and taking a firm stand with people throughout the company—at all levels, those who worked under her and alongside her as well as the top executives to whom she reported.

Equally important, she was unable to see the connection between managerial problems or problems of office politics that come up, and the need to *use* these situations to establish—at the very outset—who you are. Moving into a new job, you are constantly under scrutiny, constantly being measured, sized-up—and if you don't come down on the "strength" side, an irretrievable point is scored against you.

Mavis took for granted that she would be consulted on the hiring and firing of the heads of departments such as marketing, sales, and research that served as support systems to her own department. However, during Mavis's first week, the company president let loose with one of his periodic purges, and Mavis learned about it only after the fact, when the news went up and down the corridors. Instead of rushing in and insisting in a diplomatic yet forceful way that she should play a major role in the selection of new people—people who worked mainly with her and were crucial to her success—she did nothing.

When the new elite products line was ready to go into production, a major jurisdictional issue came up with the company's top management. The question concerned who had the final approval of the products that would actually be manufactured. The president and the two executive vice presidents both assumed that approval would fall under the aegis of the marketing director, not Mavis, although she was the head of the specialized new division. This kind of jurisdictional dispute—whether the division head or the overall marketing director has the final say in what products are to be manufactured and sold—often arises in business. Here again, instead of fighting for her right and protecting her turf—as was essential if she wanted to establish an overall position of strength—Mavis let the opportunity slip by. Her reasoning, as she later explained it to me, was: "Being new on the job, I didn't want to get into arguments about who had the final authority! I wanted to be known as a team player. I thought that when time passed and I'd proved myself, then I'd be in a stronger position to fight for it. I was sure they'd then turn over the product approval function to me." This concurred with the philosophizing and corporate party line expounded by the president himself: "We're a team of team players here at Consolidated Beautetics." What Mavis did not seem to realize was that the concessions she was making would impair her future functioning in a way that could prevent her ever being able to produce her hoped-for results.

There were numerous other occasions where Mavis neglected to take a strong stand. For example, many of her male friends advised that the best way to start a new job was to fire a few people in the first few weeks. "They have to know you mean business. They have to be afraid of you." Mavis thought this advice was horrendous, morally wrong, and also unnecessary. She thought the right thing to do was to work with the people and see how they performed. "Why should I fire someone if they don't deserve it? Maybe they're good. Let's see how they do over the next few months."

Granted, this advice was an unnecessarily brutal way of establishing a position of strength—but at least Mavis's friends were presenting her with a method that was effective. Her response to the situation—to do nothing at all for the time being—proved to be ineffective, and worse, fixed her into a position of weakness. The situation deteriorated rapidly until Mavis was asked to resign.

Here's what Mavis might have done—and what you, also, might consider doing if you are concerned that you don't look like you are on top of the job.

1. Soon after you move in, hand out short-term assignments and projects for each of the people on your staff, so that you, yourself, will be able to quickly judge each one's skills, competence, and cooperativeness.

2. Let everyone know that you are now in the judgment seat; that their previous reputations or the opinions that the other managers or supervisors had about them now do not count for very much. What counts is how *you* feel about them.

3. Be quick to praise and quick to criticize. Don't exhibit too much "feminine" patience with those who don't deliver or are incompetent or uncooperative.

4. When and if you fire or transfer someone, make sure they and others in the department (sometimes, also those above you) know that the decision has been made by you. Let the word get around that you took this action because you weren't pleased with that person's performance.

Many women simply don't understand that when you move in strongly, you are acting to minimize the possibilities of future trouble. You deliberately are not giving people around you a chance to "read out" any signs of possible weakness. If they see you as a power, they'll be apt to think twice about engaging in office combat with you—and, instead, will seek out ways and means to ally themselves with you.

Don't count on your title—or on the conditions supposedly promised in the job interviews—to anoint you with this power. You have to assume power by your own direct actions. That's what being on top of the job means.

6. I WAS BROUGHT IN FOR MY GREAT IDEAS AND NOW I CAN'T GET ANYTHING DONE

If you're "not political" • Your first concern on a new job • The importance of sizing up alliances • The strategic approach to getting things done • Diverting the office lynch mob away from you • How to get to know the right people fast • Building your company network • Approaching men

If you were hired for your problem-solving capacities and your good ideas, there was a natural assumption on the part of the people who hired you that you also have the ability to implement your ideas—to get things done. But one of the biggest single stumbling blocks to getting things done on a new job can be the inability to make the right contacts, sometimes known as being "not political."

Your first concern, therefore, on moving in to a new situation should be the people there. Put aside the temptation to blast through with your great new ideas—whether to restructure departments, revise procedures, redesign forms, introduce innovative programs, or whatever. These are great things to get you through the interview and get you hired, but before you jump in with both feet, you need to know the lay of the land—who will back your ideas, who will resist them, who is happy to see you come in, and who resents you. You do yourself a great service by taking the first few weeks to get to know the situation and the people.

Suppose, for example, your great idea for restructuring the departments had already been turned down by the divisional vice president when it was presented by your predecessor last year? Or suppose that it requires a lot of work and cooperation from the production or administration or research and analysis departments? You should get acquainted with some people in these departments first. You need to understand their goals and what motivates them before you try rearranging their lives or dumping a lot of work on them.

It's also extremely important to size up the different alliances and groupings along the corridors and in the executive suites before you get too chummy with anyone. Susan learned this lesson the hard way.

Susan's Story

Every idea of Susan's had died practically on the delivery table. It took her almost a year to realize that this was largely because of her association with the person who had brought her in—Martin. He had originally recommended her for this job, as an associate analyst with one of the Big Eight accounting firms, and he continued to take a great interest in her career. They were known as office buddies all over the company. Martin and Susan had lunch together several times a week, and she did not feel compelled to put the same effort into her other office relationships. Unfortunately, Martin was hated throughout the department and the company, and, moreover, he had fallen from power—facts that did not penetrate through to Susan until it was too late. The general attitude was "any friend of Martin's is an enemy of mine." This resulted in a virtual boycott, or sabotage all along the line, of practically every important idea of Susan's. She knew that people could be petty, but it was inconceivable to her that this kind of lynch mob virulence could be mobilized against her when she had done nothing to provoke it other than associate with Martin. It took a long, long time of sweating and failing for her to realize the depths at which these group emotions can operate in business. But, by the time full realization came, Susan had lost her job.

Ann's Story

Ann handled herself much differently under related circumstances. A finance officer in a medium-sized foundation, she had been brought in by one of the trustees, and it was clear that she had close connections with the entire board. Most people in such a position would think they were sitting pretty, but Ann was concerned that this might be the cause of problems with her colleagues—the very people she would have to work with closely in order to put into practice whatever new ideas she had. Sure enough, during the first weeks on the job, she began to pick up signals that the people around did resent her and were, in fact, lined up against her.

But Ann, unlike Susan, caught on quickly, took their antagonism seriously—and set out to do something about it. She started courting her colleagues assiduously, making lunch dates with them, throwing them ideas they could use in their own work, offering insights on how they could best deal with the board members, asking their advice on problems, and so on.

Then, after Ann had been on the job for two months, the executive director hired a new consultant with an assignment to evaluate the agency—its overall direction and goals—and make recommendations that could put it back into a leadership position. The consultant, Eugene, started off immediately in a high-handed and arrogant way. He sent a memo to the executive director recommending that the director table for "future consideration" all projects that were approved but not yet in operation. Eugene did this without so much as discussing the thinking behind the projects with the various department heads and project managers who had been responsible for developing them. He thereby succeeded in alienating them all.

That's when Ann found the device that could divert her colleagues' hostility away from herself—and toward the already disliked consultant, Eugene. She developed a series of innovative ideas that would propel the agency into an exciting new direction, one which she knew would capture the hearts of the board members. Then, she approached her colleagues one by one and explained to them that by backing up this plan, they could circumvent Eugene and leave him behind in the dust. They quickly caught the drift of her thinking and grabbed at the chance to ally themselves with her against him.

Following this, she formed her colleagues into a committee and, together, they presented the plan to the executive director—without letting a word about it get out to Eugene. In the meantime, though, Ann made sure to leak some key elements of the plan to members of the board of trustees, so that there was no chance it could be killed by the director. As she expected, the executive director was enthusiastic about "their" plan, and was also impressed that all his staff were so solidly behind it. Thus, Eugene's assignment—to give a bold, new direction to the foundation—had been done for him (and around him). His consultancy was not renewed at the end of the three-month period. More important, Ann had used the emotionality of the office to build the alliances that are so essential in order to get things done when you are moving into a new job.

A given in any new situation is getting to know the people with whom you work. It's important that you be able to take initiative. Move around. Get to know a wide range of people so that you can get help with your work, move things along, get new ideas, get information, get clients, keep abreast of what's going on in the field. Get one person to introduce you to another. Call people on some minor point and introduce yourself. Then go over to see them. Get them receptive to you and your ideas. Feel them out: see what they need, what they want, what makes them tick. If they're into cooking, bring a copy of your latest great recipe or a sample of a new herb you've discovered. Invite them to go with you to the next professional meeting. Ask them if they'd like to join you for a drink at the new posh hotel in town—and if you get one person to go with you, use the opportunity to invite someone else you want to get to know. "Jean and I are going to the Regency for a drink after work. Would you like to join us?" Stop by and say hello once in a while. If your co-worker is not busy, have an interesting story, piece of information, or joke at your fingertips. After you've done all this, *then* you can begin to think about restructuring and presenting ideas.

Don't wait for overtures. Take responsibility for getting to know people. If they aren't friendly, don't give up. Go easy, but stay in there.

Approaching men poses a particular problem. Women often feel their friendly work style will be misinterpreted, and of course it often is. You can't let that stand in your way, although with some men you have to be careful at first, until they understand your agenda. Some are ready to misinterpret everything, and some are so frightened they'll back away from anything that could possibly be interpreted as being more than business, such as taking a coffee break together. Make it easy for them. Invite them to join you when there's a group. Instead of joining a man on a coffee break where he might feel awkward, just stop in at his office with a few thoughts and a couple of friendly words, (and don't shut the door!). In general, be careful, but don't back away.

Chapter Six

I'M HAVING TROUBLE BEING THE BOSS

CONTENTS

Introduction

INTRODUCTION

One of the great facts of life in the workplace is that there is a vast arsenal of resistance to the idea of women as bosses. Resistance, rage, resentment, and envy come blasting out at the woman moving up. The thought of a woman pulling ahead, moving into a higher position, winning out, is unbearable to many of the people she works with. The usual feelings of competitiveness aroused when a new person wins out are multiplied a thousandfold when that new person happens to be a woman.

This resistance to the woman boss comes from several different sources. First and foremost, there's the resistance from the men in the company—those whom she is outpacing ("I won't work for a woman") as well as those who are over her, or on an equal level, who would rather work with one of the boys ("We need a man for this job").

Second, there is resistance from other women. ("How did *she* get that job?" "I'd much rather work for a man.")

Third, there is also a kind of "resistance" from a somewhat unexpected source: the woman boss herself—to the idea of her being a boss. It can take a long time before she becomes comfortable in the role. At some deeper level, to be a boss feels all wrong to her; for one thing, it runs completely contrary to the images of "boss" that she sees all around her. Bosses are male, strong, and aggressive. To this very day—give or take a few outstanding exceptions—the top staffs of all corporations, armies, and countries are men.

Being the boss also runs contrary to a woman's own self-image. Women (as we need to remind ourselves over and over in order to understand our own reactions) have been brought up—until very recently—to see themselves as supporters, aiders and abettors, sustainers, but not as bosses over other adults. Over children, perhaps, but other adults, no. It is completely antithetical to the way we've seen women portrayed, to the way the women around us have been.

Since we don't know how to be women and bosses at the same time, many women who do "make it" act either too soft (compliant, too understanding and sympathetic, too "nice") or too harsh (controlling, too intense, the embodiment of the traditional "tough cookie" or "hard-eyed bitch" who "thinks and acts like a man"). It takes women bosses a long time—if ever—to gain their supervisory sea legs.

In this chapter, I will take up with you the problems and situations many women face being boss, with some pointers on how you can handle these difficulties if you run into them yourself.

1. I DON'T *FEEL* LIKE A BOSS

The need for corroboration • Devices to help you get in touch with your competence • Practicing for your promotion

I've known a number of women who were hesitant to let people know about their titles and promotions because they didn't quite believe that the promotion was theirs. They were easily thrown into a state of doubt. Maybe they had misunderstood the boss, maybe he hadn't intended to deliver the full responsibility that the title implied, maybe it's not really official, maybe he's talking about what might happen in the future. They search for some confirmation of what they only half believe: that the job and the job title are really theirs; that they are expected to take over and get going.

Some women are unable to take over the reins. They don't feel like a boss, and this becomes a barrier to action. Each new supervisory activity—making decisions, acting on these decisions, handing out assignments—all seem presumptuous, and so they wait for the *real* boss to tell them what to do. Habits of a lifetime don't disappear with the acquisition of a new title.

The first step is to recognize that your unbosslike feelings have nothing to do with the realities of the present. They do not reflect your present level of competence or your ability to continue to learn. Management promoted you for what they observed in you, how they assessed you. You may imagine that somehow you fooled them into believing you are more competent than you actually are—but you may be fooling yourself by not recognizing what they recognized in you. *The fact is, they may be more objective about your abilities than you yourself are.* You may have been brainwashed by society's negative view of women and consequently can't see yourself as a leader. You should refuse in your own mind to be pigeonholed, bound, or programmed into accepting a role below the level of your abilities. Challenge all these unspoken messages that accompany your nonboss feelings, such as:

- Who am I (little me) to tell people what to do?
- Maybe I'm doing it wrong.
- Maybe I shouldn't be in charge. I don't know that much.
- I don't like asking people for favors.
- I don't like being aggressive, and I feel aggressive when I boss people around.

Now, let's look at the other side of the ledger—thoughts, ideas, reasons that can counteract these unspoken messages. The positive things to consider arise partly from your new position, partly from the new attitudes toward women, and partly from what you know about yourself, what you have experienced and learned. Consider these thoughts which may permit you to feel like a boss and to assume, as your rightful due, the full responsibilities and benefits of leadership:

- I've rarely seen women in leadership roles. Naturally it seems strange to me.
- I've learned a lot in the last few years. I have more experience than many people—men and women.
- Someone has to organize the work—why not me? I'll learn how.
- If I make a mistake, I'll find it and correct it.
- Work is an essential part of life. Someone has to supervise it, assign it, make sure it is done properly—and be the boss. Why not me?
- Maybe being the boss sounds aggressive to me. Maybe that's because I haven't had any practice at it. So now, let's start practicing—and maybe it will sound less aggressive after a while.

Putting yourself in touch with your competence will help you feel and act like a leader, at least for the moment. You may slip back repeatedly to listening to those negative messages, but for this moment you can act like a leader, make decisions, show your supervisees what you expect from them. Just as you practiced and thus feel comfortable with your old role (homemaker, secretary), you need to practice your new role. As you do this, people will see you as the boss and, more importantly, you will really feel like a boss.

To be regarded as a leader and not as an underling, you have to keep some of your feelings about yourself to yourself while you are resolving these conflicts. Revealing weakness is easy for us. Self-deprecating remarks are comfortably "feminine"—it's our strength that's hard for us to talk about. Remember that consciousness-raising groups and the analyst's couch, not your business office, are the appropriate places for insightful or candid discussions.

Getting promoted can be a judicious occasion for role-playing. Imagine yourself assuming the part of the person who promoted you or who gave you this new job. Imagine why he made you a boss. See if you can list the qualities about yourself that prompted the people who elevated you to decide that you have boss potential. Then, make an effort to use and amplify those qualities on your job.

This is particularly hard to do for those women who continue to believe that authorities are "special" people. In childhood, the authorities are the all-knowing teachers and parents. In adulthood, they are those who run things, the bosses, the higher-ups. If you are imbued with the feeling that bosses are superior beings, you are apt to become anxious when you obtain the boss title. You feel the pressure of the sudden need to become as "extraordinary" as they are.

Even before you get a promotion, try it on for size. Imagine yourself at the next level up. State your ambitions first to yourself, and then to your friends. Get used to thinking of yourself in new ways. You might even try telling people that you already are what you in fact plan to become—not to impress people, but to accustom yourself to your hoped-for new title so that when you get it, you won't feel like a misfit. As you wear your title, real or imagined, your attitude toward yourself and your "place" will begin to change.

2. PEOPLE DON'T TREAT ME AS IF I'M THE BOSS

Keeping your power visible • When *not* to delegate • How too much work can cloud your judgment

It's surprising how often I've heard from clients who, to all appearances, have been granted all the accoutrements of bossdom—who have been promoted to or hired into positions of authority over others, who emphatically have the right to hire and fire, and who have been granted exactly the office space, equipment, and salary they feel their new titles deserve—yet who find that people don't act as if these women are actually the boss.

Margaret's Story

Margaret, an account executive at an ad agency, had been given the financial go-ahead to hire a highly qualified copywriter. The copywriter would devote eighty percent of her work time to Margaret and twenty percent to assisting a more junior executive, Jim. Margaret screened and interviewed candidates and at last made up her mind about which one to hire. Having done so, she communicated her decision to Jim, who was pleased to learn that the new copywriter, Lauren, had been chosen and would soon start working. Unfortunately, on the day Margaret made her decision she was very busy getting ready to attend an out-of-town conference.

"Should I call Lauren and let her know she's hired?" Jim asked. "Great," Margaret said. "I haven't got a spare minute this afternoon. Thanks." Then she hurried off to her conference.

Jim called Lauren, informed her she was hired, and suggested they celebrate by having lunch together.

It was only when Margaret returned from her trip that she realized that she had, inadvertently, given Lauren the impression that Jim had been the one to make the final decision to hire her. After the glad-you're-aboard lunch, Jim had toured Lauren through the office, introduced her around, and in general created the impression that he was her boss.

Now, Margaret began to realize that Jim had seized the advantage over her. By turning over a key boss function, she had eroded her own authority even before her new employee had started to work.

Margaret and I moved quickly to turn the situation around.

What to do? I suggested that Margaret call Lauren immediately and also invite her to a glad-you're-aboard lunch—at a more prestigious restaurant, one where the headwaiter knew Margaret by name. During lunch, she would, bosslike, spell out in great detail the various aspects of the job, and more important, the opportunities for advancement that she, as team captain, controlled. She would quickly clarify their relationship by displaying the authority she had failed to communicate at the outset.

I suggested she say something like this: "We'll be working on such-and-such and so-and-so, and I'm expecting to get another small package-goods account in the fall. If things work out, I plan to assign you to that account so you'll be able to get package-goods experience. That was the one gap in your background that I found during our interviews.'' Lauren, the young copywriter, had to see that her assignments and her future lay completely in Margaret's hands.

After Margaret had had her power-restoring lunch and had recouped her position, she and I sat down together to examine the reasons why she had made her original mistake. It turned out that she had felt overwhelmed by having to get off to the conference. Her anxiety had made her turn over this important function of bossdom—letting the persons you hire know that *you* made the decision to hire them—to the first supposedly helping hand that was extended to her.

Hiring staff is one of the tasks that a woman boss can never afford to abdicate unless she is at a sufficiently high level in the company that her authority is taken for granted. Since women are generally seen as less important than they really are (and men as more important), you need to keep a tight rein on all functions that spell out your power position.

To be a boss may mean in some instances learning to live with over-work or even more work than you can keep up with, but you cannot afford to be so overwhelmed that you mess up your priorities. First things first. And bear in mind that a junior person's offer of assistance, regardless of intent, may not always be in your own best interests. You must play the boss role consistently; then everyone will know you are the boss—and treat you as one.

3. I HAVE TROUBLE MAKING DECISIONS

The essential difference between being an assistant and a director • Why women tend to feel their decisions need validation from higher up • Fear of making a mistake • Women's desire to do things "perfectly"

The essential difference between being an assistant director or an assistant manager and having the full directorial or managerial title is, of course, the level of responsibility that goes with each job. The boss is held accountable for the sum total of things. He's paid to make the decisions and bear responsibility for whatever happens. He's rewarded when things work out, and he risks being sacked when they don't.

Many women are beset with uncertainties about making an ultimate decision—one that fully commits them and others. To suggest, propose, argue, defend—yes, but to take complete responsibility for the outcome—no.

Lack of judgment is not the problem. If you've been promoted or brought in for a managerial job, it's very likely that you possess and have already demonstrated your good judgment. Rather, the problem is one of risk—of sticking your neck out and making decisions on your own. Women generally lack the experience of being the final decision-maker, someone who operates without an okay from a higher-up. Men know at a very early age that they will grow up to be responsible for themselves—they are the ''in-charge'' sex. They don't long for a superior species to validate their decisions—they *are* the superior species and the higher authority: the *chairman* of the board, the *president* of the company, the *head* of the family, the *chief* muckety-muck of this-and-that. Early on, they practice making their own decisions because they don't expect to find a better resource than themselves.

Women, conversely, grow up with the opposite notion—that there will always be someone to help them, and further, that they need help to cope with the ''big'' decisions. Even women who get along very well on their own will slide back into a leaning relationship after a brief stint of flying solo.

Most women are used to having their opinions validated in their helping roles—as secretaries, assistants, wives, and daughters—and they freeze when they have to count on themselves. The belief that we need an okay for everything has been too deeply ingrained.

Both men and women seek out information and opinions. Typically, men use other people's thinking as resources to help them come to a conclusion, to help them make up their own minds. Women, on the other hand, will look to others for concurrence to give them the confidence to go ahead.

Now, suddenly, as a supervisor or manager, you are expected to make more decisions, to take more initiative, to function with less direction. You may talk things over, and certainly you have to let your boss know what you've decided about the more important issues—but the higher you go, the more you have to make decisions on your own.

In addition to the dependency habit, women resist making decisions for fear of making a mistake. It's as if we believe that whatever we have to give is not enough—our value is not sufficient to offset our errors. In many women's minds, to risk being wrong is to risk being without value—perfection is the only ticket to acceptance. Like a hostess who panics at the thought of some imperfection—for example, running out of roast beef at her dinner party—imagining that this would mean that she herself is not a success—the woman boss who is "guilty" of some lapse or error in judgment imagines that she herself is a complete failure. But it's the sum total of your qualities—the entire meal, the evening, the way you operate on the job, your personality—that determines how people see you.

The unrealistic yearning for an unrealizable perfection stands in the way of getting experience. It can—and often does—make you want to work at a job below your level in order to safeguard your idealized fantasy of the "perfect" you.

Rather than become obsessed over a possible error, the trick to compensating for your mistakes is to make *more* decisions, not fewer. To protect yourself against errors is to stand still—but the more decisions you make, the more errors you will risk, and the more opportunities for success you are bound to have.

4. I DON'T HAVE THE OFFICE SPACE I NEED

Standing up for yourself • The office as symbol

You've been promoted. You've negotiated the right to hire and fire within your department, to approve expenditures, and to make crucial decisions. Still, you're in the same old cramped quarters you occupied before your promotion. Or you've been the boss for some time now, but your office space is not as prestigiously positioned as you think it should be. Or your office is not equal to those of others who are at the same level in the company as you are. What can you do?

To begin with, let's talk about the symbolism of the office. In the workplace, power and authority are usually verified by the kind of office you occupy, its location, decor, etc.—attributes such as whether it's private, has windows, has attractive furnishings, is near the boss's office, is decorated with oil paintings or has pictures of you and the president playing golf. Now, it may well be that a person can produce just as well in a shared office, or in an office without windows, or in a cluttered, shabby space—but, unfortunately, we do use office symbols to gauge the power and authority of those around us.

Inge's Story

Inge came to me after she had been fired. Two months before, she had been hired as executive editor of a major mass-circulation magazine. The only authority above her on the magazine's masthead was the publisher. Underneath her on the masthead came the managing editor, Lucy. When Inge reported for her first day at work, she found that Lucy had moved into the larger office left vacant by the former executive editor, and Inge herself was relegated to a small windowless office no different from those occupied by the rank-and-file editors who worked for her.

Although she was annoyed, Inge decided to buckle down to work—there was a magazine to get out—and to let the matter of the office wait until she wasn't under immediate pressure. She didn't feel worried. After all, she told herself, she had the leading title, and presumably, the authority—she had been told by the publisher that Lucy, the managing editor, reported to her. Inge sat down in her small office space and set to work. By the end of the first day, the magazine's staff—familiar with Lucy, whom they knew, and strangers to Inge, whom they'd never met before—seemed to have perceived a subtle (not really so subtle, after all) chink in Inge's armor. "She may *think* she's over Lucy," the staff seemed to be saying, "but if she were, why wouldn't *she* be outside the publisher's door, in the big corner office?" The staff began, on that very first day, to argue and disagree with Inge about minor matters. Subsequently, whenever Lucy suggested something, and Inge rejected the suggestion, the magazine staff supported Lucy. By the end of the first week, the two editors were at war, and the entire magazine was an armed camp.

After a month, Inge was fired. No one on the staff was cooperating with this person whom they'd perceived as a loser from the day she arrived. She had proved ineffectual, unnecessary. The staff had stayed close to the manager who seemed to have more power, as people are likely to do. The magazine went on to function without an executive editor—with Lucy, the managing editor, doing her own work and Inge's as well.

Now, I'm not certain that there would *never* have been a war between Inge, the executive editor, and Lucy, the managing editor, had the office space problem not arisen. But I suspect that had Inge occupied the prime space from her first day on, Lucy and the rest of the staff would have been much more cautious about defying her. They would have perceived her as more important than Lucy, and a person to be reckoned with.

Inge and I replayed the situation together, for future reference, to see what she should have done.

Time: her first day. Scene: Inge turns up for work at 8:45 A.M., she's led to her office. It is tiny, dark, windowless, cluttered with ancient manuscripts.

Action: She immediately marches into the publisher's office.

INGE: "I have a problem with my office. It's too small. I understand my predecessor had Room 607, and I think it would be appropriate for me to have that office."

PUBLISHER: "Don't worry about it. We'll work things out. This isn't the time to ask Lucy to give up the space now, right in the middle of our closing week." (Meaning, "I don't want to confront the managing editor; she's a tough cookie and I need her.")

INGE (thinking, "He'll have to find another way to handle this, but not at my expense"): "It's not a good idea for me to put it off. If you want me to take over and get the magazine out for you, I have to get the space and get organized and ready for action."

PUBLISHER: "Can't we just go ahead with this one issue and take the matter up afterward?"

INGE: "Maybe it would be better if I waited until the end of the week to start—when you've straightened things out." (Meaning, "No way, buster!").

She sticks to her guns, showing him that she wants everyone to understand and acknowledge her role here—including him. Since he sees there's no way he can move her, and he hired her for the top spot—she wins out.

Remember, this is just a strategy. Having a bigger or better office may help solidify your place in the company's pecking order, but keep the issue in perspective: don't fall into the trap of estimating your own worth by the size, shape, location, or accoutrements of your office. These are only to influence other people's opinion of your worth, not your own.

Nancy's Story

Another client in one of my groups, Nancy, a psychiatric social worker at a mental health clinic, was in an even tougher office space situation, but she didn't let herself be pushed around. She hit upon a rationale that kept her from losing the office she needed.

Nancy had had a private office at the clinic until she went off on her summer vacation. When she returned, she discovered that a man of much higher rank, a psychiatrist named Lew, had been moved into her office, and she had been shuffled on down the hall to a shared office. Now, according to the unwritten rules of status, Nancy hardly had a leg to stand on if she went to the director of the clinic and demanded her old space back. In the world of work, the person with the higher title usually gets the bigger or better space, and in my client's field, psychiatrists are regarded as being above social workers. But Nancy, in the course of our conversations, happened to mention to me that she had far more patients than Lew, who had been hired chiefly to do research. There was our argument. I counseled her to stress this point to the clinic director, since his own record was assessed largely in terms of the number of patients seen, treated, and discharged. She took my advice and spoke to him, saying, "As things are now, I carry a heavy case load. Lew has almost no patients. If I have to share office time, I'm going to have to drop seven or eight patients." The director was convinced. Although it was against the rules of status, he did reassign the space. He gave Nancy back the private office she needed to get her work done, and the psychiatrist ended up with the shared office.

5. I DON'T HAVE THE STAFF I NEED

Why it's essential to free up your "thinking time" • The perfect moment to make your pitch • Arguments to use

Perhaps the most irritating Catch-22 of new jobs and promotions concerns staff. You probably have an idea of what kind of staff you'll need to get the new work done to the boss's satisfaction—but when you explain to him that the present staff isn't sufficient, he resists hiring additional help, at least right away. You need more staff to do a good job, but the boss won't let you hire staff until you've proved you *can* do a good job. You have to prove you're worth the investment, but you have to prove it before he'll invest. Investments flow to projects that pay off.

If you perceived the need for additional staff at the point you were hired or promoted, you naturally should have tried to negotiate to get them at that time. But if you didn't at first realize your staffing requirements, or if you failed to negotiate successfully, you'll be in a difficult predicament. Because you'll be out to prove your worth, you'll be driving both yourself and whatever staff you do have at a back-breaking pace. Chances are you'll even be successful—so strong is the drive to prove yourself—in keeping up with all that needs to be done. But this kind of pace can only be maintained for a short period of time before causing your staff to develop resentments, or causing you yourself to get so bogged down in details that you fail to have time for overall thinking, planning, organizing, and doing all the more abstract tasks that are the true matrix of management. You'll succeed in your new position for a time—but ultimately you'll fail. Unless, that is, you select the right moment to convince your boss to let you hire additional help.

Don't assume that because you're successfully completing the work, management may be right about your not needing more staff. Understand your need for thinking time. Managers are hired for judgment. Using your judgment is as much a job function as typing, writing, selling, buying. You need time to talk, confer, listen; to make wise and thoughtful decisions; to think through the ever-changing staffing requirements of your division. Once you are convinced of the validity and the value of discussion time and meeting time and thinking time, you'll be ready to talk to your boss and prove the need for additional staff.

If you have overworked yourself and your staff and have done this impossible job for too long, you've compounded the problem. Your request should be timed to the moment when you've given more than he expected, but when there's a lot more that can be done. People like to spend money for something new. No one wants to pay more for what he already has. Don't let your boss get too accustomed to the improved department. If your timing is good you'll catch him at a moment when he appreciates—and also fears losing—the new improvements. Then, on top of that, hold out a carrot. Emphasize to your boss your plan to undertake some different but important aspect of your department's work, something no one in the company has yet been able to tackle. Use your boss's strategy on him: just as he motivates you with future rewards, you need to motivate him with promises. Bring out your graphs and charts to show your staff's high level of productivity, the improved relationships, the good reporting systems, the innovations. Your boss will see it pays to put people to work under *you*.

6. *I'M NOT THE BOSS; I'M ONE OF TWO BOSSES, AND MY WORK ALWAYS SEEMS TO GET SHOVED ASIDE*

Building your authority with staff • How to deal with your competitive co-boss

Working for more than one person provides a possibly devious employee with a built-in excuse to challenge your authority. He or she can undermine your efforts to get things done with excuses about the heavy workload from your colleague.

Even the most cooperative staff is under some pressure to cater to the most important people in the office, and they may assume that one or another boss has, in effect, more clout. Of course, if they decide in your favor, this won't create much of a problem for you. But if they decide you can be disregarded, this can result in a serious and potentially disastrous situation for you. They'll put you off by saying, "I can't do that for you right now. Ms. X is waiting for me to finish up this report for her." Or, "Can't you copy that yourself? I've got something urgent to do for Mr. Y."

You may be able to resolve this kind of problem by working out a fair and equitable assignments procedure with Ms. X or Mr. Y—but don't count on it. The pressure of work plus an ambitious drive can nudge your colleague into a self-serving frame of mind, and that's when a contest between the two co-bosses can be set into motion.

If and when this happens, it becomes important for you to remember that the staff member has a lot of power, and that you have to build your relationship and your authority with him or her. That employee is the one you have to take on now.

First, look at your image—how people around the office see you—and compare it with that of your colleague. Does your colleague have a more matter-of-fact, authoritative, assertive demeanor? In what way might you seem to be less important in the hierarchy? Are you somehow inviting the members of your joint staff to see you as less important?

If you decide that your image is strong—at least, strong enough to hold your own out in the arena with your colleagues (and/or rivals)—and that the competitive pot is actually being stirred by the staff member, you can't afford to let his or her challenges slip by, or to ignore provocations. Your answer to the implied *"Your* work can wait" should be: "I'd like you to put that aside for the moment. This letter is urgent. It must go out today. I've talked with Ms. X about it, and she agrees." Or say, "If you can't handle this right now, let's sit down and work out a schedule of priorities. What projects do you have on your desk now? Okay, schedule mine for number three. I'll be back for it tomorrow." You have, thereby, noted that there are two other projects on hand, and you've committed him or her to doing yours next. Also, you've given a deadline, based on your estimate of the time required.

If the staff member has several things to do and some of these don't appear to be terribly pressing, you can let your colleague know that you have moved your work behind some of his or her projects and ahead of the less important ones. If your co-boss raises a fuss, you're better off fighting that out with each other. Your colleague needs to know that you see your work as important—you're fair, but you're not about to let anyone push you into the background. Your recalcitrant staff member will get the message: you and Ms. X or Mr. Y are equals, and you're not letting your own needs come second.

Another possible problem when you are part of a two-boss tandem is that the party of the second part has wooed the staffer with friendship, or flirtation, or fun, or promises of tangible rewards. You may feel like the odd woman out. What to do?

Work to make that duo into a threesome—or a full-fledged group. You have to join them and strengthen your relationship with both of them. Don't let yourself get shoved aside. Take note of how your co-boss does it. You can learn to woo people, too.

Sandy's Story

One client, Sandy, had a peer who always beat her out with their staff members simply by being appealing as a man. The women who worked for both of them enjoyed being around him.

Sandy, a direct-action type, did three things:

1. She learned to establish contact on an equally interesting, if different, level, using lunches together, tips about hairdressers and physical fitness classes, investment seminars, and participation together in special women's discussion groups.
2. She filled the next staff vacancy with a man.
3. She filled the one after that with a strong-minded feminist who resented the co-boss's flirtatious humor.

7. MY BOSS BYPASSES ME AND GIVES ASSIGNMENTS DIRECTLY TO MY STAFF

How the boss sees you • Why the boss doesn't respect the hierarchy • Why—and how—to intercept the work

Nina's Story

One of my clients was floundering on her job. "My boss says I'm not delegating enough," Nina complained to me. "Yet a lot of the time, when I assign some particular job to the people under me, they tell me they haven't any time for it because the boss has gone over my head and handed them work on his own. As a result, the work I assign gets low priority. It gets done at the last minute, and the boss starts in again about how I'm not delegating enough."

I tried to help my client analyze her situation. Her boss was giving her conflicting messages. On the one hand he was saying, "Be the boss. Delegate your work." But on the other hand, he was preempting her and saying, "You're not really in charge here." I suspected that this was occurring because she struck him as weak. Her boss had lost confidence in her. He wanted her to have authority. He'd told her to delegate. But since she wasn't doing it very effectively, he bypassed her. She was floundering because he moved in on her; he moved in on her because she was floundering.

In a situation like this, the trick is to take charge so decisively that your boss doesn't feel he has to bypass you. And if he does—either because you've hesitated or because of some managerial error on his part—you need to do something about it. In most cases, a quick turnabout in style—by moving in as a leader—will set the situation right.

I suggested to Nina that she had to take charge; that she assign, schedule, and control, and then report her activities to the boss. If things were slow, she should be sure to uncover work that could be done—new projects, perfecting old ones, everything and anything she could think of to take charge of staff activities productively.

I recommended to Nina that she go to her boss and ask him to give *her* the assignments he had for her staff. I suggested that she say, "If *I* pass them on, I can keep track of what people are doing, watch deadlines, and distribute the work appropriately."

But when she did confront her boss, he argued, "You haven't been giving the staff enough to do."

She needed an acceptable way to explain her past confusion. She said, "I was feeling my way into the situation. I now know the cast of characters, who to give what, how much each person can do, and how much to push. I'll keep people busy, and of course I'll be sure the deadlines for your work are met and that important work gets done quickly. If your work comes through me, I'll be able to do that. I'll be able to keep track of the total picture."

Her boss agreed. But nonetheless, the day soon came when he again handed one of her staff members some work. This time Nina was prepared. She intercepted the work he handed out and reminded him of their agreement. He said, "You're a tough customer," but it was clear he respected her new in-charge attitude. Every time he slipped, she was quick to remind him that the arrangement she had set up worked better for him as well as for her. His slips became less and less frequent.

Paula's Story

Similarly, another client of mine dealt successfully with a bypassing boss. Paula had been put in charge of a project and had given her assistant a deadline for turning in work relevant to the project. The assistant went to Paula's boss and complained that the deadline was unreasonable. The boss gave the assistant a looser deadline.

I suggested that Paula tell her boss, "When there's a problem with instructions I've given my staff, I'd appreciate your referring the problem back to me and talking to me privately if you think I've made a mistake. If you settle my staff problems directly with them, my people will be encouraged to buck my decisions."

Using this approach, Paula was able to make clear to her boss that she had a leadership role to play. At the same time, she was careful not to present the issue as a you-or-me situation. She teamed up with her boss to supervise the staff, but let him know she considered him the senior member. She explained her complaint by referring to office hierarchy and the value of operating through regular office channels, thus showing she understood the parameters of her role. From then on, Paula made a point of reporting staff complaints and problems to her boss, along with her solutions—long before anyone under her went to him with a complaint.

If you stand up to your boss—if you fight to do the job for which you were hired—your boss will gain confidence in you. He'll be relieved that you have things under control, and respect you for it.

8. MY STAFF BYPASSES ME

When a member of your own staff competes with—or outpaces—you • The reluctance to take initiative in meeting people • The importance of having contacts • How to clip your subordinate's wings

Fran's Story

Fran, new on her job, found herself saddled with an assistant who seemed to learn all her operations with the speed of light. Before Fran even had a chance to get to know the other managers in the company on her level—with whom she would work and make decisions—her assistant started meeting with them. Fran was furious. Just when she needed to appear as if she were taking hold, he undermined her—all in the name of helping her. He was making *himself* the highly visible representative of her department. She felt helpless to rectify the situation. Each time she proposed an activity, he had already discussed, decided, and implemented it with the other departments involved.

It seemed to me that Fran had to do precisely what her assistant had been doing to undermine her: make friends. She had to establish relationships with her peers. She had to set up frequent meetings—formal and informal—with other department heads, and exclude her assistant. She had to function more independently. In addition, she had to set guidelines for her assistant's activities. She had to request daily reports on his plans so that she could monitor his activities, and at the same time indicate which functions she would take care of herself.

Fran's problem might never have developed, of course, had she immediately done these things the moment she arrived on the job. In part, her problem occurred because she'd been hesitant—and her assistant confident. Discomfort or fear stops many women from establishing relationships with people, even in business. They wait for others to make the first move because taking the initiative feels inappropriate, or because they fear they might get a cool reception. I think this reticence is often a carry-over from the idea that women who telephone men or who otherwise make the first move are too aggressive—so we wait for the call, an unfortunate residue of the custom of passively waiting to be courted. Fran's resistance to initiating business contact left a gap—and if you leave a gap, especially an interesting one, someone will fill it.

If you do get a cool reception when you approach your colleagues, you have to learn to woo them. Try to see what they might have against you. One client in this situation discovered that her colleagues hated the executive who brought her in, and got their revenge by undermining his protégé, my client. She was on the wrong team. Another client was in trouble with colleagues because she was female. A third, because her colleague was suspicious of everyone. Relationships take time to build. It's a process, not an act.

Fran had not only failed to initiate the process, but she compounded her problem once her assistant took over by talking herself out of acting, saying to herself, ''I can't tell him to stop what he's doing when I've allowed it to happen. I can't threaten to take him off the account when I permitted him to get involved.'' She felt somehow powerless—as if once she let something pass, she couldn't do an about-face; as if once she'd given something, she couldn't take it away. She was immobilized by what she imagined his assumptions and arguments would be. He could say:

- What's the big deal?
- But I've been doing it.
- You let me (led me on, encouraged me).
- Why didn't you stop me early on?
- What's changed?
- Why are you demoting me?
- You don't know what you're doing.
- It doesn't make sense.

Like a teenage girl in a sexual relationship, many women feel locked into the developing order of things. They feel they can never back up a little, even though they want to. They feel committed—obligated—to go at least as far as they went the last time around.

As many women would do in her situation, Fran worried that when you tell a person to stop what you have allowed him to do all along, it implies that you did not understand what you were doing before. She feared that her delayed action would show she was not in control of the situation; that she was naive and inexperienced.

Now, armed with these insights, Fran and I reviewed how she might deal with her assistant.

ASSISTANT: "You're cutting me back."
SUPERVISOR: "Yes. I value your work and your talent, but I think we can work more efficiently if our job functions are clearly defined and separated. We have overlapping functions."
ASSISTANT: "What's changed? I've been doing it all along."
SUPERVISOR: "I do meet regularly with department heads. I think it's inefficient for both of us to spend time with the same people. I'd like you to concentrate on blah-blah."
ASSISTANT: "You're taking away the most interesting part of my job."
SUPERVISOR: "By making sure each of us concentrates on separate job activities, we have a good chance of building and expanding this department. There will be many challenges for you."
ASSISTANT: "But I need quick feedback when I'm working on a project."
SUPERVISOR: "Good—come see me and I'll have an answer for you."

Fran never had to threaten her assistant with dismissal. She did have to clearly redefine his role, and in addition pursue the necessary contacts in her company. Perhaps most important, she had to rid herself of her own barriers to doing both.

9. I'M SUPPOSED TO BE THE BOSS, BUT THE PEOPLE WHO WORK FOR ME REALLY KNOW MORE THAN I DO

When your staff challenges your authority • How to survive while you catch up and catch on • Why you don't need to know everything they know

What do you do if you know less than your staff does? I've had a number of clients who were hired to supervise people who had been working in their particular companies far longer than my clients, and who had more experience.

If this is your situation, learn to listen. If you're embarrassed by not knowing, and if you think you have to cover up your ignorance, you'll have trouble requesting information and asking questions. Recognize right off that there is no contradiction between learning from others and being the decision-maker for them. Your staff may think this contradiction exists, but you should make it clear that providing information for you is part of their job.

Set up meetings from which you can learn, and ask a lot of questions. Take all the time you need to get the information you need—that's your priority. Your staff may knock you behind your back for your ignorance and may resent teaching you, but when you assertively request information, you'll be learning at a great clip, and you'll soon have the overview you need.

When people come to you for information and for decisions, never say, "I don't know," defensively, as if you should know. Use phrases like "I'll get back to you," "I want to think that over," or, "I need more information." Pick up on your perfect right to be new to the situation.

Keep the decision-making ball in your court at all times. While you're catching up and catching on, some people might get the misguided notion that, based on their superior knowledge of the situation, they should take over themselves and make some of the decisions that are properly yours. Don't let this happen. If someone moves in on your decision-making territory, counter their move fast. If a veteran employee sends you a memo stating, "February is my slow season. I'm taking my vacation from the 10th to the 27th," respond by telling her that you have not yet thought through vacation schedules—inform her that you will do what you can to accommodate her need. You answer as if the memo were a request. Your response is not retaliatory, it's cooperative—but clear: you are in charge.

Some of the people you supervise will always know more about their work than you do. But that doesn't mean you can't help them or even direct them. In fact, you don't *want* to know the details. Your job is to listen to their problems; to ask questions in order to stimulate a staff member to find his own answer; to make a suggestion for a helpful resource to which she can turn; to guide the department and look at the overall picture. You weren't hired to do what your staff can already do—you were hired to be a manager.

10. MY STAFF TAKES ADVANTAGE OF ME

"The nicer I am, the worse they seem to get" • The hidden contract • Nice—or weak? • The voice of authority • How to talk to a sulky assistant

One of my clients, a first-level supervisor in the telephone company, said wistfully to me one day, "What is the matter with people? I've tried to supervise by being reasonable, polite, respectful. I try to be nice, yet they really take advantage of me. And the nicer I am, the worse they seem to get. I've stood on my head to be considerate. I've even taken to apologizing for interrupting them, but nothing does any good. It's infuriating!"

We agreed that while she was indeed a considerate person, what she was doing in this instance did not stem from being considerate. Rather, she was trying to make an unstated contract with her staff, which said, in effect, "If I'm nice to you, in return you will appreciate me and be nice to me and do what I ask." Such a contract is the recourse of a person who has trouble asking for things—who ducks the direct confrontation and hopes to get what she wants by giving more and being super-nice. My client's "niceness" was really weakness, and that's why it was not working. Being nice as a supervisor is appropriate and effective, but weakness disguised as niceness is not.

Using niceness alone as a technique to control your staff's behavior simply cannot work. There are always people around who will sense that you have nothing to fall back on and who will take advantage of the situation. Like kids with a weak parent, they know they can get what they want—and your problems are compounded if your staff sees women in general as weak.

Stop hoping against hope that people will learn from you and imitate your good behavior. You have to have more effective techniques to take control of your department. Developing these new techniques will be difficult for you at first.

Here's how you can do it.

Take the apology out of your words, your voice, and your body language when you hand out an assignment.

• Words: Don't say, "I really hate asking you to do this but—" or, "I wonder if you'd mind doing this?" At the same time, don't swing to the other extreme and act like a top sergeant ("I want this by tomorrow, even if you have to stay here all night!"). You should, instead, explain the assignment, give your deadline, and, with your whole manner, show that you take for granted that both of you are doing your respective jobs—yours as a supervisor, hers according to her job description. "I need these by 11 A.M. tomorrow for a meeting at noon. I'd like you to double-check the figures. Please get back to me right away if you run into any problems."

- Voice: Keep your voice at its natural level. If you pitch it unnaturally high, it sounds as if you're uncomfortable making requests—as if you're anxious, or you need to soften the blow by being "feminine" or childlike.

- Melody pattern: Avoid making statements as if they were questions. "I need this tomorrow for a meeting?" or, "I'd like you to check the figures?" (as if to say, "Is that all right?").

- Body language: Don't stand as if you are apologetic, or are in the way, or are the bearer of bad news. You're not in the way; you're supposed to be there, organizing, directing, teaching, supervising. If work is bad news to your employee, he'll just have to cope with that. Stand straight and look him in the eye.

Keep after a person to whom you've given an assignment so he or she knows you mean what you say. If you avoid the follow-up, you're revealing once again your distaste for making requests and your fear of confrontations. Get back to the person soon after you have given the assignment ("How's it going?"). Look at the work and make sure it's well under way. The employee sees that you're not giving a chance to build up excuses. Get back as often as you think it's necessary to indicate your expectation that your deadline will be met, as well as to evaluate progress. If there are problems, and your employee is the cause, get a little tougher. "The deadline is pressing. You're going to have to push—don't forget I must have it before lunch." Your consistency, your follow-up, and your manner all convey a message—"You can't take advantage of me, because I'm on top of things"—all in a perfectly pleasant, businesslike way.

Rose's Story

Rose, a research director in an advertising agency, ran into problems dealing with a new assistant, Miriam. In general, Miriam was careless about things like showing up for meetings, or getting assignments in on time—

things one would normally take for granted in an employee. When Rose would ask Miriam for an explanation, she would add insult to injury by attempting to throw the blame back on Rose. One time, for example, when she had missed a meeting entirely, she said, "Oh, I thought you were going to confirm that meeting by phone." Another time, when she arrived half an hour after the time set for the meeting, she looked into the office, saw Rose working on something else, and said, "Oh, okay, you're busy now. I'll see you tomorrow."

She would also hand in assignments a couple of days late, saying, "I'm sorry, but I had *so* much to do." Her casual attitude about these lapses gave her an air of authority that threw Rose off. Besides, Miriam was new at her job, and Rose wanted to give her a chance. Rose made it clear to her assistant over and over again that the scheduled meetings and assignments were meant to be taken seriously; but the behavior persisted, and Rose became more and more frustrated.

That was when Rose first came to one of my career strategy groups. After she presented her problem, we tried role-playing her interaction with her assistant to see why her message wasn't getting across.

First I played the Miriam role. Rose, confronting me for failing to show up at a meeting, said, "We have work to do. Why did you miss the meeting?"

I said, "Oh, I didn't realize it was definite. I got caught up in something."

ROSE: "But this is the second time it happened. What's going on with you?"

I (parrying): "Oh, don't worry, I'll have the stuff you asked for."

ROSE: "But I gave you so much time to work on it and you haven't even started it."

I (groaning): "I'm under terrible pressure. You've got to understand. But don't worry, I'll get it done."

As Miriam, the reluctant assistant, I had gotten the upper hand. I wound up reassuring my boss instead of being reprimanded by her. In asking, "What happened?" Rose had practically invited me to give her excuses. She'd sounded plaintive, weak, and I'd used those signals to brush off her complaints regarding my irresponsibility with a breezy "Don't worry."

Rose and I then tried reversing the roles. This time I played the research director and she played the assistant. Our dialogue went like this.

DIRECTOR: "We outlined our plans together. I gave you an assignment which could be an exciting opportunity for you, but as I see it, you're blowing it. There's very little I can do for you if you don't produce the work and don't appear at the meetings."

ASSISTANT: "I didn't realize it was a definite meeting. But I do have some ideas, and the deadline isn't here yet. I am very busy on this other project. I'm new here and no one tells me who I'm working for or what comes first."

DIRECTOR: "I understand you are under pressure, and I am sympathetic. But it's still necessary to keep all commitments to me."

ASSISTANT (crying): "I am getting really lousy treatment around here."

DIRECTOR: "I see that you're upset by the pressure and I can understand that. But, as I said before, this is a great opportunity for you, and you're blowing it."

ASSISTANT: "Why? You haven't seen anything I've produced yet."

DIRECTOR: "That's exactly the problem. You miss two meetings and then you announce to me that you haven't been working on the project. If you can produce what I expect by our deadline—"

ASSISTANT: "I'll have something for you."

DIRECTOR: "Good. I'll see you Tuesday at nine."

Note that as research director in the latter scene I played it straight and frank with the assistant. I didn't get caught up in an exploration of an irresponsible assistant's problems in delivering the work; instead, I simply made my expectations clear. When the assistant presented her problems, I was sympathetic, but I did not get drawn in. I went right back to stating the terms that she would have to meet in order to succeed on the job, and ended the meeting with an agreement on what and when she would be producing.

Treating someone as a capable adult instead of going along with her helpless baby act lets her know that she can't manipulate you. If you're worried about not being nice, be reassured: it's "nice" to treat people as responsible adults.

11. I DON'T KNOW HOW TO MOTIVATE PEOPLE

Why money isn't always the answer • What else people really want • Why some supervisors criticize and blame • Seven ways to create the kind of environment that motivates

"My staff is overworked and underpaid. I've tried to get their workload reduced and their salaries raised, but management won't cooperate. Now I'm having trouble getting my people to care about the work. Morale is terrible. How on earth can I motivate them?" Money is the most obvious motivator of effort in the workplace. People should be paid what they need and what they're worth—but generally they're not. There is heavy pressure from top management, passed along at every level, to keep profits up and salaries down. If you're a good negotiator and your department is really producing, you can get enough money to keep your best people from moving out.

Even so, gripes about money, like criticism of the food along a high school cafeteria line, are catch-all complaints masking many discontents. When people are performing badly because they don't like the job, the environment, or you, it's unlikely that more money will straighten things out. You're trying to solve the wrong problem. Even with a substantial raise, people will leave or sink back into demoralization when you haven't corrected the real source of the difficulty. Money—like aspirin—provides temporary relief; meanwhile, the disease can worsen.

Another major issue—and thus, common gripe—that's tied to motivation is opportunity for promotion. When ambitious people feel they aren't getting anywhere, their spirits sag. You can, in some instances, encourage them to develop new areas, expand old ones, and enlarge the department, enabling both of you to move up. But at best the number of promotions you can give out is limited, and when ambitious people don't "make it," they become dissatisfied. If you can't meet their need for advancement, it's time for them to leave.

If you've created a positive environment, an ambitious staff member will generally work constructively and remain as long as possible, with everyone the gainer. Even less ambitious people will produce well above average in such an environment.

There are some fairly universal wants—in addition to dollars and promotions—that almost all people in the workplace have, and you won't go too far wrong by catering to these wants. Your prime key in motivating the people who work for you is in helping them feel their importance to you—letting them know that you know their contribution is worthwhile. In fact, many people live in negative environments at home, and will come to work eagerly if you establish a positive environment on the job. If you, as manager, can make them feel valued and, therefore, see themselves as better human beings—they'll *want* to come to work and to produce for you.

Why is it that we sometimes fail to see the positive qualities of people who work for us? I think it's because we become preoccupied with people's defects and shortcomings when we are in a position of being overly dependent on them. The desperately dependent supervisor or manager—particularly one who is unsure of herself—feels helpless when confronted with a large problem. Overwhelmed, she turns to others for the solution, without regard to their ability to solve it. When they inevitably fail her, she is disappointed. She criticizes, blames. The people around her never measure up, and that kind of disappointment gets communicated at one level or another and demoralizes those who work for her.

The independent supervisor, however, can weigh up strengths and weaknesses and position people accordingly. Instead of pulling on people for what they cannot or will not do, she changes job descriptions, shifts and transfers, fires and hires—always basing her decisions on people's abilities and developing strengths. When you've positioned people properly you bring out the best in them.

What, specifically, can you do to create this good environment?

- *Verbalize your appreciation of people publicly.* People want other people to know their value. (Analogy: think of how you feel when your child or husband treats you well in public as against how you feel when they criticize you. How many at-home fights are caused by a public put-down by a husband or child?)
- *Give a lot of responsibility.* Give as much as people are capable of and want (not everyone wants it). Assign tasks that people will succeed with, that keep them in touch with their competence.
- *Teach, don't criticize.* Don't make people feel inadequate or stupid. Criticism should be given in such a way that it indicates you believe the person is capable of learning. You can pass the same information along as either a critical "You should have," or a teaching "Have you thought about . . . ?"

• *If something goes wrong, don't punish with anger or threats.* If you terrify your staff, they are motivated to cover up rather than produce. A frightened employee will avoid you instead of calling on you to help straighten things out.

• *Answer questions.* Don't brush people off. If you make them feel like a nuisance, they don't feel valued.

• *Give empathy and support.* While the degree of need for assistance varies, people need to know that you recognize the scope of their problems and that you give help where feasible. Even if you can't provide solutions, you can be a sounding board. A few good questions can often help your employees find their own solutions. If you have a leaner—someone who needs constant assistance and reassurance—you have to weigh up what they're giving you versus what they're taking from you. If the scorecard looks bad, they need to be assigned to more routine work with less ambiguity.

• *Take time for fun.* You need to create a relaxed environment. Take time for a story, a joke. Don't let your anxiety about getting the job done stop you from paying attention to people. It's part of the boss's job. If people take a breather and enjoy themselves, you'll get a thousand times more work from them. The best work is done when people are motivated, and enjoyment is a major factor. Keep the big picture in mind.

Even under the most difficult conditions you can apply some of the above tools. One distressed client asked me how she could motivate a crew of busboys who had nothing to look forward to but more hard work. She actually agreed with them that the less they did, the better off they were. At my suggestion, she reminded them that many of their customers were there for a hard-earned treat, and that the busboys had a lot to do with how enjoyable that evening out was. During slow hours she made a point of talking individually with them. She also intervened actively and defended them in some of their battles with waiters.

All this takes plenty of time and thought—but there's no question that it's worth the effort—first, in terms of your own satisfaction in creating as pleasant an environment as possible for yourself and those around you, and second, when you measure it against what a motivated work force can produce.

12. I HAVE TROUBLE SUPERVISING WOMEN

The art of supervising different groups and individuals • The
woman who resents doing a service job • Why some women resent
working for a woman • Dealing with a subordinate's impatience to
advance

Your supervisory role is always the same yet ever changing. The aspect
that stays the same is that, as an effective supervisor, you are always in
charge of the shop and in charge of yourself—a pro. The aspect that necessarily changes has to do with your relationships with the men and women
who work for you.

With some of your staff people, you'll need to be more directing; with
others, less directing; and, with still others, perhaps out-and-out tough.

The art of supervising is the art of understanding the needs and talents
of the individuals you supervise. It is also the art of recognizing group, as
well as individual, differences. It doesn't follow that if you can supervise
adolescents in a camp setting, you'll have no difficulty translating your
style over to the supervision of elderly hospital volunteers; or that if you
can supervise a team of ball players, you can just as easily supervise a team
of writers struggling to put together a TV script. There are problems that
are unique to each group of people and each setting.

The complaints that follow in the next pages all deal with supervision of different groups of people. You will notice that I don't recommend your adapting a new supervisory style to cope with each complaint. I do recommend weighing the expectations of the people in each
group—how they see their jobs, their situations in the company, and
your performance and attitude as their boss—against your own expectations of them. Then see what you can do about bringing these two sets of
expectations closer together.

Supervising other women is our first concern. I often hear women say
they'd much rather hire men to work for them, that women are too difficult.
Frequently, there is a note of chagrin in the woman's voice, as if she is disappointed, that she had somehow assumed that women—being "sisters"—
would be more helpful, more understanding, more supportive of a female
supervisor.

Not so. Many women resent woman bosses far more than they do male bosses. You still hear "I'd rather work for a man" from women who toss off those words as if it's the most natural thing in the world.

It's no wonder. As a result of our female conditioning, many women have been brainwashed into accepting, even desiring, subordination to men. They'll do everything possible to help a male boss but won't lift a finger for a female boss. They have the well-known office wife syndrome. They feel important only if they serve an important man.

The reality of this syndrome was vividly demonstrated for me several years ago during a business meeting. The male representative of a consulting firm developed a headache. He phoned his secretary, who cheerfully rushed across town to deliver his aspirin to him. What struck me most strongly was that when the secretary entered the meeting room and handed her boss the pills, she displayed obvious pride and delight in being able to help him in this personal way.

I imagine some women bosses have similar relationships with their secretaries, but I also suspect that it's rare. The office wife believes she is unable to achieve on her own. She gains status by being "married" to a male boss—much as the wife at home felt in the old days (and sometimes still does). By identifying with the "superior" sex, the office wife is able to feel herself superior to the other women around her. But if she is working for a woman, the office wife doesn't have the same opportunity to shore up her ego. If she doesn't hold women in high esteem, she can't gain status by identifying with her boss. In order to hold on to her sense of importance, she attempts to bring her supervisor down to her level. She sets out to undermine her boss—either subtly through noncooperation, or harshly by open attack.

The noncooperative woman employee does not present as big a problem for women managers who are well-established in relatively high-level positions as she does for the newer women managers who are just starting to move up—and leaving others behind. These latter managers are still close enough in level to the women they are supervising to be resented. Also, they are close enough to be regarded as weak and vulnerable. Unlike the well-established woman manager, with whom the worker can identify much as she would an important man, the new manager is seen as someone whom the supervisee can compete with and possibly even beat.

What to do? If you are having trouble with a woman employee who won't cooperate *because* you are female, try to understand the self-hatred that is the wellspring of her attitude. You may not be able to change her, but you may be able to make some headway in getting her to accept your authority. The trick is to make sure that she understands that you are above her. Don't try to be equal, woman to woman.

Since the problem is caused by her seeing women—including the two of you—at very nearly the same level, you have to create hierarchical distance between you. The greater the distance in her mind, the more she'll accept you as boss. You have to be superior enough (as men are) to be respected. Remember, people who are not satisfied with what they have resent, not the queen who has palaces throughout the land, but the neighbor across the street who's living a cut above them.

Be strong. It's your strength—not your sympathy or compassion—that will encourage female-resenting female supervisees to accept your leadership. Never give way by lessening or altering your requests. Hold firm to them and *expect* cooperation.

You may even change her mind about women. After all, here you are, a woman, yet you are strong, important, powerful. Even if you don't make her view women in general in a new way, you make her see *you* differently, and you will have moved into that group of people too formidable for her to compete with.

There is another difficulty in supervising women, although this is one that male as well as female supervisors encounter. In a sense, it's the opposite of the difficulty discussed above.

Some women supervisees are highly unwilling to remain in service jobs, like that of secretary, for very long, and whatever their job, they are unwilling to do small service tasks for anyone, male or female.

As one of my clients pointed out: ''I can't seem to find a good secretary anymore. Every secretary I hire plans to use the job as a stepping-stone, and as soon as she's picked up the least bit of familiarity with the business, she moves on to another company in a more elevated slot.''

Yes—certainly. There is a leveling-out process in the works. Many women who were held back by their own lack of awareness and the world's prejudices are now leaping ahead. In addition, there has been a definite change in how women view doing service jobs. Like it or not, the rest of society has had to adjust to it.

Your best bet with female supervisees who are longing to get ahead is to recognize and credit their yearnings. Deal with their impatience. Be generous—without giving up your supervisory role. When their expectations for quick advancement are not met, explain why. Encourage those who are talented by delegating to them as much sophisticated and complex work as you can. Suggest to the women beneath you that in *your* department, under your aegis, they will have excellent opportunities to move ahead. But, in turn, they have to help build that department by making it function well at every level.

If you are in the kind of department where there is no place for them to advance, you can in this way at least create an environment that will keep them working for you for a reasonable length of time—and when it comes time for them to move on, you'll have another good contact in the industry.

13. I HAVE TROUBLE SUPERVISING MEN

"Beaten—and by a girl!" • Why the woman boss fears being unattractive • Competing with men • Building authority over men • Looking well-connected • To use—or not to use—your femininity

Many men, even those who give lip service to notions of equality, find the reality of a female boss intolerable. They simply cannot bear to play the subordinate role to a woman. Their resentment is all the worse if the woman got to where she is by competing with them. It's as if they experience a throwback to childhood fears. "Beaten—and by a girl!" they seem to be saying. They feel diminished, unmanly, and they hate you for it. They'd like to see you fail in the job that has put you ahead of them.

Women, too, feel uncomfortable with this reversal of the standard roles that both sexes learned early on. It's difficult for them to step into the male "boss" role. Women are taught that men are the leaders, and that any woman who threatens the superior male position is dealing a critical blow to his ego.

Women's problems as supervisors of men have less to do with direct resistance to their leadership than with this insidious—and internalized—belief system that holds that when you take charge you deflate the male ego. Women who make men feel inadequate are "emasculating," and just about the worst thing a woman can be is "emasculating." Women in this position often see themselves as unattractive to men and indeed often feel that they are truly unattractive human beings. The punishment, of course, for your unfeminine behavior is aloneness.

You first have to deal with your own resistance to being the boss over men by recognizing that the threat of the label "unfeminine" has long kept female behavior in a prescribed mold. Understand that you are not respon-

sible for how men react to your success. Their attitude, as well as their position, has to do with who they are—you did not cause either. For some men,
any behavior by a woman that implies equality is felt as emasculating, and
is thus considered unfeminine and labeled harshly. Some men are more
competitive, some men are more hostile toward women. Some admire
strong women and team up readily with them.

One thing is certain: you cannot allow yourself to try to protect the male
ego in business by hiding your ability, as many women do in social situations. Even if it "works" socially, the price you pay by demeaning yourself in any situation is enormous. At work, there's no gain. If you show
weakness, you'll lose respect, support, and your job. Never deal from
weakness. Resist any temptation to accommodate the male need to be a
hero. Don't dish yourself up as rescue material by appearing to be helpless.

The problem, as in competing with women, is more intense when you
beat men out in direct competition. In general, there's an easier acceptance
if you come in on a well-established high level. Therefore, the solution is
also the same as with your women supervisees: position yourself as quickly
as possible with a show of strength. Act the manager role all the way. Move
in quickly. Give men their own territory, but don't let them near yours.

Display your connections with those above you so that you appear
important—and if you don't have these connections, at least look as if you
do while you develop them. The men who work for you must see you as
part of the power structure. You cannot afford to have them see you as isolated. One client of mine was so poorly connected that she had an almost
empty datebook visible on her desk. I advised her to fill it up with names
and notations, however fictitious, while she was trying to solve the real
problem of establishing allies.

If you fail to make these moves, the men you supervise will continue to
compete with you, encouraged by their own belief that you are a weaker female—and by the evidence you've given them that supports their belief. As
one man bluntly stated, "I hate to say this about myself, but when people are
in my way I go after the women first. They're the easiest to dispose of."

Be very careful about showing any weakness that might encourage
competition. Take your place as a leader, matter-of-factly. Don't let anyone work around you. If you have to err, err on the side of strength.

Just as women try to extract cooperation from women with niceness,
the woman manager might attempt to get support from men in her company
by relying on her feminine attractiveness. If that's the way you've always
gained male attention—if men who were attracted to you did things for you,

gave you favors and gifts, advice and assistance, as men are likely to do when they're attracted to women—you might unconsciously, even compulsively, rely on that to get the cooperation you desperately need. But it won't work—certainly not over the long haul. Men put their business and professional needs first, and they won't necessarily play ball just because there's a little romantic electricity in the air.

14. I HAVE TROUBLE SUPERVISING FRIENDS AND EX-PEERS

What to do with friends who put you down • Coping with friends who won't accept your authority

When you get promoted, you may find yourself having to give assignments and criticism to people with whom you formerly had a very different relationship—quite equal and quite friendly. It can be a difficult predicament. Your friend or ex-peer may not take your requests seriously, or may not take you seriously. He or she may in every way resist the shift in rank and continue to treat you in the same old way. The company has promoted you—but your friends won't.

Acting as if nothing has changed between you and your friend or ex-peer will not make the problem go away. In fact, it will encourage it. Don't try to laugh off your new status, and don't let the friend or ex-peer mock you without responding. *Something fundamental has changed.* You must face up to this and act in such a way that everyone else faces it. You now have, willy-nilly, a new relationship to one another. Your work friendship and your equal relationship on the job are now in the past.

At work, you now must be the boss. Jump right into your new role. If your friend scoffs at your authority with inappropriate wisecracks or put-downs, or just resists cooperating with you, deal with it fast. Each time you let this behavior go by, you encourage it to continue. You may hope your friend will eventually settle into the new reality and spare you the difficult task of establishing authority, but if he or she is uncooperative at the outset, that's not likely to happen. There preexists, long before you became a supervisor, a lot of resentment in many people against being bossed by anyone—perhaps for good reasons. Many of us have suffered at the hands of overly bossy parents, teachers, siblings, previous supervisors, husbands. One place people can hold the line is with their own friends, and they might not easily deliver to you any kind of power over themselves.

You, for your part, may be afraid of engendering resentment by playing the boss role. You may be hoping that cooperation from your ex-peers will arise just naturally out of the good feelings and the friendship that you had together in the past. But when you see that your new position is not respected, recognize the failure of friendship as a supervisory tool.

You may want to continue some social interaction—but save it for after hours. Talk business during business periods and social during social periods. When and if your friend moves to personal conversations of yesteryear say, "I'd like to hear about it, but this is not a good time." When your friend says, "Now that you're the boss you're not having lunch with us," say, "Yes, things have changed and I miss those lunches." When your friend replies, "You're too good for us now," say, "I don't believe that I'm better than anyone. I do have different responsibilites and I want to concentrate on them." When your friend responds to a request from you with "Come off it. You know I can't stand that work. Give it to Jane (Jane whom *we* don't like)," say, "I don't like assigning work you don't enjoy, but I still need you to complete this project. Jane's busy. I'd appreciate it if you'd get it to me by tomorrow morning."

You don't have to be stern, angry, snobbish, or distant—just professional. You've contracted with your boss to do a job and you're doing it. What do you do if your friends persist? I doubt they will if you stick to your guns. When they see that *you* are not in a power contest—that for you the issue of your role was settled by your promotion—they will find there is no point in teasing or defying you. They can't demote you with their attitude. Your very quickness at assuming the traditional authoritative boss role will help your friends see you in a new light. Aloud they may be saying, "I wouldn't want the job, she can have it." "Did she change!" Or even, "She's only out for herself." But in no time at all they'll also be saying, at least to themselves, "No wonder they made her, not me, the supervisor!"

15. I HAVE TROUBLE SUPERVISING OLDER PEOPLE

Why family roles don't apply • How to cope with the resentment of those who didn't make it • Feeling like a kid

There may be great resistance to your authority on the part of people who have been stuck in the company on the same level for a long time, or on the part of people older than you. They may consider you an up-start. They've been up against a tough system, and if they feel they've missed out on satisfying careers, or if they feel like failures, their resentment of your success might take over. Your own attitudes can encourage or discourage the hostility of these old-timers. If *you* feel it's unfair that you've been put in charge of older or more experienced people, then you are agreeing with them that you should not be where you are. If, on the other hand, you assume—and act—as if you've been put in charge because, age and experience be damned, you have those qualities that are necessary to make things work, then they'll respect you and, in respecting you, feel less resentment.

Think about your discomfort or guilt. It may be a holdover from childhood when we learn that older people have first claim on privileges and prizes. Parents and older siblings do things long before little you. You have to wait your turn. Moreover, you're supposed to obey your elders. Your new job—supervising older, more experienced people—reverses that "natural" order of things. You feel you're not taking your turn. It seems like stepping out of the supermarket line and moving to the front—unfair. But the rules for each situation—raising kids, standing on supermarket lines, and functioning in the workplace—are different, and when you move the rules unthinkingly from one place to the other, you're stuck with misguided guilt.

There may be some logic to your discomfort. Some qualified people might have been overlooked because of discrimination against older workers. Management may have a fixed idea about the proverbial enthusiasm, energy, or commitment of the younger worker, or the supposed cynicism and feelings of defeat or withdrawal of the middle-aged employee. On this round you've benefited from prejudice against older people. But prejudices are always in operation. You yourself have probably paid the price, often enough, of one kind of prejudice or another: against short people or tall people, rich people or poor people, black, white or green people—or against women. In school, at home, and at the department store counters, we're all victims of stereotypical thinking. There are many factors to be weighed in the selection of a supervisor. Maybe management made the best possible choice, maybe they didn't—but take advantage of your break when your abilities are recognized. And remember that as you move up, you'll be in a better position to recognize and reward the abilities of those who have been overlooked because of prejudice.

It's easy to resent a supervisor whose demeanor seems to be conveying, "I don't know why it's me and not you in this slot," but it's not so easy to resent someone, however young or new on the job she may be, who takes over with confidence. While you may be tempted to say, "You're as good as I am, I'm just here by luck," it's important to assume your place, matter-of-factly, as a leader. When you do, people may decide wistfully that they've missed the boat, but instead of building up resentment against you, they'll blame fate.

I've often heard an old-timer say with envy, yet acceptance, of a bright, young, new manager: "She's that new generation. You have to admire her. She's confident and aggressive." They recognize and can accept the qualities that got you there.

16. I HAVE TROUBLE SUPERVISING PEOPLE I DON'T LIKE

What to do with an employee who's not producing • How to deal with overtalking, complaining, and other annoying characteristics

You don't need to like those you supervise, any more than they need to like you. However, you do need to work well together. As a supervisor, you can form a relationship with a person's skills—a limited relationship—not with the total person.

At work we tend to like people who are helpful and who do well, and to dislike those who don't. Watch out for mistaking personal dislike for resentment of poor work performance. One of my clients complained, "Because I don't *like* Ms. X, I can't evaluate her work properly. I find it impossible to be fair about her. She keeps trying to impress me with how hard she's working, how late she's staying, how much she's learning. But I can never accept it. I never believe her. It's because I just don't like her."

When we examined the actual situation, I discovered that Ms. X was a good talker but a poor performer. She kept telling my client about her accomplishments, what she would do and could do, but in reality her job performance was terrible. No wonder my client "disliked" her. My client was confusing dislike with disappointment. I advised her to set specific, definite goals and deadlines with this employee. This was done. The employee was asked for daily reports on her accomplishments. In addition, I suggested that my client let the staffer know she wasn't accepting words for deeds: "I know you feel you are working hard and staying late, but I'm interested in what you are producing rather than in the concentration you are devoting or the hours you are putting in." Once this criterion for evaluation was verbalized, and the expectations to meet specified goals were clarified, it became quite obvious that the employee was not doing the job. My client fired her.

What about the person who does the job but just isn't your cup of tea? You don't enjoy working with her. Now that you're sure it's not the way she does the job that bothers you—it's *her*—learn to keep the relationship limited. If qualities you find distasteful pop up in your limited interactions—if the person is petty, hostile, combative, competitive, crude, whatever—reduce your contact even more, eliminating opportunities for that person to annoy you.

You can also try dealing with the annoying quality by showing in a comparatively tactful way that you don't have much tolerance for it. For example, if the person is an overtalker, someone who spells out every last detail in her business reports, you might interrupt and say, "I'd like to explore this thoroughly, but I don't have much time. Can you formulate the problem in one sentence or send me a brief memo?" Then, stand up and usher your overtalker toward the door. If you do this consistently, the employee may learn to use his or her time with you wisely.

If you're not interested in your employee's small talk, stand up and walk toward the door, saying, "Unfortunately, I don't have time during the workday for other topics. I'd like to be able to talk, but my work is pressing."

To petty complaints or hostile remarks, interrupt with a brief nonagreeing statement or with no response, turning quickly to other subjects. Through your nonresponse, you can communicate the point that you are uninterested.

When you are not a compliant victim of other people, putting up passively with their distasteful qualities, but instead are able to guide the relationship assertively and accomplish what *you* want to accomplish, then you will find that you can work effectively with a much wider range of people.

17. HOW SHOULD I DEAL WITH SOMEONE WHO MAKES A LOT OF MISTAKES?

How to criticize people • The problem with being "nice" • When to give up on someone: a checklist

If this is your complaint, make sure that you are not inviting errors by failing either to give clear instructions to your staff or to evaluate their performance adequately. Many of us tend to ignore an error at first because we find it unpleasant to criticize. It's easier to take a wait-and-see position. We're tempted to let errors go by, hoping they won't happen again. Take, for example, a poorly organized meeting. We hope the project director who failed to organize a meeting carefully—who didn't make sure the attendance was good and the key people were present—will correct this obvious error himself, and not repeat it next time. However, when we don't offer criticism, or when we offer it weakly, we're conveying to the person who is responsible for the error that it's not very important to us. We're virtually giving him the okay to do it again. If you find calling attention to errors distasteful and duck it, the problem starts with you, not with your employee.

So first off, if you have someone working for you who makes a lot of mistakes, increase your supervision. Be on the alert for errors and the need, like it or not, to give feedback. If you feel you're being hard on someone, think about how much harder it will be for all parties concerned if you let it go and the mistakes persist. Under the impression that you are being "nice" or going easy on someone, you are encouraging a poor performance that eventually will get you both into trouble. If you tackle the problem early on and consistently, you are also establishing a basis for a performance evaluation. If he doesn't improve, you'll be on solid ground when your evaluation is negative.

How you go about pointing out people's errors to them is what really counts. Harsh criticism—"The meeting didn't accomplish anything at all. It was a complete waste of time"—can make the "guilty" party frightened, resentful, or stubborn. You give him a better chance with something like: "You had many important things to say, but the value of your work was undermined by poor attendance. It seems to me you need to strengthen the planning side of your meetings."

After you've established your standard, you're in a position to appraise someone's ability to learn. Watch his direction. Is his work getting better, or do the mistakes keep piling up? If someone is resistant to learning, you need to evaluate the requirements for the job this person is doing. Can these functions actually be adequately performed by someone with his particular background? Do you have to change the job? Or do you have to change the person who's doing the job?

Is the job too broad in scope for the kind of salary you're paying? Are you asking a secretary to be an administrator; an administrator to be a salesperson?

Are you underestimating the need for training, background, experience? Try to explore how jobs are broken down in the labor market as a whole. It's easier to find experienced people to correspond to standardized job descriptions.

Or the other way around: can you make the job uncommon? Can you keep the functions your mistake-maker is good at and hand over to someone else those she's bad at? If she is good at detail and inept with people, can you transfer the ''people'' part of the job to someone else?

If you cannot change the nature of the job itself, you will have to find the right person to do that job. Don't try too hard or too long to make things work out. It's often time-consuming and difficult to find new people, but you're better off investing in a solution. Like women who try to remake the men they marry, if you try to make people be what they obviously are not, you generally make things worse.

18. THE PEOPLE I SUPERVISE ARE SO OVERWORKED THAT *I* END UP DOING *THEIR* WORK

Why you *can't* help out • Five alternative solutions to overworking yourself

Martha's Story

Martha, an assistant sales manager in a group insurance agency, had a hardworking secretary who, when things piled up on her desk, would protest, ''I don't know how I can possibly do all this. I've got enough to keep me here until midnight every night the whole rest of the month!''

Martha wasn't angry with her secretary. She thought the woman was right—the job *was* too demanding. When Martha brought the problem to her boss's attention and asked for more help, he responded with a categorical no. "You'll just have to figure out a way to do it." With no alternatives, when her secretary complained Martha too often found herself saying, "Okay, I'll take care of it myself." As a result, the creative and developmental aspects of her job—which weren't on a day-to-day deadline—were lost in the shuffle. Her bosses became disappointed at her apparent inability to evaluate the larger picture and present new ideas, and, eventually, Martha lost her job.

Martha's basic mistake was in hearing the boss's no as closing off all alternatives beyond doing the work herself. She didn't think of the many possible solutions, depending on the situation—including making out a better case for more staff, or passing the work along to others, or even cutting down on her secretary's workload by expanding the work of her department, as Ruth did.

Ruth's Story

Ruth, an archivist, had a similar problem: a staff of exactly one overworked researcher. Her carefully documented requests for extra staff were being repeatedly turned down.

Our solution was to suggest that she add on to her small department another function. She proposed that the archives be made more accessible to the general public as a way of getting her company more well-known, a goal Ruth knew her boss had long had in mind.

Together, we drafted a memo, outlining the rationale, resources, and goals of the proposed enlarged department—also, the need for one more person on the staff. Her boss jumped at the plan. Now, with two people on her staff, Ruth was able to juggle job descriptions and thus lighten her valuable researcher's workload.

Being pressured to do more than you can handle is a difficult problem to solve, but if you want to advance, you have to protect your creative time. Here are a few things you can try:

• *Slow down the work.* Establish new, realistic deadlines for all projects. That will require standing up to your boss when he puts the pressure on you, and maybe even showing him how to get the pressure off himself. You cannot say yes to every deadline and project. Be cooperative, and on the side of management—but don't agree to unrealistic demands. Say,

"Let's talk to the client together and convince her that more time on the project will work to her advantage. She'll have a better product in the end."

• *Let an assistant absorb some of the pressure.* Or get an assistant who is a workaholic—who'd rather be at work than at home, and who will use her extra efforts to her own advantage, as a stepping-stone to a better job.

• *Sell management on giving you more help, more staff.* Present the logic of the situation persuasively or develop a strategy like Ruth's.

• *Keep management aware of the consequences of understaffing.* Set new goals, and inform them: "This staff cannot absorb any more pressure. Our volume will probably remain at around four million."

• *Do a less meticulous job.* Cut corners or lower the standards a little if you have to—but in areas that don't matter, or where no one will notice.

Or do a little of all the above.

Why did Martha fail to see these alternatives? Over and over, women's inability to "ask for" instead of "give to" leads them up the wrong path. Martha saw only one option because she was a perpetual giver. This is not to say that you shouldn't sometimes pitch in—but first things first! You need to relate your own activities to how you are being evaluated. If the job calls for creativity, good relationships, problem-solving, politicking, or whatever, you cannot go overboard on output.

Chapter Seven

PROTECTING YOURSELF

CONTENTS

Introduction

INTRODUCTION

Almost everyone understands, intellectually, that the workplace is often very rough—a jungle underneath, with a kid-glove veneer. Still, most women, when they actually encounter this roughness, are shocked by the reality of it: the amorality, the no-holds-barred competitiveness, the ruthless tactics. Too often they find themselves completely unprepared to deal with the kind of fighting and day-in, day-out jockeying for position that goes on.

Why are they so unprepared? I think it's often because the harsh reality is too much to face and too much to deal with. The moment a woman understands that she can't count on those around her to protect her interests, she has to confront the fact that she has to do it herself. If she feels helpless and unable to cope, she's likely to see things the way she needs to see them—to whitewash over and over again the unpleasant side of people and situations.

As I've mentioned earlier, women are simply not raised to fight. How many women played war games as children? How many of us grew up with the reality of fistfights—out in the school yard, the locker room, the playing field? These activities, whether we approve of them or not, serve to toughen up little boys and prepare them for the battles that lie ahead.

Because women, generally, are so unprepared for the fierce realities of the workplace, they tend to give way when the going gets rough—as it inevitably does—and, thus, they often find themselves becoming the first, and easiest, victims when the first corporate battle begins.

In this chapter, we'll look at the rough stuff together, from the day-to-day pushing and shoving to the no-holds-barred situations and problems. I'll try to show you how to recognize them and handle them—and also how to find ethical ways to do so, without having to turn into a killer shark yourself.

1. I'M BEING FORCED OUT

Women as natural targets • Being "nice" • Reading the danger signs • Fighting back • How to argue with a furious person

Over and over, I hear from women who have made it to the managerial level and then, despite their proven track records, talent, and expertise, find themselves forced out. Women are natural targets. Why? Because women, in general, have little firsthand experience with power struggles.

Welcomed into their important, new jobs with fanfare and praise, they don't expect trouble—and when it starts coming at them, they don't recognize it. They don't know how to read the signs, particularly in the early stages. Even when the signs are almost unmistakable, they still resist reading them because they don't *want* to see what's happening, as mentioned above. Quite understandably, they don't want to become embroiled in arguments, confrontations, unpleasantness, distasteful maneuverings. In short, they don't want to fight. Further, most women who are under attack in the workplace are apt to underestimate the seriousness of their situation; they can't conceive of the kind of force that may soon be directed against them. All this causes women to let a deteriorating situation go on far too long before they actually start fighting back.

Women tend to get squeezed out because they are not tough enough, soon enough. They underestimate the effectiveness of taking a consistently strong stand, and at the same time, they overestimate the persuasiveness of a reasonable, "nice" approach.

While you may get edged out even if you do take a strong stand, your chances of losing are much greater if you don't.

Here are the stories of two women who were faced with the threat of being squeezed out of their jobs, each of whom reacted in a different way.

Maureen's Story

Maureen was brought in by the chairman of a large clothing manufacturing firm to take over as creative head of one of their important, but ailing, lines. She had a good track record for spotting trends and developing products; her assignment now was to create new, exciting products to revitalize the line and turn around the profit picture of the division. She was in the number two spot, reporting to the president of the division, Hal. He was responsible for the administrative side of the business; she, for the creative side.

At the outset, Hal welcomed Maureen. They got along fine for about three months—until it became clear to him that she and the chairman of the board, who had involved himself directly in the resuscitation of the line, were spending a good deal of time together, making major decisions, and that Maureen was having a much greater say in actually running the company than Hal himself did.

Unlike Hal, Maureen had a great deal in common with the chairman: their approaches were compatible, they came from the same "class" socially, and they had similar tastes. Hal, who had been made president of the company just a few months before Maureen's arrival and had barely begun to establish his power base there, began to see Maureen as a direct threat to his position—so he went after her in the old tried-and-tested business-barracuda style.

Maureen didn't know it then, but she was involved in a full-scale war. At the time, she was totally baffled by Hal's lack of cooperation, his vindictiveness, his totally irrational decisions that were actually harmful to the company's interests. The warning signs were there—but Maureen, for all her expertise and intelligence, did not have the experience to interpret them.

As she reconstructed it for me, it all started the day she discovered that Hal had called a meeting of the sales and promotion departments without inviting her. At this meeting, key decisions were to be made concerning the marketing of new products—how they would be presented to the public, how much should be spent on launching them, where they would be introduced—all decisions that could make or break a new product. As creative head, Maureen was responsible for the success of new products. If "her" products failed, she failed, and the whole division failed. She knew it was crucial for her to be at this meeting. She therefore went, uninvited, to the meeting, and explained to Hal why it was important for her to be there—she thought he didn't understand that he needed her special knowledge of the new product line and her experience in marketing this type of product. "All right," he said, apparently convinced—allowing her to stay and to present her somewhat belated ideas. In her naiveté, she imagined she had made her point.

If Maureen had had even a glimmer of what was in Hal's mind—to tie her up in cunning, bureaucratic knots and then cause the chairman himself to toss Maureen out into the cold, with a three months' severance check in her hands—she might have acted in time. If she had seen the attempt at excluding her from the meeting in its true perspective—as the opening gun in a full-scale, unilateral state of war—she might have been wise enough to take hold much more forcefully.

She should have stepped in hard and fast by taking charge of all the meetings she needed to have to ensure the success of her products. She could have backed up her explanations to Hal at the original meeting by drawing up a schedule of future meetings and sending it out to the participants with a note: "I've set up the following tentative schedule for our planning and marketing meetings. Please let me know if you have a problem with any of these dates." Then she could have sent out invitations to each meeting, following these up with reminders, and set the agendas. Her actions would have convinced everyone involved that she was indeed someone to be taken seriously. At the same time, she should have set about to establish her own strong individual relationships with the sales, advertising, and promotional people.

If Maureen had moved in strongly, Hal might have backed down—or he might have tried to join forces with her, since she was so well-connected at the top. It's hard to know, but in any case it's unlikely that he would have pursued the course he now embarked on. Once he saw that Maureen wasn't going to be a formidable enemy, he moved in to sabotage her in every conceivable way.

At first, he just sat on her projects. All her hard work wound up in memos that were relegated to the bottom drawer of his desk, awaiting his approvals—approvals that never came. When she pressured him to set up meetings to get things moving, he would agree to the appointment and then not show up. When she protested, he threw up one excuse after another. Maureen tried everything: she called to confirm meetings in advance, she wrote memos reminding him of the important issues that had to be discussed, she proposed that they set up a weekly breakfast meeting before office hours to avoid interruptions.

Unfortunately, Maureen was trying to deal with Hal on the wrong level. She kept interpreting his behavior as ignorant and insensitive to the needs of the company. She was irritated, sometimes contemptuous, sometimes puzzled, always wondering what was wrong with him. She simply could not bring herself to believe that he was out to get her. She thought it was crystal clear that his future rode on her success with the new products, and that he would be cutting his own throat by undermining her. Her logic was: "Let's come out with winning products—and put them out right. Let's look at the bottom line.'' His barracuda logic was: "Let's look out for Number One first and get that dame out of here. Then, let's look at the bottom line.''

Meanwhile, since Hal could see there was no real opposition, his moves became bolder. Now he started to undermine Maureen with her own staff. Once he asked her for a routine confidential report evaluating the members of her staff and outlining the personnel shifts and changes she wanted to make. Then, a short time after he got the report, he called in, one by one, the staff members about whom she had made negative evaluations, saying, "Why is she trying to get you into trouble? Look at the terrible things that woman is saying about you! She's irrational.'' He actually held out the damning paragraphs to them, showing that he was on their side.

When Maureen finally heard about this some months later, she was furious—but the damage had already been done. Now, at long last, she knew they were at war.

She fought back by working harder in order to come up with even better products and, thus, better earnings. She imagined that if she had a real winner she would be safe.

What she didn't understand was it didn't matter what she came up with; Hal was undermining her ideas every time. He took her best idea—one that was exciting, new, and slightly controversial, but which had the most potential—and built up a case against it by getting his sales manager buddies to send in memos predicting consumer resistance and, thus, low sales. Then, as president, he was able to reject the idea in full equanimity.

Maureen did manage to get some excellent products out into the marketplace, but by the time these products had proved their success on the bottom line, she was long gone from the company.

In the final stage of his campaign, Hal set out to work on the chairman—to show him that Maureen's record, both in the house and in the stores, was very poor. He worked up projections purporting to show that her products would result in the company's worst sales record of the decade; he dropped hints to the chairman about the supposed low morale of her staff and how isolated she kept herself from them; he composed complaining memos to her concerning imaginary lapses and errors on her part, diligently passing carbons along to the chairman.

His campaign proved effective. The chairman grew more and more disenchanted with Maureen and the formerly excellent relationship between them cooled. Hal had won out—he had gotten past his main obstacle. Now, he informed Maureen that the chairman no longer wished to be involved in the day-to-day operations of the division—and that from now on she was not to deal directly with him. She should go through channels—that is, through President Hal himself.

It now became clear to Maureen that the situation was hopeless. She resigned, deciding that the company was totally mismanaged; that the chairman was subject to irrational mood swings and was unable to sustain a good opinion of anyone for any period of time; and that President Hal was a vicious shark and not too bright.

Her opinions of these people were undoubtedly close to the truth, but it is a fact of life that in this world there are difficult and unethical people, and women must learn how to deal with them. The first step is to learn to recognize the early warning danger signals.

What could Maureen have done if she had understood early on what she was up against? She could have worked through Hal, making him part of everything and, thereby, making herself seem less of a threat to him. Or she could have forced the issue. She could have taken a stand, insisting on the conditions under which she could and would do the job. She could have let him know that there was a risk in trying to cut her out—that he'd have a fight on his hands, one that he might lose. Even though he was over her, she could—since he was uncooperative and hostile—have competed with him for the territory she needed to put her products over, and she could have refused to let him into her territory. In fact, she could have used her good relationship with the chairman to undermine Hal and to get more autonomy for herself.

There's no guarantee that Maureen would have won out, no matter what she did, but by following the no-contest course she guaranteed that she would lose.

Although in retrospect the outlines of what happened and why it happened seem starkly clear, the fact is that until Maureen and I analyzed the situation together two years later, she had no inkling of the real reasons she had been attacked so ruthlessly by Hal and later abandoned by the chairman. She had buried all thoughts of that unhappy period in her life, yet had lived with tremendous anxiety for these past two years. When what had happened and, more important, *why* it had happened, became clear, her first reaction was "I feel like a fool!" Most people who have had comparable setbacks feel this same way—that there's something wrong with them. As I explained to Maureen, it was important for her to realize that she wasn't just "dumb," and that Hal wasn't just diabolical, and the chairman wasn't just neurotic—rather, that there was a complex, yet typical, dynamic in motion here, and she'd had no preparation to cope with it. When she accepted the fact that, given her inexperience, she couldn't have understood what was going on—any more than someone can understand calculus without studying it—she was enormously relieved.

Norma's Story

Norma also found herself being edged out, but fortunately, unlike Maureen, she realized what was going on in time for her to mount a late, yet nonetheless effective, defense.

Joe, an aggressive and ambitious director of sales, clearly wanted to get rid of Norma, the company's bright young technical director, and replace her with his own candidate—an outside consultant whom he felt would be more sympathetic and amenable to furthering his interests.

Some departments, such as the sales and technical development departments, have conflicting interests, and the result is a natural antagonism. That's what had happened here. In this instance, sales (Joe) would come up with new product ideas for his clients, then sell the clients on these new products—and then put pressure on technical development (Norma) to get the products worked out and on the market so he could deliver on his promises. Technical (Norma) would say, ''It's not that simple—there are a lot of technical problems to be worked out. It will take time.'' Whereupon, sales (Joe) would see technical (Norma) as uncooperative, and probably inept. And technical (Norma) would see sales (Joe) as out for a quick buck—and as undermining the long-range need of the company for solid products.

After several such tangles, Joe came to regard Norma with unconcealed hate. She just plain wasn't delivering, and he was no longer interested in cooperating or communicating with her. Now when he had a new product idea, he skipped Norma entirely and conferred instead with the consultant to the technical department, Phil. Likewise aggressive and ambitious, Phil had originally been brought in by the company's president to help Norma. By now, he was thinking about how he could get rid of Norma and take over her job. He was, therefore, only too happy to cooperate with Joe and would invariably come up with quick, seemingly sound solutions to Joe's requests for new products. Most of the designs, modifications, and innovations that Phil sketched out so speedily proved to be impractical from a technical point of view, but that didn't bother him one bit. Putting them into production was Norma's problem, not his. Over and over again, Norma found herself coming to Joe and trying to explain why Phil's ideas could not be implemented; how, after painstaking checking and testing in her laboratories, her engineers had discovered they simply did not work out. But Joe didn't accept her explanations. He thought that she was being totally uncooperative—and was out to get him.

By this time, Joe had built up quite a case against Norma, and because he had a lot of power in the company—not only was he a big producer, but he was a good buddy of the president's—her job was in serious danger.

The first question I asked myself when I heard her story was why did Norma have so little credibility? Why did Joe believe Phil and not her—especially if she had the evidence that the product couldn't be made according to Phil's specifications? Before I could know the reason, I had to examine more closely what went on among the three of them.

I asked Norma if she had ever thought of meeting with both men and trying to prove, right then and there, that Phil didn't know what he was talking about. She could show that Phil hadn't taken into account the real problems involved in implementing the design: the length of time it took to run the requisite experiments, to get delivery on certain scarce components, the shortage of staff, and so on. Norma explained that she had tried to do that, but Phil had a furious temper—"He started yelling and screaming and pounding the table. I thought he would break the table! He goes out of control." So, she went on, when a difference of opinion came up in a meeting, she would keep quiet and later try to catch Joe and explain the problems to him privately. Where the real debate took place—in the meetings with the Joe and the consultant—she faded every time. She kept quiet because she was frightened of anger; but Joe interpreted her silence to mean that she didn't have good reasons for her position. He concluded she was just being obstructionist.

Like many women, Norma backed away from arguments. She was afraid of confrontations. She was more comfortable having a little private talk, like a wife talking to an understanding husband. Norma had to learn how to argue and speak up on her own behalf wherever and whenever it was necessary. We worked out possible dialogues to help her learn how to hang on to her position in the face of Phil's fury.

PHIL (screaming): "Of course it can be done! It's done every day. Don't you understand theory?"

NORMA: "Hold on, now. Let's think this through together. If we—"

PHIL (interrupting, screaming louder, pounding the table): "What the hell is there to think about? It's in every high school textbook!"

NORMA (still calm and collected): "Yes, I understand the theory and I still have two problems. One, the test model overheated, and two, even if we can find a way to make it there's a minimum of a—''

PHIL: "You screwed up the test. I've checked similar ones hundreds of times with no problems."

NORMA: "Well, let's settle it. I am convinced that it won't work, but come into the lab tomorrow morning and let's check it out together, step by step, and by late afternoon, we can bring our findings back to Joe. We still have other problems—the components you want to substitute are difficult to obtain and will take at least six weeks for delivery."

PHIL (mumbling, and looking a little less arrogant): "I don't know where you get your information."

NORMA: (Silence.) She doesn't answer; she drops the argument because it's clear that Phil is beginning to back down, and that this would mark the beginning of her new credibility with Joe.

Because Norma finally fought for her views, she, unlike Maureen, was able to stop the squeeze play and regain her solid position within the company.

2. I'M UP AGAINST A NO-HOLDS-BARRED BARRACUDA

Barracuda behavior • Strategies to dispose of an enemy

When an out-and-out barracuda comes along, you have to get him or her away from your particular section of the water—diverted upstream or downstream, or tossed up onto the beach, but off and away from where he or she can do you any harm. That is self-preservation rule number one.

It's very important that you understand just what I mean by a "barracuda." I'm talking here about someone who is so ruthless, so vicious, so without principle that he or she will try to destroy anyone who stands in the way. Barracuda behavior goes way beyond everyday, garden-variety nastiness, bad-mouthing, a push here, a shove there (for example, the kind of behavior described in Norma's story earlier), which you can handle by being assertive, clever, and strategic. Barracuda behavior calls for much rougher solutions than would be justified in the normal course of business.

Here is how one woman managed to get rid of her no-holds-barred enemy.

Erika's Story

Erika was the director of market research in a medium-sized New York advertising agency. As the agency grew and the work piled up on her, she prevailed upon the president and his two partners to let her hire a highly experienced person to serve as associate director—to act, in effect, as her deputy, taking the day-to-day contact work with the agency's other departments—the creative people, the account executives, etc.—off her shoulders.

The person she hired to be her associate director was a young, bright, and (as it turned out) ruthlessly ambitious man named Max.

Max pitched into his new job with a vengeance. He quickly established himself as one of the boys in the departments he was working with—and then, as is often the case with a hungry, fledgling barracuda, he saw his opportunity in the form of his woman boss.

Since he met with the people in other departments on practically a daily basis, while Erika's own contacts with them were at the more formal weekly staff meetings, Max was able to set into motion a subtle undercover campaign on his own behalf, designed to sabotage the supposedly vulnerable woman boss.

Almost everything he said and did was intended to let his cronies know that they had to protect themselves against the ineptitude, errors, and cover-ups of his, he hoped, soon-to-be-displaced boss.

"The reason your commercial didn't pass Erika's copy test is she didn't interview among the right people." (This to people in the creative department.)

Or, "Keep this to yourself, but let me tell you that you paid too much for that positioning study. Maybe Erika is using her friends as suppliers. I'm certain that study could be done for a lot less money." (This to an anxious account executive.)

Or, "You know, it's highly likely you might have gotten the answer you needed if the questionnaire had been worded differently." (This to creative.)

Or, "The numbers from that study Erika just did are a bit misleading. Ask her to let you read the actual questionnaires. You'll get a much better sense of how consumers really feel about our advertising." (To both account executive and creative.)

Meanwhile, Max was inflating his own role, taking credit for Erika's projects and viciously undermining her at every turn of the road, taking every thought, distorting it, twisting it. When "the boys" didn't like something that came out of his department, when the work of the department created problems for them, he always managed to make it appear as if the trouble had been caused by Erika's errors—or by Erika's lack of concern. She was just not a "team player."

But he had underestimated Erika—and Erika's own, considerable contacts in the other departments. The "vulnerable" woman boss soon got wind of what was going on. (It pays to have a grapevine of your own!)

What could Erika do? She could not very easily fire her seemingly energetic and efficient deputy at this point. Max had too many supporters and probable defenders who saw him as an important ally. They wanted to see him rise to the top in Erika's department—even to supplant Erika herself. Also, Erika realized that by now her deputy looked very impressive to the agency's top brass as well.

She therefore decided to solve the problem within the confines of her own departmental operations, where she could exert control. She set about finding a research project for her deputy—one that was long-range, highly visible, and guaranteed to fail. And, preferably, one that took him out of the office on extended trips.

Soon she hit on the perfect project. She called Max into her office and said, "I want you to drop your regular work and take on this very special assignment." He was being attached to the agency's biggest account, a household products company that Erika knew, from her private conversations with the agency's top executive on the account, might not renew their contract when this year's budget had run out. Max's assignment, to run for the next three months, was to think up a list of imaginative new products for the company to manufacture and to test these product ideas in six key market areas throughout the country. Then he was to write a report, based on his findings, that would be part of the agency's presentation when renewal time came at the end of the year.

Max jumped gleefully at what he saw as his great chance to show his stuff. He spent two full weeks interviewing supermarket customers and then developed his list of imaginative new products for the client: an antidust furniture polish, a nonallergenic household cleanser, a cold-water dishwasher detergent, and so on. Then came six weeks of diligently testing these ideas out in the key market areas. Finally, a last flurry of writing up his history-making report.

The report was used as part of the agency's end-of-year presentation to the client, as Erika had promised, and after the last storyboard, graph, and chart had been packed away, the client turned down each and every one of these new product ideas, good or not. Some days later, as Erika had guessed would happen, the client also sent a "Dear John" letter to the agency president, informing him that they had decided to withdraw the account and try their luck with another, larger agency.

As is often the case when an agency loses a major piece of business and has to cut back, nearly everyone connected with the account was fired—including our young barracuda.

If you, like Erika, are on a ruthless competitor's hit list, here are some other possible solutions you could use to get the barracuda out of your waters.

- *Steer a barracuda down a wrong channel.* Give him or her misinformation so that the project he or she takes off on can never reach fruition.
- *Use the old spring-a-leak gambit.* Make sure the barracuda's competition gets wind of his or her best ideas—so they can get there first. Also, be sure that the top brass hears about all the barracuda's errors, but be careful about bringing the news to them directly. It may be unwise if (as in Erika's case) they favor the barracuda. If they don't have firsthand knowledge of the situation, they might see *you* as a self-serving barracuda.
- *Palm him or her off on a "buddy."* Give the barracuda a raise and a fine performance report and make a gift of him or her to some other highly deserving barracuda in your company. This is a case of wedding one barracuda to another.
- *Recommend your barracuda to a headhunter you can trust.* Say, "Don't quote me, but I think this guy might be interested in leaving." Executive search firms are always on the lookout for talent. With the help of your tip, your headhunter might find the barracuda a job somewhere else.

Some of these solutions are pretty rough. You might not want to go this far, and it would be understandable if you decided to quit your job instead. I believe what I am suggesting, however, can be morally justified in certain situations. And I don't think we should allow ourselves to be outmaneuvered by unscrupulous operatives. We should no longer retreat and leave the field to the bad guys.

3. HOW DO I HANDLE THE FAIR-HAIRED BOY (GIRL)?

How a boss's favorite gets squeezed out • A way to use the fair-haired person to your advantage • How to keep him or her out of your territory in the first place

Enemies are one thing. You have a right—in fact, a responsibility to yourself, if you want to keep your position intact—to "take care" of them. But what about the "fair-haired" boy—or girl? The person who has been brought into the company with the blessings and sponsorship of some higher-up, possibly the president or chairman of the board? The person who may be related to someone up top? The person who is the cynosure of everyone's eye—and is obviously being groomed for a top-executive role? He or she presents an altogether different problem, one that can be a great deal stickier for you to handle—particularly if the fair-haired one is treading on your toes, edging into your turf, or has picked you as the one standing in the way of his or her progress.

Here's a classic story. It plays out again and again. The president of the company meets a bright young star—who's clever, articulate, charming (perhaps with a fine backhand)—through friends who loll around the pool at his summer estate. He takes a shine to this guy, and he wants him in his company. So he picks up the phone and tells his vice president: "I've found the perfect assistant for you." There's the birth of the company's fair-haired boy.

The president proved to be right on the nose in his snap assessment of the young chap. He was perfect for the job—and, for that very reason, the vice president didn't want him around. The president liked and admired the kid too much. Who wants to have someone working under him in the department who has a direct daily pipeline to the boss on his seven-acre estate? Is this young man being groomed for *my* job? Who is this snotty little kid, anyhow? I want the people in my department loyal to me, dependent on me, and I want the power to hire them and fire them. A vice president can get ticked off like anyone else when the new little baby is brought home from the hospital and gets all the attention. The vice president is quite capable at this time of acting like a three-year-old sibling rival. In addition, there's the real political element involved here.

So the vice president sets out to make sure the kid fails. He gives him assignments that no one can handle—that are undoable, difficult, unpleasant—and the fair-haired boy begins failing. The vice president makes sure that the failures are highlighted publicly at meetings: "John, why don't you give us your report on the interview with so-and-so?" John begins to get shaky, to feel self-doubt. On the one hand, he knows there's something wrong with the way the company is functioning and with what is going on, but at the same time, he's doing badly. After several such experiences, he becomes demoralized enough to quit his job.

In my career workshop groups, we found a better way—more ethical and much more effective for all concerned—to handle a fair-haired boy or girl. It calls for self-confidence on your part. I try to teach women to function not out of weakness but from a vantage point of building on their very real strengths so that they do not have to resort to punishment of another human being.

Rachel's Story

Rachel had nothing against Steve, the fair-haired boy who had come in last month as her administrative assistant. He was guilty of nothing at all except being a friend of the president's—and the fact that Rachel had been virtually forced to take him aboard.

Rachel had made a big investment in developing her career strengths —in building her professional talents, her assertiveness ability, her people relationships. Her staff was outstanding in their loyalty to her; the productivity of her department was at the top of the company chart. She was secure both in her job and in herself as a human being. Therefore, she didn't panic at the thought of Steve being a possible threat. Instead of trying to force him out—as many less confident managers might be inclined to do when a fair-haired boy or girl appears on the scene—Rachel and I worked out a way for her to use Steve to her own advantage as well as to his. In the process, she would teach him a good deal about the company's business and the business world in general; and, also, make him an ally and friend rather than an enemy and potential rival.

What she did was to convert Steve into a public relations vehicle for her department. Since he had direct access to the president, she used him as a personal pipeline to get her messages over to the company's top brass. Here's how she did it. She handed him first-rate assignments, gave him valuable pointers along the way, acknowledged his good work, and gave him helpful feedback. In sum, she created an ideal work situation for him and got him on her side. She knew that any news about her that he brought to the top would be cast in a favorable light. Now, when she wanted the president to know about something, she found ways to talk to Steve about it. She would invite him into her office to have a serious discussion, asking for his opinion or his suggestions, or she would simply share the good news with him. After some eighteen months, when he was ready to move ahead, together they dreamed up a new department, with Steve himself as its head. Now, in addition to having a pipeline to the president, she had a good friend and ally in an important position in the company.

Moral: the stronger you are, the nicer you can be.

If you're not as confident as Rachel was, or if you think the boss's protégé really does present a clear and present danger to you, there still may be a chance for you to handle the situation in a humanistic way. Head him off before he gets into the corral—get rid of him at the interview stage. That, in fact, might be the kindest thing you can do.

When the word comes down from above ("I've found this perfect person for you. I want you to see her.") you should be totally cooperative, even enthusiastic, about interviewing the fair-haired candidate. You should go on to have a friendly, receptive interview during which you thoroughly question the candidate and learn as much about the person as possible. The lengthy interview will make the candidate feel attended to, respected, and, at the same time, it will give you the opportunity to discover the excuse for not hiring him or her. You report back to the president, "She's a lovely woman, but she's overqualified. The work here is much too detailed." Or, "He's everything you say and more, but he doesn't have the mathematical aptitude for this job. I think he'd do better starting as a such-and-such. Maybe we can refer him to so-and-so." You've been totally cooperative and helpful—and you've spared yourself and the candidate the unpleasantness of the next months during which you would have to force him or her out.

4. *I'M THE FAIR-HAIRED GIRL*

The Mary Cunningham story • The dependency trap • Why your
sponsor can't transfer his power to you • When the lynching in-
stinct is directed at you

Now, the tables are turned. *You* met the president at the country club or
you are the favorite niece of the controller, the friend of the best friend of
the sales manager. The president ''suggests'' that the vice president in
charge of sales or the production chief or whoever take you on as deputy or
administrative assistant. You come into the office or the plant on a made-to-
your-measure red carpet. Perhaps you see mind-reeling opportunities opening before you (you wouldn't be human if you didn't—coming in this way,
with so much clout behind you). You find yourself immediately on the
spot—everyone is eyeing *you* now, seeing *you* as treading on *their* toes,
edging into *their* turf (''What's she doing here?'' ''Is she after my job?''),
or they see you as the one standing in the way of their progress.

You are in the fair-haired girl spot. What do you do when people are
threatened by you before they even know you?

Women come to my career counseling groups with various types of
''boss's protégée'' or ''fair-haired girl'' problems, and at various stages of
their fair-haired girl lives. Some come in when they are still at the interview
stage—and are wondering why they haven't yet been offered a job. Others
come in when they've been on the job just a few weeks and have found their
backs riddled with flak from co-workers. Still others have been on the job
for a disillusioning year or more and are engaged in life-or-death struggles
with the boss who was forced to hire them. And there are a few who come
to our groups after they have been eased out of their jobs and, riddled now
with self-doubt and wonderment, are asking: ''What happened?'' They
don't know what hit them.

Rosemary's Story

The executive director of a voluntary agency had been searching for a long
time for a top-notch conference coordinator, someone who could set up
conferences and round-table seminars, using the knowledge and talents of
the agency's major officers and professional staff to educate other profes-

sionals and establish the agency as a leader in the field. After weeks of interviewing candidates, the director hit upon Rosemary, who had been recommended to him by his ex-college roommate. She seemed perfect for the job. He was impressed with her personality, proven track record, ideas, and enthusiasm. He immediately hired her.

Rosemary plunged in with zest, and, as the director had expected and hoped, had a series of uninterrupted successes with the dozen or more conferences she organized and ran during the first year. Each new idea she came up with was supported by the director with enthusiasm and budget, staff, space—the works. He worked directly with her (no roundabout, time-consuming, going-through-channels was necessary) and cooperated fully with her. Everyone was aware that the director had made Rosemary his protégée—his fair-haired girl.

By the end of the year, it was clear—at least to the director—that Rosemary could handle much more than the job she was now in. He called her into his office to discuss his plans for her. He had mapped out a very bright future for this fair-haired girl of his. He wanted her to launch a new program to train personnel, which would be, he felt, a natural extension of the work she was now doing. She would set up and run in-house training meetings and seminars for the staff at various levels—in *all* departments—where they would learn more about the functions and aims of their own departments, as well as of the agency in general, and where, conceivably, they would be groomed for more advanced future jobs. This personnel department, the director explained to Rosemary, would be combined with her present conference department into an entire new training and conference division, with herself at its head.

At the next directors' meeting, the executive director made the happy announcement, enthusiastically presenting his plan for developing the new division. The announcement was met with cold silence—and then some hostile questions. "Why do we need this?" "Each of our departments is already training its own people." "Just what kind of training would she be doing?" "What are *her* qualifications?" There was absolutely no support for the director's proposal.

Almost immediately after they stepped out of the conference room, The Treatment started. Not surprisingly, the various managers saw all too clearly that where previously Rosemary's job had been to provide a platform for them, where they could show themselves off to best advantage, now—under this proposed new plan—she would, in a sense, be training them (that is, telling them what to do), and would have a centralized function affecting *all* their departments. They thereupon no longer invited her to meetings. They gave very polite but ineffective responses to her inquiries, proposals, etc. They rerouted or bypassed her memos; instituted a slow-down on passing along important information; and, worst of all, they came in one by one to the director's office, each to express in his own way his objection to the plan and his subtle criticism of Rosemary as a person.

But, unexpectedly, The Treatment was also levied against Rosemary by the director himself. Suddenly, she was no longer his protégée—the fair-haired star-to-be. To her astonishment, he pulled the rug completely out from under her. From full support—budget, resources, frequent meetings with her (an open door), praise, promotions—he suddenly became distant, icy, even insulting. He launched into a cruel (and to her, inexplicable) cam-paign against her—even to the extent of entering a roomful of people and greeting everyone but her. He nit-picked her offhand comments, even criti-cized her use of language and made unfavorable physical comparisons be-tween other women and herself.

Rosemary retreated into a shocked silence. Her air of bubbling sponta-neity left her. Her ideas died before they even got to the vine—she kept them to herself. By spring, she had resigned her job—as everyone, includ-ing the director himself, had hoped she would.

What happened? It is the simplest story in the world. Much as the exec-utive director had originally favored Rosemary and had appreciated her tal-ents and her value to the company, he couldn't stand up to his managers' unified opposition. Even though he was the chief executive, he just didn't have that much power. Indeed, it is unusual for any one person to have that kind of power in a large organization. The directors under him control the vast complex network that *is* the agency. If it comes to a showdown be-tween the entire management group and the chief executive, the chief exec-utive will be forced out. The board of trustees or governing board will back the management group. If the president cannot get the cooperation of his staff, he becomes useless.

Thus, the executive director had no choice. He had to get rid of Rose-mary.

Rosemary's story is similar, in its basic components, to a much more publicly expounded "fair-haired girl" story of the early 1980s. I'm referring to the all-too-well-known Mary Cunningham case.

Mary Cunningham, you may recall, had come into the Bendix Corpora-tion equipped with a Harvard M.B.A. and an incisive, no-nonsense mind.

Her first job was that of executive assistant to William Agee, the company's board chairman and chief executive officer. She proved so efficient and compatible at this job that within fifteen months she received two promotions, first to vice president for corporate and public affairs, and then to vice president for strategic planning. Her duties now were to evaluate the operations of all the divisions of this Fortune-500 corporation and figure out new ways and means to increase its profitability—this at the age of some twenty-seven years.

The corporation's top brass saw red (and blond) and turned on her with a vengeance. The ensuing corporate infighting hit the headlines. According to the press, after Cunningham's promotions rumors began buzzing up and down the corridors of Bendix about an intimate relationship between her and Chairman Agee. Agee himself tried to halt these innuendos by meeting first with Bendix's top management, then with the executive committee of the board, and finally with six hundred company employees, avowing that Cunningham's promotions had been totally justified. He described her contribution to Bendix as outstanding, and denied that her advancement had anything to do with their personal relationship. But his efforts to defend her—and himself—failed. Shortly afterward, she resigned.

What could these two women—the high-positioned, highly visible Mary Cunningham and the relatively lower-level, unknown Rosemary—have done to avoid their "fair-haired girl" problems? Had they themselves committed any errors that had contributed to their downfalls?

What could they have done against the powerful emotions of envy and resentment? The tremendous force with which these lynching emotions operate in competitive situations cannot be exaggerated. In Cunningham's case, the envy and resentment were masked by what is a more acceptable excuse in our culture for ganging up on a woman in the workplace: intimations of "immorality." ("What? Sleeping with the boss? Out!")

It seems likely that both these women felt too safe under the seemingly protective wing of the strongest man in the company. Women tend to be too oriented to "pairing"—the natural order of things, man and woman together—a tendency they carry over into the workplace. They also tend to overestimate the power of men in general, and in particular, in the workplace, the power and protective capacity of the one big man at the top. They imagine this is all they need. Thus, they very often fail to develop other relationships beyond the boss-protégée one.

This places them in a very vulnerable position as they move further up the office pyramid—being promoted to higher jobs, but without allies; without a power base of their own. I know that Rosemary was "guilty" of just such a sin of omission—and, from what I understand of Mary Cunningham's situation at Bendix, I think she probably was, also.

I think that both these women should have refused their promotions and thereby decelerated the process of advancement until they had built up their own personal power bases—with allies who would themselves have benefited through their advancement. This would have gotten the women out of their isolated positions in the office and their dependency on a single person, however loyal and supportive.

5. I'M EXPECTED TO DO THINGS THAT DON'T SQUARE WITH MY VALUES

The issue of payoffs • Why advertising your values can cut you off • When your employer is not interested in quality • If you've gotten entrapped in something shady • When to resign

Most of us who work sooner or later find ourselves in the situation of being called upon to do something that offends our sense of right and wrong—from lying on the boss's behalf (telling his wife he's tied up in a business meeting), to padding a client's bill, to participating in something that endangers the health of workers or consumers.

When you are faced with a serious issue that might compromise your moral standards, you might have to resign from your job, but sometimes you can manage to maintain your own standards by going a quiet route or a clever route.

Rhoda's Story

Rhoda, a purchasing agent with a large manufacturer of stationery and other paper products, had been on the job for some six months when a supplier from whom she was considering buying certain chemicals in quantity sent a $400 camera to her home. The very next morning, she stormed into her boss's office, set the camera down on his desk, and reported the attempt to buy her off. Her boss had, just the past week, written a memo to the staff, reminding them that it was against company policy to accept gifts. She expected him to take immediate action. She also wanted to make clear to him where she stood—that she wasn't accepting any payoffs, that she ran a clean ship. When her boss responded with a shrug of his shoulders and then changed the subject, Rhoda was dumbfounded. As she was leaving, he told her to take the camera with her.

Rhoda was thoroughly confused. She thought she was being a hero—and here she was getting rebuffed, and even, in a way, rebuked.

If Rhoda had stopped to think strategically before she marched into her boss's office, she might have asked herself some pertinent questions. Could it be that her boss was taking payoffs himself? Was his memo simply the standard pro forma notice that was never intended to be followed? What was really her point in going public? What were her chances of accomplishing whatever it was she wanted? What would she be communicating to her boss about herself? How would he regard her in the future?

If Rhoda's boss was taking payoffs himself, her indignation might make him very nervous. Even if he weren't, he might get nervous, thinking that if there ever were a scandal—or even the hint of one—Rhoda might prove to be trouble. He might see her as one of those self-righteous women who appoint themselves as guardians of morality and who kick up a fuss every time someone does anything wrong, big or little. Men tend to stereotype women as overly moral in the best of times; Rhoda's behavior in this instance might reinforce this already distorted stereotype. Further, by presenting her boss with evidence, only a few days after his big antipayoff memo, Rhoda was putting him on the spot. If he in fact didn't want to launch a clean-up campaign, she had put him in the position of appearing to support and condone the supplier's action. She might find herself isolated and alone, cut off from the daily goings-on in the department, possibly blocked from moving ahead, and even eased out completely. She had a lot to lose by bringing the issue to him.

And what did she have to gain? Her expectation was that he would launch a clean-up campaign—but that's not likely to happen. Many people don't feel strongly about such things, and indeed, even if they do, they may not be ready to stick their necks out. It seems to me that this is the kind of issue that one has to handle alone.

Rather than present the camera—and the problem—to her boss, Rhoda would have done better to return the camera to the supplier, explaining diplomatically, "There's a company policy against accepting gifts from people we do business with. I appreciate your sending this, but unfortunately I cannot accept it." In this way, Rhoda would have behaved in accordance with her own standards while avoiding an outspoken public judgment. She would have extricated herself without alienating either the supplier or her boss.

If you really want to change the status quo, you are going to have to develop a well-thought-out, strategic, and full-blown campaign in order to even have a chance of achieving your goal without losing your job.

While Rhoda could have maintained her own moral standards by handling the issue quietly and directly, the solution for Audrey, a client whose boss had a self-serving agenda that wasted the time, money, and resources of the community, was to maneuver him around to more worthwhile endeavors.

Audrey's Story

"I've got to leave this job," Audrey said when we first met. "I'm supposed to be the director of strategic planning of X (a large metropolitan hospital), but my boss is totally self-serving, and if a plan of mine doesn't enhance his ambitious drives, that's the end of it. He couldn't care less about sick people and good medical care."

From Audrey's point of view, good hospital care was the primary consideration, and she objected to her boss's self-aggrandizing goals. Her boss, the overall administrator of the hospital, supported projects that were more in the best interests of his career than in the best interests of the community.

Finally, when he suggested buying a multimillion-dollar piece of nonessential equipment that was very much in the news but which was already in use in a hospital only a few miles away, Audrey took a stand. She presented her case at the next directors' meeting, and spoke privately to several members of the board of trustees, arguing that there were other, more urgent needs. Her point of view was rejected. Her boss's ambitions fit right in with those of the other directors and the board members: they all wanted *their* hospital to be the largest and most impressive facility in the community, and wanted to offer services that seemed to put them at the forefront of medicine.

Audrey was outraged; she felt she had no choice but to resign. "There are alternatives," I suggested. "You argued, and that's fine. But you're giving up too soon. Why couldn't you join your goals with his goals and find projects that would be meaningful to the community and at the same time fulfill your boss's need to have his hospital be the jazziest in the city?'' She could focus her efforts on developing activities that would pass her boss's test of being newsworthy, flashy, and impressive and, at the same time, pass *her* test of being needed, helpful, and significant.

The solution seemed obvious, but Audrey and I agreed that she had been unable to arrive at it because she was stuck at the level of moral indignation—immobilized by the shock of seeing that hospital workers didn't put the community's need for good medical care first. She had chosen her field because she wanted to help people. She simply did not realize that, in some ways, social service institutions and businesses were very much alike. Both are driven by the dynamic of competition. Hospitals compete with each other for funding and patients, just as businesses compete with each other for shares of the market. Admirable or not, what they are both concerned about is whether the company's product or institution's service will get established, whether it will grow in importance or popularity, whether it will sell. Often, the extremely ambitious and self-interested individual serves these goals while serving himself. His personal needs coincide with the needs of the organization.

Once Audrey was able to confront the facts—that this was reality, that one doesn't easily come by the ideal that she had in mind, and, further, that she actually had a chance to accomplish her goals—she was able to start thinking along the lines of the solution I had proposed. Instead of settling for the easier road of sitting back and being morally superior (''I'm right, but he's got all the power—so what can I do?''), she could try to take hold of the problem and maneuver her boss into a more worthwhile course of action.

We've seen how it's possible to find ways to maintain your own standards and avoid doing things that don't square with your own value system. But when there is no way out—if, in order to hold on to your job, you have to violate your own sense of morality or do things that border on illegality or are out-and-out illegal—I'd suggest you resign. If you have already gotten entrapped in something that might be illegal, see a lawyer right away—*before* you resign. Together you can work out a way to protect yourself.

The possibility of your ever being engaged in shady activities on the job may seem remote, but this problem has a way of sneaking up on people, as it did in Helene's case. It has to do with inexperience, fear of losing a job and compliant behavior.

Helene's Story

Helene was a grants administrator in an institute for geriatric care. All projects that were funded by grants were processed through her department, from the development of the initial concept for the grant to the disbursement of the monies after the grant was awarded. Helene was responsible, among other things, for overseeing the expenditures of the grant monies. She approved expense vouchers and watched to see that the expenses were in line with the funding proposals.

Helene's dilemma arose when her boss charged the cost of equipment for his own personal use against various projects throughout the agency. Over a period of some months, he gave her vouchers for a word processor, video cassette camera and recorder, and personal trips, lunches, and cab fares. From time to time, when she expressed concern that the money that he withdrew was not being used for, say, a particular research project, he would counter with: "I've cleared it with the project director. Don't worry, I'm doing some work with them." Helene was not assertive enough to counter his reassuring words with: "I *am* worried and I would rather not sign vouchers for things I'm not familiar with. I would appreciate it if you would handle these yourself."

She didn't have the experience to argue with him and it seemed inappropriate to confront him. She was also afraid of losing her job. She wanted to believe him—it solved her problem—so she allowed his reassuring words to lull her suspicions. But each time he submitted some new, improbable expense, her anxiety resurfaced. She was worried—and with good reason—about being caught in an indefensible position.

Finally, when her anxiety was intolerable, Helene came to me for counseling. I advised her 1) to see a lawyer immediately, and 2) to resign. Her attorney, in turn, suggested that before she resigned she should build up a record to protect herself by making copies of her boss's requests for monies from the grants funds. When her boss put in new requests, her lawyer helped her draft written responses, expressing her opinion that such expenses were not allowable under the terms of the particular grant. She would now be protected in the unlikely event that she would ever be dragged into an investigation.

If you find yourself involved in issues that cry out to be exposed—where for example, the health of workers in the plant is being jeopardized, or a dangerous product is coming off the assembly line—you may want to conduct a public fight. This option has great risks and great rewards—much like those involved in engaging in an open fight against company policies that discriminate against women.

Chapter Eight

SURVIVAL TACTICS

CONTENTS

Introduction

Part 3: Operating Style

1. Don't Get Caught Reading Papers Left Lying on Someone's Desk
2. Don't Isolate Yourself
3. Give In on Small Issues
4. Tell Jokes
5. Say No—a Flat No—When You Are Told to Work Under Someone Who Is at the Same Level You Are
6. Don't Take No for an Answer
7. Step In and Take Over When Things Aren't Moving
8. Don't Brag About Being a Smart Operator

INTRODUCTION

Here is a list of survival tactics and useful hints and strategies that, over the years, I have added to my repertoire and that I think will be helpful to any woman in the workplace. Some of the following devices come from hard-learned experience, others from advising and observing my clients. Taken together, these principles add up to an effective operating style. As you put them into practice, you will find that you will not only have an easier time, but also will become a smarter operator in the workplace.

Although these pointers are presented in a slightly different format than the advice in the rest of the book, they derive from the same basic principles: the need to understand the hidden dynamics of the workplace, the need to abandon a ''good girl'' attitude toward rules and regulations, the need to be assertive and speak for yourself, and most of all, the need to *think* for yourself.

PART 1
POLITICKING

How to line up supporters • Making—or placing—friends in the
right places • Leadership style • How to get support at a meeting

1. "RUN FOR OFFICE"

You have to influence people—get them (your office constituents) on your
side. Some wheeler-dealers report they follow the eighty-twenty rule—that
is, they spend eighty percent of their time politicking and twenty percent
doing the actual work. I have trouble convincing women to spend even
twenty percent of their time politicking.

2. GIVE INFORMATION TO GET INFORMATION

Bring in interesting items of news, ideas, etc., that will engage and involve
the other person. Soon, he or she will start sharing information with you.
That's how you get an information exchange going.

Take responsibility for forming the relationships you need. Take the
lead and find a way to develop fruitful interactions with other people.
Sometimes it takes a bit of fishing around—questioning, probing—before
you hook on to the topic, the occurrence, perhaps the item of gossip, that
will result in this necessary interaction between the two of you.

3. "BANK" A FAVOR

Favors between co-workers can be essential in the workplace. It pays
therefore, for you to "invest" in a colleague by "banking" a favor on his
or her behalf. Help her get the raise she wants, if you can, by pointing out
the boss's vulnerability or sharing good arguments with her. Help him work

out some technical problem, if it falls within your area of expertise. Then, when the time comes, you will be able to collect on your investment, receiving a favor in return. This is an application of the principle of one good turn deserving another—and in the workplace, it really counts.

4. BE NICE TO PEOPLE IN LOWER POSITIONS

Treat them as well as you would anybody else. Don't take advantage of your position. Treating everyone well is good for your reputation and it's good for your soul. You'll also get more cooperation. And if you don't treat them with respect, they might look for ways to get revenge. (Your order disappears, you don't get a messenger, your mail gets lost.)

5. HELP PEOPLE GET JOBS

Wherever you land people, you've got a friend. Anita found a top-flight secretary for her department, but the day her secretary started work, the secretary to the company's president resigned. Anita, learning about this, proposed that her new secretary work for the top boss. She thus was doing her boss a favor, doing the secretary a favor, and also doing herself a favor. She got two for one—the president was grateful and the secretary was grateful. Now when Anita wants something from the president, her requests are no longer shoved to the bottom of the pile. She has a very cooperative friend in court.

6. MAKE EVERYONE YOUR "MENTOR"

Popular wisdom says "get a mentor"—a combination teacher-sponsor-champion—but this may be putting your precious egg (your career, your future with the company) into a single basket, however high-and-mighty a one. I think it is much better to seek out *many* mentors, relating to a number of people in the company who can teach you, help you, sponsor you. To strain a metaphor, take pieces of your egg (or make an omelet out of it) and spread them, strategically, in many baskets. This can serve to broaden your options *and* your power base.

7. TRY TO SET UP THE OUTCOME OF
MEETINGS IN ADVANCE

If you want things to go your way, don't rely on persuading people at the formal, decision-making meeting. There's too much going on at such a meeting—people showing off, people currying favor, people jumping on bandwagons.

The time to line up your key potential allies is before the meeting. Lay out your persuasive arguments, but don't stop there. The trick is also to present the opposition's strongest, most convincing case, and then explore and discover the weaknesses of your adversary's position *with* your hoped-for allies. This approach ensures that they won't be surprised and over-whelmed with the other person's logic at the moment of decision at the meeting. Also, by drawing your allies into the whole back-and-forth process of the debate this way, you've made them think their positions through. They are now thoroughly committed because, in a sense, they have persuaded themselves.

PART 2
PLAY IT COOL AND SHREWD

What to keep to yourself • Business deals and contracts • When a business partner says, "Don't you trust me?" • Hiring secret consultants • When to put it in writing • The art of "killing" a project • When *not* to involve your allies • The importance of job mystique • When—and how—to throw a fit

1. TURN DOWN THE CORPORATE PHYSICAL EXAM

At higher levels, the physical is thrown in as a perk. While these exams are supposed to safeguard the health of people the corporation considers important—this precious resource—it also tips off the chairman, the president, and the chief executive officer to any ailments that you might develop. You can count on the doctors clueing them in on your physical problems, and these may very well be used against you to limit your movement up the corporate ladder. Saying no to these extensive, comprehensive physical examinations may be a lifesaving strategy as far as your career is concerned. Since this is being offered to you because you're a big shot, be a bigger shot—saving a couple of hundred dollars doesn't matter to you. "That's taken care of. I prefer to stay with my personal physician who has been giving me a comprehensive checkup every year."

2. KEEP YOUR DISABILITIES TO YOURSELF

Don't reveal any physical problem or history of illness that isn't apparent. You might as well own up to problems they'll discover if you're required to undergo a physical, but otherwise, keep your troubles to yourself.

3. MUM'S THE WORD ON YOUR
"PEOPLE" TROUBLES, TOO

There are always sharpies looking for weak spots, sizing up workplace alignments (who are your enemies, who are your friends), ready to step in and take advantage of any situation. Take the case of Pat, the perfidious assistant. Her boss, Elise, confided in her about the difficult relationship she had with the vice president of her division. From then on, when something had to be discussed with the vice president, Pat offered to relieve Elise of the strain of dealing with this difficult man. Four months later, Pat had Elise's job.

4. DON'T MAKE BUSINESS DEALS WITHOUT
CONTRACTS—EVEN WITH FRIENDS

That doesn't mean that without a contract the deal won't work out—but, in most situations, you are taking a big risk. It's not that the parties of the other part are always "dishonest," but even the most ethical people can get caught up in a self-centered point of view. And misunderstandings can arise, even among the best of friends.

Women, in general, shy away from asking for a contract because it doesn't seem "nice." They think it will look as if they don't trust the other person to stick to his word. ("He will be insulted.") They have difficulty just saying, "I want to get this in writing, and this is how I think we should structure the deal . . ."

If the party of the second part brushes this off ("Let's just work it out as we go along," or, "What's the matter, don't you trust me?"), that's the time to declare yourself. Say, in effect, "Yes, of course, I trust you—and I want the deal in writing." Then, give your reasons: "I don't want to leave room for misunderstandings," Or, "Putting it on paper will force us to clarify all the details of the deal as well as our respective obligations." Where you don't have a basis for trust, say so: "This is an area in which we don't have much experience together. We don't really know how things will work out."

Don't fall victim to arguments that emphasize the pressure of time. "Let's get down to work or there won't *be* any sales. If we waste all our time on these details, we'll be out of business before we start." It's tempting to bury your concern about a difficult negotiation and get on with the work, but the price you pay for the time you gain may be too high.

The fact is, if you show you are businesslike and "want it in writing," the other person is apt to take the deal much more seriously—and you, as well.

5. DON'T ASK FOR A RETURN CALL WHEN YOUR MESSAGE IS IMPORTANT

When you have a speech all primed up, a pitch to make, or an important point to get across, and the other person isn't in, don't leave a call-back message because, when the return call comes, it will be at a time of his or her choosing, not yours—and you may have already put your just-right speech onto a back burner of your brain. If he or she is not there, you should call back yourself. Do it again and again—but always on your own time. That way, you'll be able to make your pitch and try to get your point over when *you're* in the right mood.

6. HIRE SECRET HELP

If you can't get the help you need from friends, spouses, whoever, then pay people to help you—and present the work as your own. You can hire any kind of off-the-premises help—consultant, expert, editor, whatever you need. It may sound outrageous, but when you think about it, we accept it as standard operating procedure for high-up executives and politicans who use "secret consultants" and take credit for the consultants' ideas. Sometimes it's paid help, as in the case of the corporation president's hired speech writer, and sometimes it's not—you come to work with a proposal you've written with your spouse's help, or with your friend's terrific idea for a new product line, or with your cousin's solution to a knotty distribution problem. But if you don't happen to have someone on hand who can give you the kind of help you need for free, why not pay for it?

Winifred's job was to open up a new territory in the southwest. It was going too slowly to satisfy her—so she hired herself a young salesman to help her, without informing the company. Result? She developed the territory twice as fast as expected. She was given new areas, and ultimately became the regional director of the whole southwest. The new salesman paid for himself, although his commissions were in Winifred's name since no one back in the home office knew of his existence.

What do you think the company would have thought if they had known? Was what she did unethical?

I'm not so sure the company would have been disturbed by her "lie." Chances are her boss, the company's sales manager, would have seen what she had done (hired somebody on her own to help boost the sales of company products) as a potent manifestation of the very qualities of assertiveness, toughness, and just plain business "smarts" that the job required. Besides, it was also making him look good with his own superiors, since the department's overall sales records had been enhanced.

7. DON'T COUNT ON "COVERING YOURSELF" WITH MEMOS

Putting things in memos—getting a record in writing—may settle minor disputes, but in major disputes, you'd better have a lot more than your memos to back you up. As in a war, nobody is much interested in who did what, why, and when. There is no judge or jury, no impartial hearing where you can present your memo as evidence to prove you were "right." What counts is *who wins*—and that has more to do with who has the power, who has allies, who makes the right strategic moves. The memos may be a good backup, but don't think for a minute if you are standing alone, or are in a weak and vulnerable situation, that the written record will be enough to protect you.

8. MASTER THE ART OF "KILLING" A PROJECT

When a project comes across your desk—or when you are asked to do something—that you feel is inadvisable, it might be wise to let it die unobtrusively, or to "kill" it with kindly fingers—instead of getting embroiled in a big fight over it. The best ways to do this are to entangle the project (the proposal, the key memo, or whatever) in bureaucratic delays, or put it in the far-back reaches of a bottom drawer, or on the bottom of your "to-do" pile—or, simply, to let it twist slowly in an ineffectual breeze.

9. GUARD YOUR PRIVACY

Whoever is typing your letters can talk about them. If they go through the typing pool, believe it or not, copies might also be going to the president. If your phone is on a switchboard, or if you have an extension, give a thought to a possible eavesdropper at the other end, or, if you are high enough in the company, to the possibility that you might be wiretapped. Don't leave notes and papers on top of your desk or in unlocked drawers or even in the wastebasket unless you want someone to read them. You have to assume that there are people who have an interest in poking into your affairs.

10. DON'T HAVE PARTNERS IN CRIME

If you are going to do something you don't want known, do it alone.

11. DON'T ENTRUST PEOPLE WITH CONFIDENCES

If you can't say it to everybody, don't say it to anybody. There are people who will use what you have to say to undermine you or ingratiate themselves with someone else. Sometimes, you may reveal things thoughtlessly, or inadvertently. If you ever find yourself saying, "Don't tell anybody, but . . ." leave the sentence unfinished unless your strategy is to get them to pass the item of information or juicy bit of gossip along.

12. DON'T TELL ALL

If you want to make yourself seem indispensable, keep some key parts of your job to yourself and create a mystique about them—even if the "key" is the simplest thing in the world.

Pina, for example, succeeded in being invaluable to her department in large part because her press contacts kept their achievements in the public eye. "How did you get that write-up? How do you know that reporter?" other people in the department would ask. She would answer breezily: "I get around—I meet a lot of people." She didn't tell them that anyone could do it if they had the gumption—that she had made her "special contacts" by picking up the phone and calling someone whose by-line she had gotten from a newspaper page or the masthead of some magazine.

Then there was Selma, administrative assistant to the production manager, who had a special list of suppliers who could come through with twenty-four-hour delivery of essential spare parts in emergency situations. "You're doing a great job," her boss complimented her. "But I'd sure like to know how you get those emergency deliveries. I can't get them myself."

Selma had "gotten" to these special suppliers through her brother-in-law, who was a retired spare-parts manufacturer, but she wasn't about to tell her boss that. She wanted to keep the "mystique" intact. Her answer, therefore, was: "They treat me well, what can I tell you."

BOSS (persisting): "Oh, come on. Who do you know? Suppose you're out of the office someday, or on vacation, and we run into trouble?"

SELMA (standing fast): "Well, as a matter of fact, I do have personal channels to the suppliers—and I'm afraid that if someone else tried to use these channels, the supply of spare parts would just plain dry up. I don't want to jeopardize our situation."

Many women feel compelled to answer a direct question. They hear the question as a *command* for them to respond. It's as if the questioner is setting the rules—and these women feel they have no right to reverse the situation; to say, in effect, "No—we're not playing by your rules, we're playing by mine." It's important to remember that you have no obligation to answer each and every question put to you—and especially no obligation to answer it directly and fully. You want to appear as cooperative as possible, but being cooperative doesn't mean giving away all your methods, your sources of information, your special suppliers, or whatever.

In such cases, you should stand fast. Bear in mind that a broken record, with embellishing variations on the same theme, can be your best response—and your best defense. Just keep saying no diplomatically, and in different ways.

13. KNOW WHEN TO THROW A FIT

Dorothea's request for funds to hire a consulting group to test-market the new product she had suggested and painstakingly checked out for ten months was shot down in a meeting by the vice president of marketing because "the whole company is cutting back on expenses." Dorothea had confidence in her idea and she wasn't going to let it die. First, she tried arguing her case in her usual assertive, reasonable manner, the manner that more often than not won the day for her. But when she saw that she wasn't getting anywhere—that the vice president was holding firm to his decision—she switched gears. She threw a fit. She stood up, slammed down her papers, and said, "What's the matter with you people? It's the best product idea we've had in sixteen years. This is a disaster." And she stormed out without a backward glance. A couple of hours later, the vice president appeared in her office and said, "Let's talk about product X," and proceeded to make a quick concession to her wishes. As often happens when someone throws a fit, he had gotten less sure of himself. People see the firmness of your belief, and thus their own view is shaken. Moreover, the passion of your reaction will make them concerned about the possible disruption of a good working relationship. Rather than worry about your anger, they will try to appease you.

Throwing a fit can be a very powerful move, but to be effective, tantrums should be few and far between. And don't attempt to throw a fit if your company is one of those uptight outfits that don't permit disruptions of its even-tempered atmosphere.

14. SEARCH FOR THE MOTIVE

Look for the self-serving angle of others. What is the other person after? Why is he taking the stand he is taking, making this point or that in the discussion or meeting? What's his angle?

Example. The art director is trying to convince you that her "artistic" layout will sell your company's product more than the "hard-sell" layout that you favor. She may be thinking more of her portfolio than of your advertising campaign—her main interest might be in creating work that would impress interviewers on future job hunts.

Example. The production man always wants to deal with the same supplier, who—he says—is more efficient and more cooperative about deliveries. Is this true? Or is he saying it because he's a friend of the manager there, or because he's thinking about the big Christmas gift that comes every year—or simply because he's too lazy to try elsewhere?

Knowing the other person's motive can be an important "weapon" in your hands. It can help you shape your own strategy, your actions and counteractions, so that the company's best interests—or your own—can be served.

PART 3
OPERATING STYLE

Keeping your information pipeline going • The pitfall of seeming too intense • Taking a stand on work you shouldn't be doing • Not taking no for an answer • Stepping in and taking over

1. DON'T GET CAUGHT READING PAPERS LEFT LYING ON SOMEONE'S DESK

2. DON'T ISOLATE YOURSELF

Keep your door open. Although the "rules" of hierarchy say that you are supposed to deal only with the people who report to you, and they in turn communicate your messages to the people who report to them, I think it's important for you to break this rule. Don't depend entirely on the people directly under you for information and for communicating with others. Develop some direct channels to the people below them and, in fact, to people all around the company. Keep these channels free and open so you can form your own firsthand impressions—that way you avoid the danger of having information inadvertently filtered out or deliberately colored by your staff.

3. GIVE IN ON SMALL ISSUES

In the long haul, you get more that way. Don't strive after perfection—the one hundred and ten percent solution. Giving in when the issue doesn count for too much—when it's not a matter of life and death—will get your subordinates (as well as people on your own level, or above you) more cooperative, more motivated to work along with you when it really counts.

4. TELL JOKES

Lighten up the atmosphere with a wisecrack, a funny line. Store up the good jokes you hear and pass them along later. A playful style can imply a relaxed confidence in your own ability—and that of others—to get the job done. An intense, deadly serious style, however, can imply that you lack confidence, that you believe that you and your group need every second, nose to the grindstone, to produce work that measures up.

5. SAY NO—A FLAT NO—WHEN YOU ARE TOLD TO WORK UNDER SOMEONE WHO IS AT THE SAME LEVEL YOU ARE

If you are on a downskid and you say no, you'll probably get fired—but you are on your way out anyway, so you have little to lose. If you're not on your way out but are caught in some kind of power play or reorganization, you had better hold your own with a refusal. I'm not, of course, talking about the standard back-and-forth help that colleagues are expected to give each other—but don't say yes to anything else, no matter how "reasonable" the request sounds.

BOSS: "I want you to help Susie service her accounts. She's overwhelmed with work. She's sold more than she can handle."
YOU: "I need my time to develop my own accounts." (In other words, no.)
BOSS: "Well, a bird in the hand—we'd better take care of what we've got." (Here's where so many women get stopped. They don't feel entitled to take care of their own needs, and therefore get completely caught up in the boss's thinking.)
YOU: "I want to build my own accounts—then we'll have two birds." (Sticking with your belief that you have a valuable contribution to make, and with your right to build your own future.)

6. DON'T TAKE NO FOR AN ANSWER

When you need something from a co-worker, a superior, or one of the other departments, don't be put off by a stall, a refusal, or unreturned phone calls. The smart operator tries to find a way to get the other person lined up on her side.

Harriet, a junior sportswear buyer, could never seem to get the mannequins she needed for her displays from George, the department store's display manager. Each time she tried, George would explain how short of mannequins they were and why he couldn't give her one—excuses that added up to a big, fat no—and each time she'd give up in disgust and try to make do with her display minus the mannequin.

Somehow, Jill, Harriet's opposite number in misses sportswear, always managed to get mannequins for her displays. How did Jill get around George and his excuses? She wouldn't take no for an answer. When George put her off, Jill would cajole and joke: "Gee, George what can I do to get a mannequin—can I bribe you with an ice cream soda?" And she'd appear down in the display department in the next day or two and pay him off: "Come on, I owe you an ice cream soda. What bar do we go to?" Jill's conversations with George were never limited to just getting or not getting something. To her, every conversation was part of forming a working relationship. The other person was always a part of the picture; the relationship was always in the process of developing. As Jill proved, it is well worth the effort.

7. STEP IN AND TAKE OVER WHEN THINGS AREN'T MOVING

Don't wait around. Learning to intervene in a situation at the right moment is a skill that doesn't come naturally to many women. In general, we seem to stand too much in awe of the "expert," whether official or self-proclaimed, even when said expert is in the process of falling on his or her face. If your expert is doing badly or not doing anything at all, you have nothing to lose by taking the reins yourself. At the least, you'll get an understanding of the issues and you *and* the expert will come up with better judgments. By taking hold, you can often bypass the impasse and get things moving again.

8. DON'T BRAG ABOUT BEING A SMART OPERATOR

Don't wear an "I'm a Smart Operator" T-shirt. Desist from telling people about stunts you've pulled off or clever deals you put through. That's not to say you should stop publicizing your achievements, but when your means are in danger of being misunderstood—of causing people not to admire you, but to become suspicious of you—keep them to yourself. Above all, don't give anyone advice about possibly "sneaky" strategies they might employ with their own problems; they just might reach the conclusion that you are simply a sneaky, not a smart, operator.

CONCLUSION

Throughout this book, I have emphasized the need for women to take hold; to count on their own judgment; to listen to others, but not lean on them; to make their own decisions and take a chance on them; to move ahead when everything around them stops. It's through this taking of full responsibility—this independent stance—that one achieves career success and, indeed, success in life.

This is a formidable task for the countless women who were not raised to take charge of their own lives. They have to master the skills of negotiation, of speaking up for themselves, of arguing—sometimes fighting—of selling and persuading, of being a leader. They have to become sophisticated rule-breakers, develop a sense of strategy, learn how to promote themselves, and learn how to establish their own authority.

As you strive toward these goals, it's quite unlikely that you will progress in a straight line. You'll undoubtedly find yourself slipping back into some of the old habits of compliance, or its opposite—outbursts of inappropriate or impatient anger. You may find yourself backing away from problems; or being a good girl, or a helpmate, or a perfectionist; or waiting for direction. You may despair ("What's the matter with me? I should be able to do all this.") or fear that you'll never learn ("It's too hard. I'll never be able to do it."). At times it will feel as if you haven't learned anything, as if you haven't progressed, as if you're back where you started.

Bear in mind that slipping back to old, familiar patterns is a normal part of the learning process: two steps forward, one step backward. The danger lies in getting mired in the feeling that there is something innately wrong with you instead of realizing that this is a moment when you are lost—but only temporarily. Remind yourself that you have a bank of new approaches and new solutions available to you. As you practice these over and over, the moments of feeling lost will be replaced with a confident sense of yourself as an in-charge, strategic woman.

VOLUME CONTENTS

*A chapter-by-chapter, section-by-section
summary and guide*

APPENDIX A

Part 2: Match Your Image to Your Job   212

1. How to Publicize Yourself   213
   The danger of assuming people know who you are and what you have
      achieved
   Overcoming modesty
   How to toot your own horn without bragging
   How to impress the people above you when your boss won't let you
      near them
   Measuring the risk of bypassing your boss

2. What's the Right Image for You?   217
   What image will get you what you want?
   How to sound, look, and act the part
   The pitfalls of looking too rich—or too poor
   How to look well-connected when you need to

Part 3: Your Professional Self-Image   220

1. I'm Afraid of Losing My Femininity   220
   What kind of a woman does a man really want?
   The new femininity
   Why being strategic feels unfeminine

2. I'm Afraid of Becoming a Cardboard Corporate Character   223
   How the pressure is exerted
   How to resist it
   How to make concessions without paying a price

CHAPTER 5: MOVING IN 225

Introduction   227

1. The Job Isn't What I Thought It Would Be   228
   How to claim the job you were promised
   When cooperation does not earn respect
   How to create your own job description

2. They Don't Want to Announce My New Title--Yet   232
   The hidden danger in accepting the delay
   When a woman is promoted over men
   Arguments that make a good case for your title
   When to announce it yourself

What to keep to yourself
Business deals and contracts
When a business partner says, "Don't you trust me?"
Hiring secret consultants
When to put it in writing
The art of "killing" a project
When *not* to involve your allies
The importance of job mystique
When—and how—to throw a fit

A LIST OF THE MAJOR TOPICS INCLUDED IN THIS BOOK

Following is a cross-referencing guide, broken down by topic. Entries indicate where in the text you will find related discussions—examples, solutions, analyses—that will help you understand the topic.

CONTENTS

Alliances and Networks

Ambivalence about Working and/or Moving up

The Ambivalence Block

Asserting Your Authority

Asserting Yourself

Being "Nice"

The Competence Block

Competition

The Competition Block

See also Appendix B listing: *COMPETITION*

The Compliance/Aggression Block

See also Appendix B listing: *COPING WITH YOUR ANGER*

Confusing Family Roles with Work Roles

Coping with Your Anger

Criticizing Others

Dealing with Other People's Anger and Resentment

The Dependency Block

The Efficiency Block

The Empathy Block

Evaluating Your Own Performance and Abilities

"Failure" and Mistakes

Fear

Getting a Raise

Getting Bypassed, Excluded, or Ignored

Getting, Giving, and Withholding Information

Getting Off the Defensive

Getting—or Creating—Better Assignments

Getting the Right Job Title

Handling Both Job and Home

Handling Criticism

Having Too Much Work

The Helplessness Block

The Helpmate Block

The Honesty Block

*How the Nature of the Work—and the Abilities Needed—Change as You
Move Up*

How to Argue

The If-You-Can't-See-It, It-Isn't-Work Block

The I-Hate-to-Fight Block

The I-Have-Trouble-with-Authority-Figures Block

Jumping Your Job Description

The Like-Me Block

Male Chauvinism: The Hidden Effects

Mentors and Protégés

Problems with Self-Image

Proving You're Promotable

Publicizing Yourself

The Put-Yourself-Down Block

See also Appendix B listing: *EVALUATING YOUR OWN PER-
  FORMANCE AND ABILITIES*

The Security Block

See also Appendix B listing: *FEAR*

Seizing the Initiative Versus Being Dependent

Sex and Work

Sex Discrimination

Sexism

Using a Boss's Ambition—or Weaknesses—to Your Advantage

The Virginity Block

The Waiting Block

What to Do with Your Good Ideas

When Your Boss Is Blocking Your Progress

The Work-Is-Like-Family Block

Your Values and Morals